Biblical Exegesis

Biblical Exegesis

A Beginner's Handbook

THIRD EDITION

John H. Hayes
Carl R. Holladay

Westminster John Knox Press
LOUISVILLE • LONDON

Scripture quotations from the New Revised Standard Version of the Bible are copyright © 1989 by the Division of Christian Education of the National Council of the Churches of Christ in the U.S.A. and are used by permission.

Book design by Drew Stevens
Cover design by Mark Abrams

Third edition
Published by Westminster John Knox Press
Louisville, Kentucky

This book is printed on acid-free paper that meets the American National Standards Institute Z39.48 standard. ♾

PRINTED IN THE UNITED STATES OF AMERICA

Library of Congress Cataloging-in-Publication Data is on file at the Library of Congress, Washington, D.C.

ISBN-13: 978-0-664-22775-3
ISBN-10: 0-664-22775-9

Contents

Preface

When this book originally appeared in 1982, there were few such handbooks available. Since then, several have been published. Some focus on doing exegesis of either the OT or the NT. Others presuppose knowledge of Hebrew or Greek. Still others provide detailed, step-by-step "how-to" instructions. Some are collections of essays by scholars treating different approaches to exegesis.

From the outset, we thought an exegetical handbook should treat both the OT and the NT; provide simple, helpful information and guidance about doing exegesis, without being overly prescriptive; introduce students to various methods succinctly; provide basic bibliography that would take students beyond our introductory discussion; and emphasize exegesis as an everyday activity based on commonsense principles rather than as an esoteric academic discipline.

Over the years, our approach seems to have worked. Our book has been used in undergraduate Bible survey classes, in seminary courses—both OT and NT introductions and exegesis courses on individual biblical books—and in various church settings. It has also been used in high schools. It has had a wide reach internationally. Readers seem to appreciate that it is substantial but nontechnical, comprehensive but not inordinately lengthy, helpful but not pushy, and readable.

In our second edition (1987), we retained the format of the first edition but included new chapters on structuralism and canonical criticism. In this edition, we have retained all of the chapters of the second edition and added a new chapter, Exegesis with a Special Focus: Cultural, Economic, Ethnic, Gender, and Sexual Perspectives. We have been selective not comprehensive, realizing that much has occurred over the last twenty years. We do think, however, that these new perspectives illustrate some of the most important developments.

The appendix, Using Electronic Technologies in Exegesis, acknowledges the technological revolution that has occurred since our book first appeared. Over the years, we have accommodated to these new technologies in our teaching. Mainly, we have learned from our students,

who know far more about these things than we do. Rather than including this appendix as another chapter, along with other chapters that discuss exegetical approaches and methodologies, we have located it at the
end of the book. We do this, not because we think it is less important,
but to signal that we regard these technologies as new tools that can
benefit us in any approach that we use. Here again, we have tried to
make our treatment simple, informative, accurate, and helpful. Knowing how rapidly technology changes, we realize that some of this information will be dated when the book appears. Even so, we believe our
observations will remain true for the foreseeable future.

Besides adding this new material, we have worked through the second edition completely. We have retained some of it, reworked other
parts, and completely rewritten still other parts. The result is a thoroughly revised book. We have tried to retain the simple, uncluttered
style that commended the earlier editions. We have added some details
and examples that we believe give more texture to our discussion. We
have updated and expanded all of the bibliographies. Because the field
of biblical studies has grown enormously over the last twenty years, we
decided to include only books in the bibliographies. Removing some of
the articles was a painful decision, since several of them were seminal in
their own right. The bibliographical data provide the names of the publishers and the dates of the current or the latest publication of a work.
Dates in parentheses are those of the original publications.

Along the way, we have accumulated debts, mainly to our students.
Derek Olsen scanned the second edition and reworked and updated it.
He contributed the core draft of the appendix on computer technology.
Since his initial draft, however, John Weaver and Richard Wright of
Pitts Theology Library have made further refinements. Eric Barreto
and Kevin Muñoz also shared with us their considerable knowledge of
computer technology, and wrote some of the new sections. Amanda
Stephenson read through the entire draft and provided many helpful
editorial suggestions, which we followed. At the last stages, Bo Adams
generously shared his impressive knowledge and experience of computer and Internet technology, in addition to performing a lot of the
grunt work on bibliography, diagrams, and general editing. Peter
Trudinger extended a helping hand in the final process. Drew Denton,
Jason Bethel, and Robert Williamson Jr. also assisted in the final editing, especially in preparing the indexes.

We are especially indebted to the students we have taught over the
last thirty or so years at Emory University's Candler School of Theol-

ogy. It has been a special delight for us to introduce the Bible to them, spark their interest in exegesis, and teach them different approaches to biblical interpretation. We think they are better interpreters of the Bible because of our efforts. Whatever form their exegetical efforts take—and many of them have become ministers in local churches—we think those who listen to them teach and preach are better off. At least, we hope so.

J.H.H.
C.R.H.
JUNE 30, 2006
ATLANTA, GEORGIA

1

Introducing Exegesis

Exegesis as an Everyday Activity and as a Specialized Discipline

Exegesis is a normal activity all of us practice every day of our lives. Whenever we try to understand something we have heard or read, we are doing exegesis.

The term "exegesis" comes from the Greek verb *exēgeomai*, which literally means "to lead." Its extended meaning is "to relate in detail" or "to expound." When applied to texts, the term refers to an interpretive exercise in which we explain a passage. Broadly speaking, the noun "exegesis" can refer to any act of interpretation or explanation. Ordinarily, we may not refer to our many efforts to interpret spoken or written language as "exegesis," but it is an appropriate term to describe such activities.

Understanding any form of communication inevitably involves exegesis. When someone speaks to us, we must listen to what is said and decide what is meant. We ask automatically, even unconsciously: Is it a question or a statement? What is the speaker trying to communicate? Should we take the words literally or nonliterally? Is the speaker joking or being serious? Does the speaker's language fall into a conventional pattern of usage? Do the words take the form of a greeting, a sales pitch, a formal demand, a lecture, a sermon, or a threat? How should we respond? Should we laugh, cry, take notes, hand over our billfold, respond with a statement, or ask a question?

Because we spend so much time speaking and listening, we process many of these questions intuitively. Facial gestures and body language may communicate as much as spoken words, perhaps more. As we interpret a "speech act," we trigger a multifaceted, complex range of responses that may seem second nature to us. We may not even give much conscious attention to how we respond. Even so, when we participate in such acts of interpersonal communication, we are using our exegetical skills.

Oral communication generally takes place in familiar situations with persons we know. This enables us to assess the context and intentions of the speaker as well as to analyze the spoken words themselves. The context helps us to determine the larger social framework in which the event of communication takes place and thus to understand the words spoken. Is it someone in an official position who is giving commands, offering directions, supplying information, or making suggestions? Are the words spoken in a formal, highly structured situation, or is the setting more casual? Does the communication occur at a wedding or in a bar? Is it conversation between friends? Were the words spoken under normal or abnormal conditions? Engaging in oral communication involves more than paying attention to a speaker and listener—the communicators; it also requires us to understand the context in which the words are spoken.

Although some of these dynamics are also present in written communication, there are some important differences between oral and written communication. Since the writer is generally not present when we read a written text, the words assume a greater importance than is the case in oral communication. Through imagination and prior knowledge, we may re-create in our mind a picture of the writer and the situation in which the text was written. If we receive a letter from a friend, we have prior knowledge about the person. We often know something about the situation in which the letter was written. But even when we read a letter from someone we know, we must engage in exegesis. We may know the letter writer intimately, but we still have to interpret the written words to understand what is said. The written text is the medium through which we interpret the person's words and seek to understand what is being communicated.

At a minimum, interpreting written texts presupposes that the writer and the reader share a common world, a common frame of reference, and a common understanding of language. To this extent, the writer and the reader are not remote from one another.

And yet we interpret many written communications in which we have little or no knowledge about the writer. In such cases, the act of interpretation occurs primarily between the text and the reader. Unlike the speaker in oral communication, the writer becomes less important.

When we read a highway sign or a traffic direction, it matters little who wrote these words. What matters is that the reader and the words on the sign share a common linguistic field of reference. It is only necessary that the written directions or the symbols painted on the sign make sense to the reader and lend themselves to exegetical understanding. But even highway signs may not be easy to understand. If we see a sign that reads, "Road Construction 1500 Feet," does this mean that for the next 1,500 feet a driver should expect construction activity or that after traveling 1,500 feet a driver should expect to encounter construction activity? Even this seemingly simple written message requires exegesis. Meaningful exegesis requires prior experience in understanding such signs.

We constantly read and interpret multiple forms of written texts. On any given day, we may read an assignment in a scientific textbook, a short story, a poem, a label on a food container, announcements of meetings and other events, a newspaper, a letter, an advertising brochure, the telephone directory, and a traffic sign. These texts employ different forms of communication. They also represent different literary forms, or genres, of written documents. Since these texts are part of our normal culture, we have been socialized into how to read and understand them in spite of their diversity. We do not read and interpret a poem as we would a recipe. In the former we expect metaphorical language, in the latter simple, straightforward instructions. Neither do we read the front page of a newspaper in the same way we read the editorial page.

In our culture, some types of writing require close, intensive exegetical work. Every profession has a body of specialized, technical literature that must be mastered and constantly consulted. Lawyers and judges spend much of their time interpreting laws and law codes. Such exegesis typically requires legal experts to examine how laws have been interpreted and applied in the past. So important are these previous rulings that the history of interpretation of laws is a central element in the legal profession. In particular, constitutional lawyers specialize in the exegesis of the constitution and the history of its interpretation.

The same is true of other professions. For accountants, tax codes are the definitive texts that must be interpreted and applied. In the health care professions, scientific articles in specialized journals, along with standard textbooks on different topics, constitute the texts that inform daily medical practice. Diplomatic language and treaties often require a special exegesis, since communication in this area is frequently sensitive and deliberately ambiguous.

What is required for the exegesis and interpretation of texts varies greatly, of course, depending upon the nature of the texts and their relationship to normal communication. Some texts need merely to be read to be understood. Others require detailed analysis. Some use normal, everyday language, grammar, and sentence structure. Others use specialized vocabulary, involved grammatical and sentence structure, and distinctive forms of expression. Some texts employ symbolic and metaphoric language. Others employ language that severely limits the range of meaning, thus reducing the potential for multiple interpretations and misunderstanding. Some texts seek to clarify. Others are intentionally ambiguous. Some texts seek to persuade. Others seek merely to inform. Some texts are produced to entertain, others to sadden.

The difficulty we may experience as we interpret such a wide range of oral and written statements depends on two variables: (1) the commonality of experience and language between speaker and listener or between writer and reader, and (2) the technical level of the language.

1. A major consideration is the degree to which the sender (the speaker, author, or editor/collector) and the receiver (the hearer or reader) share a common world of discourse and experience. When two familiar persons from a common background talk with each other or exchange letters, very few, if any, problems of communication develop. When there are differences between their forms of discourse and their range of experiences, difficulty in understanding each other may result.

Two persons from a similar rural environment usually experience little difficulty communicating with each other. The same is true with two persons from a similar urban environment. But misunderstanding often occurs when a city dweller and a rural person try to communicate with each other. So different are their range of experiences and forms of discourse that it may be nearly impossible for them to understand each other. To explain this communication breakdown, we sometimes say that they live in two "different" worlds.

2. A second factor that affects understanding is the extent to which a particular form of communication involves specialized content and forms of expression. This point can be illustrated by using examples drawn from letter writing. Personal letters, one of the most common means of personal communication, are generally written in a straightforward manner. They vary in content and form, depending upon the degree of familiarity between the sender and receiver and the content to be communicated. It

usually requires little effort to understand letters from a friend or a parent. But a specialized letter from a technician describing some mechanical or chemical process, or from an accountant explaining a bookkeeping procedure, is a different matter. Understanding also relates to content. An essay on Paris in the springtime would probably present fewer interpretive problems than an essay on the influence of Renaissance architecture on nineteenth-century building construction in Paris.

Factors Affecting the Exegetical Process

So far, we have considered exegesis as an everyday, normal activity. It may occur in simple or complex forms, depending upon the nature of the communication. When we examine the exegetical process more closely, however, we notice that further levels of complexity are introduced by several factors.

Third-Party Perspective

Quite often, the interpreter is not one of the primary or original parties in the communication event. In these cases, the interpreter is neither the sender nor the receiver of the communication but a third party who in one sense is an outsider, an observer, or even an intruder.

Letters are more difficult to interpret when being read by a third party. The persons involved in the original communication may be totally unknown to the interpreter. Generally most documents are best understood when the sender has some prior knowledge of the receiver and the receiver has some prior acquaintance with the sender. By imagining how the communication will be received and understood, the sender can shape the message accordingly. Similarly, the receiver can imagine the sender in order to understand better both the content and the shape of the communication.

In order to understand a communication between two other parties, however, a third-party reader must imagine, even empathize with, both the sender and the receiver. In one sense, the third-party interpreter must assume the identity of both the sender and receiver and read the document from these perspectives. The third-party interpreter first assumes the role of the sender, then that of the receiver, and out of this imagined situation tries to understand the communication between them. This requires the interpreter—the third party—to search out information or use informed imagination about both the sender and the receiver and their situations. When the content or form of the document is specialized, unique, or ambiguous, this process is even more necessary and imposes greater demands.

Communication in a Different Language

Further complexity is introduced when a text is composed in a language different from that of the interpreter or exegete. Here a language barrier intrudes into the interpretive or exegetical process. If an English-speaking person receives a letter written in German, or wishes to read a German-language textbook, special problems arise. The English-speaking person must acquire sufficient knowledge of German to read the text or resort to a translator who can aid in overcoming the language barrier. In both cases, ascertaining the meaning of something written in another language is not always easy. Since each language has its own distinctive structure, grammatical features, and vocabulary nuances, it is difficult for a translation to convey exactly what the original language expresses. For this reason, translations are always interpretations to some extent.

Once a passage is translated into another language, this introduces another level of complexity. Interpreting a text translated into another language might be called a second-level interpretation. A first-level interpretation would be an interpretation of a text in the original language. It might be done by a native speaker or hearer or by someone who has acquired knowledge of the original language. A second-level interpretation occurs when an interpreter seeks to understand the content of a translation. At this level, the interpreter is always one step removed from the original, regardless of how well the text has been translated. When we interpret texts that have been translated from another language, we inevitably confront a communication gap, however small, between what the translation says and what the writer originally expressed.

The Cultural Gap

Writings produced in one cultural context and interpreted in another setting present special problems. There are two reasons for this. First, a document may mention, describe, or allude to special ideas, practices, and customs that would be clearly understood by a person reading the document in the original culture but that baffle a reader in a different culture. Second, communication within a culture frequently assumes a shared body of cultural understanding. This general reservoir of experience, worldview, and perception that lies behind the text would not be shared by the cultural outsider. A document, for example, reporting the actions and outcome of a particular sporting event, say a baseball game or a cricket match, would present difficulties in interpretation for a person living in a culture in which the sport and its rules of play were unknown.

Differences in culture are not just related to ideas, concepts, and worldviews. Also involved are differences in the way things are said and written and the customary way of reading and interpreting. In some cultures, for example, when one tells a story, the first character to be mentioned is always the villain. Generally, the more remote the culture reflected in a given document, the greater the difficulty the exegete encounters in interpreting it.

The Historical Gap

When we study a document from the past, we must move mentally from our own time to an earlier period. The chronological gap between the reader and the text being interpreted does not have to be great for there to be interpretive difficulties.

Reading a fifty-year-old newspaper can be a fascinating experience. We notice, for example, differences in clothing fashions, in prices for advertised items, in issues that were the concerns of the day, and in the style in which articles were written. Questions arise immediately. Why were things that way? Why were certain issues and events considered important? How could prices have been so low? How could people have thought and reacted the way they did?

When we read documents from the more distant past—for example, from the days of ancient Greece and Rome—we often encounter persons, places, practices, and perspectives that are a "world apart" from our present situation. This is why editions of the ancient classics often contain notes that explain historical persons, events, or customs that were familiar to persons who lived at that time but are no longer part of our modern frame of reference.

Writings That Developed over Time

The exegetical process is sometimes more complicated because the documents being interpreted are the products of collective authorship and historical growth. Simply put, a writing may not have been written by a single author at a particular time. Instead, it may be the result of editorial activity that occurred over a long period of time. Rather than being produced by a single author, it may have been written or edited by multiple authors. This is what is meant by collective as opposed to individual authorship. By historical growth we mean that a writing may have been composed over a long period of time rather than at one particular point in time.

Many writings in our own culture result from collective authorship and historical growth. The United States Constitution, for example, was produced by a constitutional convention. Many people contributed to its formation. Over time, the original document has been expanded through the addition of amendments.

We are all familiar with different editions of textbooks. Often a textbook will be written by one author and then revised by the author or even by a second author. The later revisions may make it impossible to distinguish original material from later, added material. Unless we have access to the various editions, we cannot easily detect the various strata of editorial composition.

College and university catalogs are typically writings that have developed over time and are the result of collective authorship. Ordinarily, different people have written different sections, and these have gone through many editorial revisions. Some of the information in a current catalog may have been there since the first catalog was published by the school. Other items may have resulted from recent policy decisions. If a researcher wished to explore the development of the school's policies and curriculum but possessed only the current catalog, it would be difficult. By comparing the current catalog with earlier editions and information gained from other sources, however, we can draw firmer conclusions. For example, we can determine when courses in computer science or liberation theology were introduced or when coeducational dormitories became permissible.

In the ancient world, books were often produced through collective authorship. Even in medieval times, writers often avoided originality. Instead, they frequently combined older works that had already been compiled and edited from previous works. Ancient works were frequently the products of a long and complex editorial process and contained layers of materials and traditions. The ancient Jewish historian Josephus (ca. 37–100 CE), for example, utilized assistants in his writing, which means that some of his works were really the product of a joint effort. In addition, he frequently incorporated or rewrote earlier sources without acknowledging that he was actually doing so, much less naming his sources. In defense of Josephus and many of his ancient counterparts, however, it must be noted that borrowing the work of one's predecessors was fairly common practice in ancient times. Our sensitivity about property rights of individual authors and how these are protected by copyright laws is more typical of modern times.

Even today, the term papers we write in academic settings are often composite. We quote words and borrow ideas from others. When we do so, however, we are expected to acknowledge our sources in footnotes to indicate that we are "accumulating" previous work as we develop our interpretations.

When working with ancient writings, we can usually detect the results of this process of growth and historical development by locating literary "seams" in the material—places where different blocks of material have been edited together. Other indicators of editorial activity include the presence of anachronisms in the text, differences in style, and even contradictions in the contents. In our exegetical study, we must always be open to the possibility that a given ancient writing might have resulted from such collective authorship and editorial activity and take these considerations into account in our interpretations.

Another consideration should be noted about literary productions in antiquity. Works were sometimes produced as if they were the work of another person, generally some venerable figure from the past. A writer would sometimes produce a work and attribute it to a person of the remote, or even recent, past. Such writers possibly thought they were expressing the views of the one under whose name they wrote, maybe even preserving some authentic material from that person.

Sometimes such works were produced by students or followers of important figures in order to pass on the legacy of their teacher. Works produced in this way tended to be associated with and attributed to the revered personality rather than to the person's students or followers. Some philosophical treatises that were attributed to the eminent Greek philosopher Aristotle (384–322 BCE) are now known to have been written many years after his death, sometimes by his own students.

Written works attributed to a revered figure of the past possessed an aura of authority. We see this in the large body of literature that was written under the name of Enoch, to whom the Bible gives only incidental notice (see Gen. 4:17–18; 5:18–24). None of these Enochian writings made its way into the Scriptures although they are referred to in the little NT book of Jude (vv. 14–15). Generally the nature of such works, called pseudepigraphs, can be discovered by analyzing the texts from literary, linguistic, and historical perspectives.

Multiple Texts or Editions of the Same Writing

A sixth factor that can make the exegetical process more difficult is the existence of multiple texts of the same documents. Frequently two or more copies of a given document exist but exhibit considerable differences. At this point, the interpreter is confronted with the problem of determining the actual wording of the text to be interpreted. Differences between copies of the same work are more common for ancient than for modern works.

Divergent texts of the same work, however, are an issue even after the use of the printing press became widespread in the fifteenth and sixteenth centuries. For example, many of the plays of Shakespeare (1564–1616) exist in such different forms that the study of these texts and their textual history has been a popular, highly controversial field.

Before the use of the printing press, copies of texts were always made by hand. Even copies of short texts generally contained numerous differences from the original, including misspellings, omitted words or units, and repeated words or units. We possess few texts from antiquity in their original form, the so-called autographs. Most often we possess copies of copies of the original. Since no one copy of any text of major size agrees exactly with another copy of the same text, this requires the exegete to inquire about the text in its original or authorial form.

The problem of multiple texts of the same work becomes more complicated when those texts have been preserved in several languages. If differences between various copies exist, but all the copies are in the same language, this presents the problem in one dimension. If there are diverging copies of the same work in several languages, this adds another dimension. Copies of manuscripts of Aristotle's works, for example, exist in Greek, Latin, and Arabic. Where there are significant differences among these, the exegete must work across language boundaries in order to discover what appears to be the most likely reading.

Interpreting Sacred Texts

Exegetical practice is further complicated when the text being studied is considered sacred. Many readers treat such texts differently from other texts, even from the same historical period. Regarding a text as sacred usually involves more than treating it as good literature or as a classical work.

We are all familiar with the concept of the classical works of Western literature reflected in introductory English literature anthologies. There are certain well-accepted criteria by which literary works are recognized as classics. Among these are the following: (a) a work is well written and a good example of its genre; (b) it engages issues and concerns that are reflective of recurring human conditions; and (c) it possesses a quality that invites multiple if not infinite interpretations.

A sacred text may possess some or all of the characteristics of a classic. Other dimensions enter the picture, however, when the work falls into the category of the sacred. We hold opinions about classical works; about sacred texts, we hold beliefs and convictions.

Sacred texts belong to the category of Scripture, which has several distinguishing characteristics. First, Scripture possesses an authority for individuals or groups that exceeds normal conditions. In popular parlance, we sometimes speak of a sportsman's "bible" or some other authoritative text, such as Guinness's *Book of World Records*, to which final appeal is made. By this we mean that its authority exceeds that of other books. It can be used to resolve disputes or controversies. By analogy, religious groups usually possess their own distinctive set of Scriptures, whether it is the Muslim Qur'an or the Jewish and Christian Bibles.

Second, Scriptures occupy an official position in the life of the groups that regard them as authoritative. They are sources to which appeal is made and whose contents inform in a special way the lives and thoughts of communities and their members.

Third, Scriptures are understood to embody a truer reflection of reality than other writings. This higher reality is thought to have been expressed through the voice, thought, or word of God in a way that is not true of other writings.

By their very nature, Scriptures bear special relationships to the communities that consider them sacred. The communities have frequently participated in the production and formation of their Scriptures. The sacredness of Scriptures is based on community decisions that assigned them a special role in their lives. In addition, the manner in which the communities have understood and interpreted their Scriptures becomes a decisive influence in how they are assessed. Communities of faith often bring assumptions to their Scriptures from which they develop systems of thought and religious practices. Interpreting the Scriptures becomes a central feature of their life together. Traditions of interpretation that develop around the Scriptures sometimes become as important as the Scriptures themselves. Exegetes of a sacred text must take into account the mutual influence between Scripture and

tradition. They must recognize that the Scriptures have informed traditions of interpretation and practice, but also that those very traditions
also shape how the Scriptures are read and interpreted.

Summary

In this section, we have noted that exegesis is an activity in which all
people engage when they interpret oral and written texts. Second, we
have noted that some conditions and texts require special efforts at
interpretation and that some exegesis must therefore have special qualities. Third, we have discussed several factors that can complicate the
exegetical process and require interpreters to acquire special training
and employ special tools.

The Bible and Exegesis

Biblical exegesis belongs to the category of specialized exegesis. Interpreting the Bible differs from reading a letter from a friend, an article in
a contemporary magazine, a newspaper account of some event, or a
modern novel or short story. The various complexities that can influence the exegetical process noted in the previous section are all related
in one way or another to biblical exegesis. Let us note how all seven of
these factors pertain to biblical exegesis.

1. The Bible was originally addressed to ancient readers. None of us
was involved in the original communication events as either senders or
receivers. Paul's letters, for example, were written to the Romans, the
Galatians, the Corinthians, and other early Christian communities and
individuals. When we read Paul's letters, we are reading somebody else's
mail. The books of Luke and Acts were accounts written for someone
named Theophilus (Luke 1:3; Acts 1:1).

Many other examples could be adduced, but these illustrations
remind us that when we interpret ancient biblical writings, we are
doing so from the perspective of a third party—someone who is overhearing and trying to understand an earlier conversation.

2. The Bible was composed in ancient languages. The OT was written in Hebrew and Aramaic and the NT in Greek. Even the modern
Israeli who speaks Hebrew or a Greek citizen whose native language is
modern Greek recognizes that the languages of the Bible are not the
same as modern Hebrew and Greek. As modern exegetes of the Bible,

we must take into consideration the language barrier that separates us from the original biblical writings.

3. As modern readers of the Bible, we are separated from the original authors and readers of the texts by an enormous cultural gap. The culture presupposed by the Bible is that of the ancient Mediterranean world in general and Palestine in particular. One has to note only a few general characteristics of biblical culture to sense its difference from much modern culture.

The social structures presupposed by the writers of biblical materials were patriarchal and authoritarian. The dominant economic system was based on agricultural production, which was closely related to village life. Diets were seasonal. Medical arts were primitive. Machines were little developed. Slavery was widespread. Mortality rates were high, especially for infants. Travel was slow and difficult. Life was rather simple and characterized by stability and similarity rather than change. Human life was oriented to the cycles of nature and climate. Entertainment was limited. Good artificial lighting did not exist. Animals were slaughtered, dressed, and burned on altars as an integral part of worship. Divine beings, both good and bad, were assumed to be participants in the ongoing course of life and history.

4. Modern readers of the Bible also experience a historical or chronological gap that ranges from almost twenty centuries to over three millennia. The biblical writings were composed over a period of twelve centuries. Since biblical writings originated over such a long period of time, informed interpreters must understand the different historical contexts within which the various books and traditions of the Bible came into being.

In addition to the length of time over which the Bible was written, there are two other historical considerations. First, much of the Bible takes the form of historical narrative. To call the Bible a history book is a misleading simplification, but much of it is concerned with historical matters. Interpreters cannot ignore this pervasive historical dimension of the biblical writings. Second, biblical writers often express their thoughts and develop their theology using the categories of past, present, and future. Not only do they take seriously the course of historical events, but they also operate with categories that are dependent upon historical perspectives.

5. Collective authorship and the gradual growth of biblical traditions are clearly evident in the Bible, especially the OT. Since we do not know for certain who wrote any of the OT books, it is impossible to

speak of individual authors of these writings. Instead, most of the OT writings appear to have developed over time, with many persons probably contributing to their formation.

For centuries, Moses was assumed to have been the sole author of the Pentateuch, with the possible exception being the account of his death and burial in Deuteronomy 34. In the twelfth century, the Jewish exegete Ibn Ezra (1092–1167) hinted, in a cryptic fashion, that some of the material might be post-Mosaic. Gradually the idea of multiple sources and authors behind this material was explored. In the eighteenth and nineteenth centuries, scholars developed the theory that four major sources, none written by Moses, had been combined to produce the Pentateuch. These sources were: (1) the J source, so-called because of its use of the name Yahweh for God (spelled Jahweh in German) and its assumed connection with Judah; (2) the E source because of its use of Elohim to refer to God and its possible connection with the northern tribe of Ephraim; (3) the D source found primarily in Deuteronomy; and (4) the P source, found primarily in the second half of Exodus and the books of Leviticus and Numbers. These sources, J, E, D, and P, were assumed to have been combined late in history to produce the Pentateuch.

If we take Amos as a typical example of a prophetical book, the diversity of material in the book makes it impossible to speak of Amos as the author. In the book, we find four types of material: (a) a superscription provides some historical data about the prophet (1:1); (b) much of the book consists of oracles or speeches attributed to the prophet (1:2–6:14; 8:4–14; 9:5–15); (c) some material is biographical, like the superscription, and speaks of the prophet in the third person (7:10–17); (d) other material reports visions by the prophet and appears to be autobiographical with the prophet referring to himself in the first person (7:1–9; 8:1–3; 9:1–4). These diverse elements in Amos suggest that it was an edited work produced by someone other than the prophet himself. Practically all of the prophetic books manifest this same type of diversity.

Evidence of collective authorship and historical growth is also reflected in thematic changes and the different political situations that are presupposed in a given OT writing. Since the Middle Ages, scholars have noted that the historical conditions, the style of the speeches, and the content of the first part of Isaiah differ from those in the second part. Isaiah 1–39 presupposes a struggling state of Judah defending itself against the aggressive and powerful Assyrian Empire. Isaiah 40–66 assumes that the Judeans are in exile and that a faltering Babylonian Empire is the major political power. The former presupposes the historical conditions of the eighth century BCE, while the latter reflects conditions of the sixth century BCE. To interpret the latter half of Isaiah as though it came from the eighth century BCE would be like interpreting a twenty-first-century writing as though it came from the nineteenth century. Like many portions of the OT, the book of Isaiah must be viewed as an anthology of materials coming from different periods.

6. As with most documents from antiquity, the oldest manuscripts of the OT and the NT we possess are copies that were made long after the original documents were written. The oldest complete manuscript of the Hebrew Bible dates from the Middle Ages (the copy was made in 1008 CE). The oldest complete manuscript of the NT dates from the fourth century CE. About 5,000 different Greek manuscripts or fragments of the NT are known. Of these, no two are identical. The manuscript copies of the Hebrew Bible or parts thereof are less numerous. In recent years, however, older fragments and almost complete manuscripts of some books of the OT have been discovered in caves and other places in the Dead Sea region of Palestine. Some of these show considerable differences from the standard Hebrew texts.

Since the Bible was translated into other languages, such as Syriac, Latin, and Coptic, these early versions must also be taken into account in our interpretations. This is particularly the case with the OT, which was translated into Greek and Aramaic during the last centuries BCE and the early centuries CE. In addition, the first five books of the OT (the Pentateuch) also exist in an early Hebrew form known as Samaritan, which differs frequently from the standard Hebrew text. All of this means, of course, that ancient translations of the original Hebrew, Aramaic, and Greek writings into other languages can provide valuable information for biblical exegetes.

7. That the Bible falls into the category of sacred Scripture needs no special comment. Two matters, however, should be noted, one positive and one negative. Positively, today's biblical exegete has been preceded by centuries of biblical study and interpretation that can be drawn upon for perspectives and insights. Negatively, the Bible as sacred Scripture is surrounded by various traditions and traditional interpretations. The exegete is frequently tempted to read the text in light of these traditions—what we were taught it meant—without exercising any critical judgment or allowing the text to speak on its own terms. To do this is to engage in what is called "eisegesis," an interpretive practice in which we read our own traditions and opinions into the text, rather than listening to what the text itself actually says.

The above considerations might suggest that exegesis of the Bible is a formidable if not impossible task. In one sense it is, but in another sense it is not. If the Bible in its manuscript and translated forms were newly discovered, and we had to approach its interpretation as a completely new endeavor, we would face a truly overwhelming challenge. Critical tools and resources would have to be developed, along with methods of approaching these new materials.

Fortunately, modern exegetes are in a different position. Probably no other book has been studied as extensively as the Bible. Through the centuries thousands of people have interpreted the Bible, developed special methods of interpretation, and prepared study resources that are now available to us. Tools for biblical study have also been prepared by scholars who have spent their lives engaged in biblical exegesis and interpretation. These scholarly materials have always been available in libraries, and now, modern technology makes them even more accessible. Having these rich resources at our disposal gives us an enormous assistance in our exegetical work.

Biblical Exegesis through the Centuries

From their earliest days, Judaism and Christianity have sought to understand their Scriptures, to explain their contents, to appropriate their meaning, and to apply and embody their teachings. The manner in which this has been done has varied through history. Some have suggested that the history of Judaism and Christianity is, in many respects, the history of how they have interpreted their respective Scriptures. How these two closely related religious communities have understood the task of interpretation says a lot about their religious self-consciousness and their relationship to the cultures within which they existed.

Broadly speaking, the history of biblical exegesis may be divided into three major periods, each of which reflects particular interests and characteristics. These are (1) the early and medieval period, (2) the period of the Reformation, with its roots in late medieval Jewish scholarship and the Renaissance, and (3) the modern period, in which earlier methods of interpretation were refined and new ones were developed. While this threefold classification oversimplifies many historical complexities, it provides a useful framework for understanding how biblical exegesis has developed.

The Early and Medieval Period

In the early phase of biblical interpretation, readers tended to assume that the faith and practices of their communities were identical with, and directly authorized by, the teachings of the Bible. Since they believed that the Bible was divinely given, they assumed that their appropriation of its teachings was divinely ordained. Interpreters of the Bible believed that they were discerning the will of God as it had been given to the biblical writers and embodied in the texts. They thought that everything in the Bible, even its difficulties and problematic texts, was divine revelation. One rabbi advised, "Search it and search it, for everything is in it."

Recognizing that biblical exegesis was a specialized discipline, ancient interpreters developed special rules for its interpretation. Rabbi Hillel (d. beginning of the first century CE) formulated seven rules for interpreting Scripture in order to determine normative practices. These were expanded to thirteen by Rabbi Ishmael in the second century and were subsequently modified and enlarged. The Christian scholar Tyconius (d. about 400) also formulated seven rules to be used in understanding biblical texts.

Generally, however, the theology of the interpreters and their respective communities influenced the results of their exegesis in this early period. This was especially the case with the Christian use of the OT. In describing how the Bible should be interpreted, Augustine (354–430 CE) wrote:

> Every student of the Divine Scriptures must exercise himself, having found nothing else in them except, first, that God is to be loved for Himself, and his neighbor for the sake of God; second, that he is to love God with all his heart, with all his soul, and with all his mind; and third, that he should love his neighbor as himself, that is, so that all love for our neighbor should, like all love for ourselves, be referred to God.

If a text did not teach love, Augustine insisted, it should not be interpreted at face value: "Whatever appears in the divine Word that does not literally pertain to virtuous behavior or to the truth of faith you must take to be figurative." This often meant ignoring the "precise meaning which the author . . . intends to express." Augustine further advised his readers that "when investigation reveals an uncertainty . . . the rule of faith [the content of Christian faith] should be consulted as it is found in the more open places of Scripture and in the authority of the Church."

When Augustine talked about the figurative meaning of texts, he was referring to the practice of finding a hidden or secondary meaning behind statements in Scripture. The practice of finding several levels of meaning within texts was widespread in the ancient world. The Greek Stoic philosophers employed allegorical interpretation to explain problematic features of Homer's *Iliad* and *Odyssey.* This enabled them to account for offensive behaviors attributed to the Olympic deities. Using allegorical interpretation, readers found philosophical and ethical teachings in the text that were not obvious in a literal reading.

This allegorical approach was greatly developed in the Egyptian city of Alexandria and was applied to the OT by the Jewish exegete Philo (d. ca. 50 CE). The Christian scholar Origen (ca. 185–254 CE) argued that all biblical texts could have more than one meaning. "Just as man consists of body, soul and spirit," Origen wrote, "in the same way so does the scripture." Because the literal meaning of some texts did not agree with accepted theology or ethics, Origen said that such texts "have no bodily sense at all, [and] there are occasions when we must seek only for the soul and the spirit, as it were, of the passage." All texts could thus be taken as having a special, secondary spiritual (symbolic, typological, or allegorical) meaning and at times the straightforward meaning could be totally ignored.

Allegorical interpretation could be applied not only to difficult and unedifying texts but also to other texts in order to edify believers. The classic example of this is Augustine's analysis of the parable of the Good Samaritan (Luke 10:29–37). Augustine said the man who went down from Jerusalem to Jericho refers to Adam. Jerusalem is the heavenly city of peace from whose blessedness Adam fell. Jericho means the moon and stands for human mortality, for the moon is born, waxes, wanes, and dies. The thieves who attacked Adam are the devil and his angels. They stripped him of his immortality and beat him by persuading him to sin. They left him half dead. The priest and the Levite who passed the man by without helping him are the priesthood and ministry of the OT which cannot bring salvation. The term Samaritan is taken to mean Guardian; thus it refers to Jesus himself. The binding of the wounds is the restraint of sin. Oil is the comfort of good hope, and wine is the exhortation to work with fervent spirit. The beast on which the man was placed signifies the flesh in which Christ appeared among men. Being set on the beast means belief in the incarnation of Christ. The inn to which the man is taken is the church, where persons are refreshed on their pilgrimage of return to the heavenly city. The two pieces of money that the Samaritan gave to the innkeeper are the promise of this life and of life to come, or else the two main sacraments. The innkeeper is the apostle Paul.

Not everyone in the early church favored this type of allegorical interpretation, in which readers looked for multiple levels of meaning in the biblical text. A group of interpreters associated with Antioch of Syria, such as John Chrysostom (ca. 347–407) and Theodore of Mopsuestia (ca. 350–428), emphasized the literal meaning of Scripture. Rather than looking for the hidden (allegorical) meaning behind a biblical statement, they sought to understand the inspired writer's intended meaning. For the Antiochian school of interpretation, a typological or nonliteral reading of a biblical text was permissible only when it did no violence to the straightforward or literal meaning.

Eventually the interpretive approach of finding multiple meanings in texts dominated. The standard practice throughout most of the Middle Ages was to look for four meanings in a text: (a) the literal (straightforward or historical) meaning, (b) the allegorical (spiritualized or symbolic) meaning, (c) the tropological (moral or ethical) meaning, and (d) the anagogical (eschatological or heavenly) meaning. A short medieval Latin poem gave expression to this approach:

> The letter shows us what God and our fathers did;
> The allegory shows us where our faith is hid;
> The moral meaning gives us rules of daily life;
> The anagogy shows us where we end our strife.

While Jewish exegesis developed in many directions, it tended to adhere more closely to the literal meaning. Perhaps this resulted from Jewish resistance to interpretive approaches influenced by Greek philosophy, or from a greater desire to follow the explicit edicts and teachings of the biblical texts. Nonetheless, even Jewish exegesis eventually devised a fourfold interpretation of texts: (a) *peshat* (the plain meaning), (b) *remez* (allusion or allegory), (c) *derash* (the homiletical appropriation), and (d) *sod* (the mystical or secret). This fourfold interpretation of a text came to be referred to by the acronym PaRDeS, which means "Paradise."

Late Renaissance and Reformation

In the fifteenth and sixteenth centuries, important shifts of perspective occurred in biblical interpretation and exegesis. The impetus for some of these shifts came from Jewish scholarship of the eleventh and twelfth centuries. Scholars like Ibn Ezra (d. 1167) and Rashi (d. 1105) stressed the grammatical analysis of texts, which had as its goal the elucidation of the plain meaning (*peshat*) of texts. Renaissance scholars of the fourteenth and fifteenth centuries rediscovered early classical texts, and they formulated new approaches that took these new discoveries into account.

1. Interpretation played down the desire to find multiple meanings in biblical texts while still holding to the inspiration of the Scriptures. Martin Luther (1483–1546), for example, declared: "The Holy Spirit is the plainest writer and speaker in heaven and earth, and therefore His words cannot have more than one, and that the very simplest, sense, which we call the literal, ordinary, natural, sense."

2. There was a break with traditional interpretation as the best means of understanding texts. Throughout the Middle Ages, interpretation often meant nothing more than noting what the church fathers and earlier authorities had said about a text. The new impetus tended to bypass tradition in order to let the texts speak for themselves. This emphasis they designated as *ad fontes* ("to the sources").

3. Translations into the common languages meant a break with the Christian custom of using the Bible only in Latin. This development raised the problem of which text was to be used in making translations. It also stimulated the study of Hebrew and Greek and the printing of texts in the original biblical languages.

4. The freedom granted interpreters in Protestantism, rather than producing the unanimity of opinion that the Reformers had rather naively assumed would result, led instead to a multitude of opinions believed to be based on sound exegesis and interpretation. But it soon became obvious that the theological stance and historical situation of the interpreters played an important role in exegesis.

5. The development of secular learning—philosophy, science, and general humanistic thought—meant that the Bible was no longer taken as the final, exclusive authority on many matters. Reason came to occupy an important role in the wider culture. New rationalistic explanations of history and human behavior came into conflict with systems of thought based on the Bible, revelation, and ecclesiastical tradition.

6. A new understanding of history, especially as it related to the Bible, affected interpretation. In the medieval world, the past and present tended to blend into a unified whole. Rather than viewing the past

as a previous, distinct period, medieval thinkers often saw the past as an earlier expression of the present. With the development of history as an academic discipline, scholars drew attention to the chronological and cultural gaps between the present and the past. Firmly anchored in the past, the Bible was increasingly seen as a book that originated in the distant past and reflected an archaic outlook.

The Modern Period: Post-Enlightenment to the Present

The modern period of biblical interpretation, extending from the Enlightenment to the present, was characterized by one general aim: to study and understand the biblical documents as one would any other set of documents from antiquity. The historical setting of the biblical writers and their compositions received increased attention. Interpreters emphasized the relationship between content and context. The message of the biblical writings was examined in light of the ancient contexts in which they were produced.

Because of this new emphasis, the Bible was studied from many new perspectives. It was also subjected to a variety of methodological approaches. It was used to reconstruct the history and religion of Israel and the early church. It was also compared with the literature of other early cultures. Many interpreters were also attracted to the Bible because of its aesthetic and artistic values. These new approaches took their place alongside study of the Bible for its religious values and theological insights. Throughout this period, the Bible continued to serve as the foundation document for both Judaism and Christianity. Today the Bible is often studied and taught in contexts that are strictly academic, without a community of faith. In subsequent chapters of this handbook, we will examine some of the approaches that developed out of this period.

The Task of Biblical Exegesis

Exegesis should be seen as a systematic way of interpreting a text. As noted earlier, everyone engages in exegesis, but biblical exegesis has its own specialized needs and disciplines. Its goal, however, is quite simple: to reach an informed understanding of the text. This is different from saying that the exegete seeks to determine *the* meaning of the text. A biblical text can be meaningful at different levels, depending on the interpreter's perspective and goals. Different types of exegesis have been developed to address these multiple dimensions of meaning.

Because texts yield meaning in different ways, we can never produce an exegesis as though it were the final word. Each time we return to a classic text such as the Bible we can expect to find fresh meaning. With each new encounter, our goal is the same: to develop a coherent, informed interpretation that is based on the best knowledge available to us. Even if we have read a biblical text many times, with each new reading we may see it from a different perspective and experience new insights. Exegesis does not allow us to master the text so much as it enables us to enter it.

Exegesis may be thought of as learning how to interrogate the text. Our questions arise in different ways. We may bring certain questions to a text before we read it. Or reading the text may prompt new questions. We can put many questions to a text, but doing exegesis is often a matter of knowing which questions to ask. As we gain experience in interpreting texts, we realize that some questions are worth pursuing, while others are not; or that some questions are answerable in ways that others are not. As a rule, certain types of interpretation have arisen in order to address a specific set of questions. The questions we ask of a text determine what methods we employ to interpret it.

We can appreciate the multiple aspects of exegesis by drawing on the study of linguistics. One way of understanding the process of communication is through the "communication triangle." In highly simplified form, it can be depicted as follows:

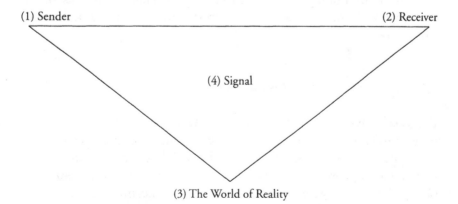

(1) Sender   (2) Receiver

(4) Signal

(3) The World of Reality

In this diagram, the sender represents the speaker, writer, or artist with whom the communication originates. The receiver is the audience, listener, hearer, or reader to whom the communication is addressed or is of interest. The world of reality denotes the universe of objects, ideas, and meanings that are shared by the sender and receiver and make communication possible. The signal is the means of communication. For the artist, the signal is the work of art; for a writer it is the text.

A similar schematic diagram, which is widely used to illustrate various literary-critical theories, offers some close parallels to the communication triangle. This second diagram is as follows:

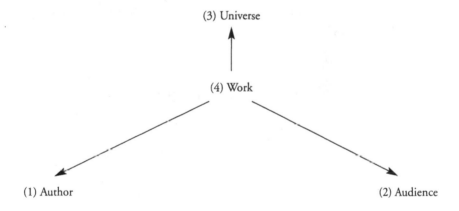

If we apply the first model to biblical interpretation, the following triangle would result:

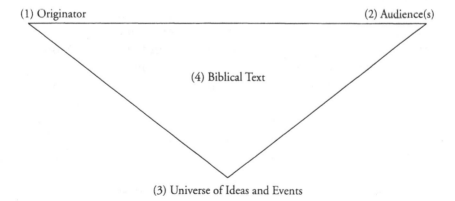

The originator of the biblical text may be an author, editor, or redactor. Or a given text may have had numerous authors, editors, or redactors. In some cases, the originator is best understood as a community, for example, a group within Israel responsible for producing certain psalms. The audience may be the original hearer or reader, but it can also include subsequent hearers or readers. The universe of ideas is the thought world, perspectives, and understandings that are shared by the originator(s) and audience(s). This shared universe of ideas, which is mirrored within the biblical text, enables communication to occur. The signal is the medium of communication, which originally may have been oral or written but now exists in written form.

If we apply the second diagram to the process of biblical interpretation, it looks as follows:

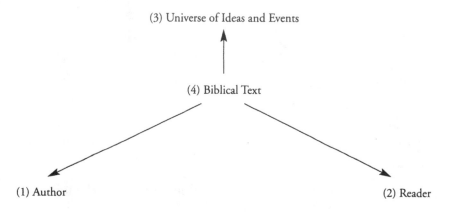

(3) Universe of Ideas and Events

(4) Biblical Text

(1) Author   (2) Reader

Problems that confront us as modern exegetes may be classified according to which part of the model our questions address. We can also use the model to illustrate the ancient or modern communication process. We can interrogate the text in terms of the author's initial communication, the (hypothetical) original shape of the text, the world of ideas shared by the original parties to the communication, and the original audience's hearing, understanding, and reception of the communication. Or we can ask about later forms of the text, later audiences, and later understandings of reality. As modern readers, we can see ourselves as an audience, reading the text in an even later form (generally in translation, for example) and in the context of a universe of ideas that differs significantly from that of the original participants.

Specific types of biblical criticism have been developed to answer certain questions or solve certain problems in the task of biblical exegesis. In the remainder of this book, we will be discussing some of these methods: what questions they intended to address and how they developed. Our choice of topics to treat is not arbitrary. Over the centuries, a broad consensus has developed among biblical interpreters about the kinds of questions to ask, the problems to be encountered, and the methods to be employed. Debates still continue about the value of asking certain questions and the usefulness of various types of biblical criticism. But we cannot pretend that these questions have never been asked before or that our predecessors have not worked hard to formulate meaningful ways of responding to these questions.

Like all historical processes, this centuries-long discussion has registered gains and losses. Some methods of interpretation are no longer in vogue, while others have endured over time. The variety of methods to be discussed attests to the richness and diversity of the biblical documents. Often, these methods of interpretation complement each other. This reminds us that there is not just one approach to a biblical text but many. Even when we employ several methods, we still cannot establish a single meaning for a biblical passage.

We treat these different approaches as types of criticism, which is a technical expression used by scholars to denote a field of study in which some clearly defined principles and techniques have been developed. The word "criticism" derives from the Greek word *krinein*, meaning "to judge" or "to discern." It refers to a process of thinking in which discerning judgments are made. A literary critic is one who studies literary documents, attempting to make intelligent and informed judgments about them as literature. In the end, such judgments may be negative or positive, complimentary or uncomplimentary, but "criticism" per se is a neutral term. Biblical criticism, as a broad category, encompasses many subdisciplines and a wide variety of interpretive activities that seek to make discerning judgments about the Bible. As such, "being critical" is not equivalent to "being destructive." Rather, it signifies an attempt to reach an informed judgment about a creative work or writing.

Most of the questions that arise when modern readers engage in exegesis can be classified under one or more of the types of criticism. When we discover a variant reading within a text and wonder what the original wording might have been, we are addressing problems that are dealt with in *textual criticism*. Before interpreting any biblical text, we must decide at the outset the wording of the text to be considered.

Another set of questions pertains to the historical, geographical, and cultural setting of the text: the context of the original author(s) and audience(s). If certain customs, events, places, and names mentioned in the text are unfamiliar to us, we must gather information about them in order to develop an informed understanding of the text. This applies not only to matters referred to in the text itself but also to the setting in which the text originated and its history of transmission. Determining the chronological period, geographical locale, and authorship of the document can be equally important. Such questions fall under the rubric of *historical criticism*.

Grammatical criticism deals with questions relating to the language of the text. This includes the words themselves, either singly or in phrases, as well as syntax—the way in which the words are put together in sentences or paragraphs. Understanding the grammar of a passage may require us to become familiar with the rules of grammar that were in effect at the time the passage was written. Often interpretive questions can be resolved only through grammatical analysis.

Concern with the style, character, compositional techniques, and rhetorical patterns constitutes the field of *literary criticism*. (Frequently, in biblical studies, literary criticism has been too narrowly identified with source analysis, which comprises only one aspect of literary criticism.) Where the passage is located and how it functions within the larger literary document are often crucial for understanding a text. Since most of the biblical documents originally existed in oral form or were written to be read aloud, ancient authors usually gave close attention to how the material should be arranged for maximum effect upon listeners. For this reason, we must also attend to rhetorical features of a text.

If literary criticism deals with how the passage is structured and how it relates to its larger literary unit, *form criticism* focuses more narrowly on a single passage or subunits in a passage. Special attention is given to the literary form, or genre, of the passage. Here we ask, for example, whether a passage is a narrative, a story, a parable, a prophetic speech, or a hymn. These questions have become important to biblical interpreters because of the close relationship between form and meaning. We read a poem one way, prose another. The literary form of a passage creates certain expectations for the interpreter. Form criticism also deals with the social context in which texts originated. These "life settings" include such varied activities as worship, teaching, preaching, and debate.

It is now widely recognized that the Bible, in many of its parts, resembles an anthology of sacred writings in which revered stories, traditions, and sayings uttered by individuals and preserved by various communities have been collected, edited, and formed into a single text.

Many of these texts have a "prehistory," which means that they were spoken or written much earlier than their incorporation into the biblical text itself. Efforts to uncover the earlier stages of development through which a text has passed are dealt with under *tradition criticism*.

Even though a text might have a prehistory, we find it located within a specific biblical writing. For this reason, we also ask how the author(s) or editor(s) intended a passage to be understood in its final literary form. *Redaction criticism* focuses on the changes or redactions a text underwent in reaching its final form. It assesses the significance of such changes and how these reveal the theological outlook of the author or editor.

Some interpreters read the biblical text without regard to such historically oriented matters as the origin of the text, the intention of the author, and the original audience. Such approaches focus on the structure of the text and how universal beliefs are embodied within it. *Structural criticism*, an approach that draws heavily on literary and philosophical theory in nonbiblical disciplines, addresses these dimensions of the text. This form of biblical criticism uses the structure of a text as a clue for deriving its meaning.

Over the centuries, the various biblical writings have been compiled into defined collections from which certain writings have been excluded. These prescribed lists of writings constitute the Jewish and Christian canons. When several sacred writings are collected into a single book, the Bible, the whole becomes more than the sum of the parts. Individual writings are read not only in their own right but in light of each other and in light of the whole. *Canonical criticism* explores how the Scriptures were transmitted and shaped by believing communities to produce a canon and how these texts are to be read and understood as parts of a collection of sacred writings.

By distinguishing these different types of biblical criticism, we do not imply that exegesis is a mechanical undertaking that occurs in a stair-step fashion, as if one method or stage of exegesis always leads to the next. Depending on the nature of a particular text, questions may arise in different ways. Initially we may be puzzled by literary or historical features of a text and only later discover that an important textual variant within the passage needs to be clarified. Even though questions may arise from the text in a somewhat random fashion, they need not be pursued randomly. Even the novice interpreter soon discovers that there are systematic ways of tackling various exegetical questions.

Exegesis generally occurs in two stages: analysis and synthesis. At the outset, we examine different aspects of the passage, including historical, grammatical, and literary questions related to the text. This helps us "break down" the passage into its component parts. We address individual problems and investigate discrete units of material. Even though we may pursue these questions separately, they often relate to each other, even inform each other. As we analyze a text, our understanding of the passage gradually increases. Here we are laying the groundwork for synthesis.

By synthesis we mean the process by which we pull together the results of our investigation. In analysis we deconstruct the text; in synthesis we reconstruct it. In the latter, our goal is to relate our analytical investigations to each other, weigh the significance of individual findings in light of the others, and decide how all of these contribute to our overall understanding of the passage.

As exegesis takes place, we discover that it has both a positive and a negative function. Positively, we are able to make certain claims about the text that were previously unknown or uncertain to us. In this way, exegesis produces new knowledge, at least for the interpreter. Negatively, we may succeed only in determining what the text *cannot* mean. Sometimes the most productive part of exegesis is exposing false understandings of a text. We may discover that what we thought a text meant is not supported by the evidence we have uncovered. But even negative knowledge can be positive.

We may employ the tools, methods, and approaches of different forms of biblical criticism, such as lexicography, textual criticism, and historical analysis, all of which can be highly technical, even scientific, in nature. But exegesis is as much art as it is science. It requires both imagination and creativity, not only in learning how to put questions to a text, but also in learning how to answer these questions. Above all, exegesis requires that we synthesize our answers into a coherent, meaningful interpretation of the passage. Exegesis may draw on several theological specialties, many of them highly technical, but it also challenges us to draw on our creative capacities in developing informed, imaginative, interesting, and compelling interpretations of the Bible.

BIBLIOGRAPHY

(Items marked with an asterisk are especially recommended as additional reading for beginning students.)

Bibliographies

*Bauer, David R. *An Annotated Guide to Biblical Resources for Ministry.* Peabody, MA: Hendrickson, 2003.

Carson, D. A. *New Testament Commentary Survey.* 6th ed. Grand Rapids: Baker Academic, 2007.

*Childs, Brevard S. *Old Testament Books for Pastor and Teacher.* Philadelphia: Westminster, 1977.

*Danker, Frederick W. *Multipurpose Tools for Bible Study.* Rev. and exp. ed. Minneapolis: Fortress, 2003.

*Fitzmyer, Joseph A. *An Introductory Bibliography for the Study of Scripture.* 3rd ed. Rome: Editrice pontificio istituto biblico, 1990.

France, Richard T., Graham N. Stanton, and Alan R. Millard. *A Bibliographical Guide to New Testament Research.* 3rd ed. Sheffield: JSOT, 1983.

Glynn, John. *Commentary and Reference Survey: A Comprehensive Guide to Biblical and Theological Resources.* 10th ed. Fully revised and updated. Grand Rapids: Kregel, 2007.

Hurd, John C., Jr. *A Bibliography of New Testament Bibliographies.* New York: Seabury, 1966.

Longman, Tremper. *Old Testament Commentary Survey.* 4th ed. Grand Rapids: Baker Academic, 2007.

Marrow, Stanley B. *Basic Tools of Biblical Exegesis.* Rome: Biblical Institute, 1978.

*Martin, Ralph P. *New Testament Books for Pastor and Teacher.* Rev. and updated. Eugene, OR: Wipf & Stock, 2002.

Scholer, David M. *A Basic Bibliographic Guide for New Testament Exegesis.* 3rd ed. Grand Rapids: Eerdmans, 2002.

Stewart, David R., and John A. Bollier. *The Literature of Theology: A Guide for Students and Pastors.* Rev. ed. Louisville, KY: Westminster John Knox, 2003.

Wagner, Günter, ed. *An Exegetical Bibliography of the New Testament.* Macon, GA: Mercer University Press, 1983–.

Biblical Exegesis

*Barton, John. *Reading the Old Testament: Method in Biblical Study.* 2nd ed. Rev. and enl. London: Darton, Longman & Todd; Louisville, KY: Westminster John Knox, 1996.

Brettler, Marc Zvi. *How to Read the Bible.* Philadelphia: Jewish Publication Society, 2005.

Brown, Raymond E. *Biblical Exegesis and Church Doctrine.* Repr. Eugene, OR: Wipf & Stock, 2002 (1986).

Broyles, Craig C., ed. *Interpreting the Old Testament: A Guide for Exegesis.* Grand Rapids: Baker, 2001.

Carson, Donald A. *Exegetical Fallacies.* 2nd ed. Carlisle, UK: Paternoster; Grand Rapids: Baker, 1996.

Conzelmann, Hans, and Andreas Lindemann. *Interpreting the New Testament: An Introduction to the Principles and Methods of New Testament Exegesis.* Peabody, MA: Hendrickson, 1999.

Erickson, Richard J. *A Beginner's Guide to New Testament Exegesis: Taking the Fear out of Critical Method.* Downers Grove, IL: InterVarsity, 2005.

Fee, Gordon D. *New Testament Exegesis: A Handbook for Students and Pastors.* 3rd ed. Louisville, KY: Westminster John Knox, 2002.

Fee, Gordon D., and Douglas K. Stuart. *How to Read the Bible for All Its Worth.* 3rd ed. Grand Rapids: Zondervan, 2003.

Gorman, Michael J. *Elements of Biblical Exegesis: A Basic Guide for Students and Ministers.* Peabody, MA: Hendrickson, 2001.

*Haynes, Stephen R., and Steven L. McKenzie, eds. *To Each Its Own Meaning: An Introduction to Biblical Criticisms and Their Applications.* Rev. and exp. ed. Louisville, KY: Westminster John Knox, 1999.

Kaiser, Otto, and Werner G. Kümmel. *Exegetical Method: A Student's Handbook.* Rev. ed. New York: Seabury, 1981.

Kaiser, Walter C. *Toward an Exegetical Theology: Biblical Exegesis for Preaching and Teaching.* Grand Rapids: Baker, 1998.

Kee, Howard C., Eric M. Meyers, John Rogerson, Amy-Jill Levine, and Bruce Chilton, eds. *Cambridge Companion to the Bible.* 2nd ed. Cambridge: Cambridge University Press, 2008.

Klauck, Hans-Josef. *Ancient Letters and the New Testament: A Guide to Context and Exegesis.* Waco, TX: Baylor University Press, 2006.

Marshall, I. Howard, ed. *New Testament Interpretation: Essays on Principles and Methods.* Carlisle, UK: Paternoster, 1985; Grand Rapids: Eerdmans, 1997.

McKenzie, Steve L. *How to Read the Bible.* Oxford and New York: Oxford University Press, 2005.

McKnight, Scot, ed. *Introducing New Testament Interpretation.* Grand Rapids: Baker, 1989.

Porter, Stanley E., ed. *Handbook to Exegesis of the New Testament.* Leiden: Brill, 1997.

Schertz, Mary H., and Perry B. Yoder. *Seeing the Text: Exegesis for Students of Greek and Hebrew.* Nashville: Abingdon, 2001.

*Soulen, Richard N., and R. Kendall Soulen. *Handbook of Biblical Criticism.* 3rd ed. Rev. and exp. Louisville, KY: Westminster John Knox, 2001.

Steck, Odil H. *Old Testament Exegesis: A Guide to the Methodology.* 2nd ed. Atlanta: Scholars, 1998.

Stuart, Douglas. *Old Testament Exegesis: A Handbook for Students and Pastors.* 3rd ed. Louisville, KY: Westminster John Knox, 2001.

Tate, W. Randolph. *Interpreting the Bible: A Handbook of Terms and Methods.* Peabody, MA: Hendrickson, 2006.

Williams, David M. *Receiving the Bible in Faith: Historical and Theological Exegesis.* Washington, DC: Catholic University of America Press, 2004.

Yoder, Perry B. *From Word to Life: A Guide to the Art of Bible Study*. Scottdale, PA: Herald, 1982.
Young, Frances M. *Biblical Exegesis and the Formation of Christian Culture*. Cambridge and New York: Cambridge University Press, 1997.

Annotated Study Bibles

Attridge, Harold W., Wayne A. Meeks, Jouette M. Bassler, Werner E. Lemke, Susan Niditch, and Eileen M. Schuller, eds. *The HarperCollins Study Bible: New Revised Standard Version, including the Apocrypha/Deuterocanonical Books with Concordance*. Fully revised and updated. San Francisco: HarperSanFrancisco, 2006.
Barker, Kenneth L., John H. Stek, and Ronald Youngblood, eds. *TNIV Study Bible*. Grand Rapids: Zondervan, 2006.
Berlin, Adele, Marc Zvi Brettler, and Michael Fishbane, eds. *The Jewish Study Bible: Featuring the Jewish Publication Society Tanakh Translation*. New York: Oxford University Press, 2004.
Coogan, Michael, Marc Zvi Brettler, Carol A. Newsom, and Pheme Perkins, eds. *The New Oxford Annotated Bible: With the Apocryphal/Deuterocanonical Books*. Augmented 3rd ed. New York: Oxford University Press, 2007.
Harrelson, Walter J., Donald Senior, Abraham Smith, Phyllis Trible, and James C. VanderKam, eds. *The New Interpreter's Study Bible: New Revised Standard Version with the Apocrypha*. Nashville: Abingdon, 2003.
Kee, Howard C., ed. *The Cambridge Annotated Study Bible: New Revised Standard Version*. Cambridge and New York: Cambridge University Press, 1993.
Kroeger, Catherine C., and Mary J. Evans, eds. *The IVP Women's Bible Commentary*. Downers Grove, IL: InterVarsity, 2002.
NIV Archaeological Study Bible: An Illustrated Walk through Biblical History and Culture. Grand Rapids: Zondervan, 2005.
O'Day, Gail R., and David Petersen, eds. *The Access Bible: New Revised Standard Version with the Apocryphal/Deuterocanonical Books*. New York: Oxford University Press, 1999.
Saint Mary's Press College Study Bible: New American Bible. Winona, MN: Saint Mary's Press, 2007.
Senior, Donald, and J. J. Collins, eds. *The Catholic Study Bible: New American Bible*. 2nd ed. New York: Oxford University Press, 2006.
Suggs, M. Jack, Katherine D. Sakenfeld, and James R. Mueller. *The Oxford Study Bible: Revised English Bible with the Apocrypha*. New York: Oxford University Press, 1992.

History of Biblical Interpretation

Ackroyd, Peter R., C. F. Evans, G. W. H. Lampe, and S. H. Greenslade, eds. *Cambridge History of the Bible*. 3 vols. London and New York: Cambridge University Press, 1963–1970.

Baird, William. *History of New Testament Research.* 3 vols. Minneapolis: Fortress, 1992–.

Bray, Gerald Lewis. *Biblical Interpretation: Past and Present.* Downers Grove, IL: Inter-Varsity; Leicester, UK: Apollos, 1996.

*Clements, R. E. *One Hundred Years of Old Testament Interpretation* = *A Century of Old Testament Study.* Rev. ed. Guildford, UK: Lutterworth; Philadelphia: Westminster, 1976.

"Cook, John G. *The Interpretation of the New Testament in Greco-Roman Paganism.* Peabody, MA: Hendrickson, 2002 (2000).

———. *The Interpretation of the Old Testament in Greco-Roman Paganism.* Tübingen: Mohr Siebeck, 2004.

De Hamel, Christopher. *The Book: A History of the Bible.* New York: Phaidon, 2001.

Evans, Gillian R. *The Language and Logic of the Bible: The Earlier Middle Ages.* Cambridge and New York: Cambridge University Press, 1991.

———. *The Language and Logic of the Bible: The Road to Reformation.* Cambridge and New York: Cambridge University Press, 1985.

Fishbane, Michael. *Biblical Interpretation in Ancient Israel.* Oxford: Clarendon Press; New York: Oxford University Press, 1985.

Froehlich, Karlfried. *Biblical Interpretation in the Early Church.* Philadelphia: Fortress, 1984.

*Grant, Robert M., with David Tracy. *A Short History of the Interpretation of the Bible.* 2nd ed. Rev. and enl. London: SCM; Philadelphia: Fortress, 1984.

Greer, Rowan. *Anglican Approaches to Scripture: From the Reformation to the Present.* New York: Crossroad, 2006.

Hahn, Herbert F., and Horace D. Hummel. *The Old Testament in Modern Research.* Exp. ed., with rev. bibliographical essay. Philadelphia: Fortress, 1970.

Harrisville, Roy A., and Walter Sundberg. *The Bible in Modern Culture: Baruch Spinoza to Brevard Childs.* 2nd ed. Grand Rapids: Eerdmans, 2002.

Hauser, Alan J., and Duane F. Watson, eds. *A History of Biblical Interpretation.* 3 vols. Grand Rapids: Eerdmans, 2003–.

*Hayes, John H., ed. *Dictionary of Biblical Interpretation.* 2 vols. Nashville: Abingdon, 1999.

Kugel, James L., and Rowan A. Greer. *Early Biblical Interpretation.* Philadelphia: Westminster, 1986.

Kümmel, Werner G. *The New Testament: The History of the Investigation of Its Problems.* Nashville: Abingdon, 1972; London: SCM, 1973.

McAuliffe, Jane D., Barry Walfish, and Joseph W. Goering, eds. *With Reverence for the Word: Medieval Scriptural Exegesis in Judaism, Christianity, and Islam.* Oxford and New York: Oxford University Press, 2003.

Morgan, Robert, with John Barton. *Biblical Interpretation.* Oxford and New York: Oxford University Press, 1988.

*Neill, Stephen, and N. T. Wright. *The Interpretation of the New Testament, 1861–1986.* 2nd ed. London and New York: Oxford University Press, 1988.

O'Keefe, John J., and Russell R. Reno, eds. *Sanctified Vision: An Introduction to Early Christian Interpretation of the Bible.* Baltimore: Johns Hopkins University Press, 2005.

*Pelikan, Jaroslav. *Whose Bible Is It? A Short History of the Scriptures.* London and New York: Penguin, 2006.

Porter, Stanley. *Dictionary of Biblical Criticism and Interpretation.* London and New York: Routledge, 2006.

Reventlow, Henning G. *The Authority of the Bible and the Rise of the Modern World.* London: SCM, 1984; Philadelphia: Fortress, 1985.

Riches, John. *A Century of New Testament Study.* Cambridge: Lutterworth, 1993.

Rogerson, John. *Old Testament Criticism in the Nineteenth Century: England and Germany.* London: SPCK, 1984; Philadelphia: Fortress, 1985.

———, ed. *The Oxford Illustrated History of the Bible.* Oxford and New York: Oxford University Press, 2001.

Sæbø, Magne, ed. *Hebrew Bible/Old Testament: The History of Its Interpretation.* 3 vols. in 5. Göttingen: Vandenhoeck & Ruprecht, 1996–.

Sandys-Wunsch, John. *What Have They Done to the Bible? History of Modern Biblical Interpretation.* Collegeville, MN: Liturgical Press, 2005.

Simonetti, Manlio. *Biblical Interpretation in the Early Church: An Historical Introduction to Patristic Exegesis.* Edinburgh: T. & T. Clark, 1994.

Smalley, Beryl. *The Study of the Bible in the Middle Ages.* 3rd ed. Oxford: Blackwell, 1983.

Trebolle Barrera, Julio C. *The Jewish Bible and the Christian Bible: An Introduction to the History of the Bible.* Leiden: Brill; Grand Rapids: Eerdmans, 1998.

Yarchin, William. *History of Biblical Interpretation: A Reader.* Peabody, MA: Hendrickson, 2004.

2
Textual Criticism
The Quest for the Original Wording

When studying the Bible, we often discover variations in the wording of the text in ancient manuscripts. The technical terms used to describe such variations are "textual variants" and "variant readings." The field of study that is devoted to this aspect of biblical interpretation is known as textual criticism. Scholars who specialize in this area are called textual critics.

Textual criticism is one of the oldest forms of biblical criticism. Many ancient authors, such as Origen of Alexandria (ca. 185–254 CE), were keenly aware of the different forms in which biblical writings were written and preserved. They recognized the implications of this complex textual situation for interpreting the Bible. By devoting extensive attention to the study of how these various texts and translations of the Bible were transmitted, they became pioneers of textual criticism. Origen, for example, placed six different versions in parallel columns, creating an enormous "parallel Bible" (Hexapla), which has survived only in fragments. The first printed edition of the Bible to note variant readings from different manuscripts was an edition of the NT published in 1550 by Robert Estienne (1503–59). By the time John Mills (1645–1707) published his edition of the NT in 1707, more than 30,000 variant readings were included.

Discovering Textual Variants

As modern interpreters, we encounter textual variants in different ways. Sometimes this occurs when we read the same passage in different translations. For example, reading the story of the Ethiopian eunuch's conversion in Acts 8 in the King James Version, we notice his confession given in verse 37. Reading the same account in the New Revised Standard Version, we discover that this verse is missing from the text. Instead, it is placed in a footnote and prefaced with the remark: "Other ancient authorities add all or most of verse 37."

One of the most famous textual variants occurs in 1 John 5:7. In the King James Version, the text reads: "There are three that bear record in heaven, the Father, the Word, and the Holy Ghost, and these three are one." When Erasmus (ca. 1466–1536) published the first edition of his NT in Greek (1516), he omitted these words, although they were found in the Latin Vulgate, because they were not in any Greek manuscript available to him. They were later included in Erasmus's third and subsequent editions, because a Greek manuscript "turned up" that included them. Thus they were later translated as part of the King James Version. Modern translations, like the New Revised Standard Version, relegate this obvious Trinitarian gloss to a footnote.

We may also detect variant readings in a passage even if we are working exclusively with one of the major committee translations of the Bible, such as the New Revised Standard Version (NRSV), the Revised English Bible (REB), the New Jerusalem Bible (NJB), the New Jewish Publication Society Translation of the Hebrew Text *Tanakh: The Holy Scriptures* (NJPS), the New International Version (NIV), or the New American Bible (NAB). Reading a passage in one of these modern translations, we may be referred to a footnote in which we find unfamiliar symbols and abbreviations.

For example, in the NRSV text of Micah 4:13, we read: "you shall beat in pieces many peoples, and shall devote their gain to the LORD." In the footnote attached to the word "shall" we find: "Gk Syr Tg: Heb *and I will.*" This note tells us that the NRSV wording follows the Greek translation of the OT, also known as the Septuagint, here abbreviated as "Gk"; a reading found also in the Syriac translation (Syr); and the Aramaic translation of the Hebrew Bible, commonly designated

Targums (Tg). The text of the Bible in Hebrew, here abbreviated as "Heb," has a variant reading, which is given in italics: *and I will.*

Another example is Genesis 10:5, in which the NRSV has: "These are the descendants of Japheth in their lands." The footnote attached to the word "Japheth" says: "Compare verses 20, 31. Heb lacks *These are the descendants of Japheth.*" This footnote tells us that the italicized phrase, which is found in the NRSV text of Genesis 10:5, does not appear in the Hebrew Bible. But when we compare verse 20, "These are the descendants of Ham," and verse 31, "These are the descendants of Shem," of chapter 10, we see that the NRSV translators concluded that a similar phrase was found originally in verse 5 but dropped out for some reason. They decided to include the phrase in verse 5 even though it is not found in the Hebrew Bible or in any ancient translation.

A striking example of a modern translation adding a section to the text can be seen at 1 Samuel 10:27 in the NRSV. An entire, previously unknown, paragraph has been added:

> Now Nahash, king of the Ammonites, had been grievously oppressing the Gadites and the Reubenites. He would gouge out the right eye of each of them and would not grant Israel a deliverer. No one was left of the Israelites across the Jordan whose right eye Nahash, king of the Ammonites, had not gouged out. But there were seven thousand men who had escaped from the Ammonites and had entered Jabesh-gilead.

This addition is made on the basis of the reading of one Hebrew manuscript discovered among the Dead Sea Scrolls. This is indicated in the NRSV footnote by the abbreviation "Q Ms," which stands for a Qumran manuscript discovered near the Dead Sea. The reference to Josephus (ca. 37–100 CE) acknowledges that this Jewish historian may have been familiar with such a text (see *Antiquities* 6.5.1 [68–71]). The final note "MT lacks *Now Jahash . . . entered Jabesh-gilead*" indicates that this paragraph is absent in the Masoretic Text (in pointed Hebrew) of the OT.

Sometimes, the reader encounters differences among translations that are not based on any ancient version. A translation may include a term or phrase not found in the original or any version. (The original KJV printed all of these in italics.) In Psalm 109:6, for example, the NRSV adds "they say," but reports in a textual note that this phrase is not found in Hebrew (or in any version!). The translators here have inserted an "interpretive variant" since they believed that, beginning in verse 6, the psalmist began to quote what others said about him. Such readings are generally noted as "Cn," that is, "Correction" (see note attached to the word "father" in v. 14 of the same psalm). Such readings are not textual but interpretive variants and are always open to question.

As interpreters, we frequently find textual notations about variant readings in modern translations of the Bible. As we encounter them, we are led to ask: What accounts for these variations of wording within a text? Which of the variants represents the original reading? Or can we even determine the original wording of a text? Understanding the nature of our earliest biblical manuscripts (handwritten texts) can help us appreciate why such notations occur, what they mean, and how to use them.

How Biblical Texts Were Preserved and Transmitted

None of the original manuscripts, or autographs, of any biblical writing has been preserved. So far as we know, no firsthand, or even second-hand, copy of any of the original manuscripts has survived. What have survived are manuscripts, written much later than the original, in which scribes have copied earlier copies. These copies vary in date, but the oldest are usually copies of single books of the Bible. Quite often, only small parts, even tiny fragments, of individual writings have survived.

The oldest surviving manuscript fragment of an OT writing in Hebrew dates from the third century BCE, while the earliest extant NT manuscript is a fragment from the Gospel of John dating from the early second century CE. Since there is a chronological gap between what was written originally by a biblical author (or what was compiled by an editor) and the earliest surviving copy, it is probably an illusion to assume that we can ever recover with certainty the original wording of a biblical text.

Thousands of copies of biblical writings have been preserved from ancient times. Some of these are complete manuscripts containing the entire Hebrew OT or Greek NT or major portions of each testament. Many others are manuscripts of individual books that are either complete or virtually complete. Still others are manuscripts containing only portions of single books. No two of these manuscripts are identical in every detail.

As early as the third century BCE, the OT began to be translated into Greek. Later, it was translated into other languages, including Syriac (a Semitic language akin to Aramaic) and Latin. Shortly after the NT was written, it began to be translated, first into Syriac, later into Latin. It was also translated into other languages that were more regional, such as Coptic, an Egyptian dialect. Often manuscripts of these translations, even in the same language, differ significantly from one another.

We often find considerable differences between the translations of biblical writings and their original Hebrew or Greek counterparts. For example, the Hebrew version of Job is one-sixth longer than the Greek version. The Greek version of Jeremiah is about one-eighth shorter than the Hebrew version, and much of the material in the Greek version is arranged in a different order.

Because of the popularity of the biblical writings, they were often quoted in commentaries and other written works that dealt with biblical topics. Quotations of the same biblical passage vary from one writer to another, or even within the same writer. These biblical quotations by later Jewish and Christian writers sometimes differ considerably from what we find in the original manuscripts in Hebrew and Greek, or in the translations of these manuscripts into other languages, such as Syriac, Latin, or Coptic.

Types of Textual Variants

Since ancient biblical writings were preserved in these different forms, we can identify four types of textual variants: (1) variations among manuscripts in the original languages, (2) variations among the early translations of biblical writings, (3) variations between the ancient manuscripts in the original languages and manuscripts of early translations, and (4) variant quotations in early nonbiblical Jewish and Christian writings.

Once we understand not only how ancient writings were originally composed but also how they were copied, preserved, transmitted, translated, and quoted, it is easier to explain how such variations in the wording of a biblical passage could result.

Many of the varying quotations in rabbinical and early Christian literature arose because writers were frequently quoting from memory. Major differences between early translations and original-language manuscripts, as in the case of Job and Jeremiah, probably resulted because different textual traditions or different versions of these books lie behind the surviving Hebrew and Greek texts. The Greek text of some OT passages may be closer to the original than the known Hebrew texts.

Textual variants within biblical manuscripts written in the original languages often reflect corruptions in the text. Generally speaking, textual critics have detected two types of changes that were made by scribes as they copied manuscripts: (a) unintentional and (b) intentional.

Unintentional errors include both hearing and reading mistakes scribes made as they copied manuscripts. The former could occur as several scribes, assembled in the same scriptorium (a room in which scribal copying occurred), listened to a single scribe reading aloud from a master copy, and then copied what they heard. While this ancient form of multiple copying was more efficient than a single scribe sitting at a desk copying a manuscript, it also yielded hearing errors. A scribe might correctly hear a word read aloud, and then record it incorrectly; or he could mistakenly record a word because he failed to hear it correctly in the first place. Either way, what he wrote differed from what the scribe in the front of the room saw written in the manuscript from which he was reading.

Visual errors occurred when a scribe produced a fresh manuscript by looking at a master copy, and then writing what one saw or thought one saw. In this form of producing a new manuscript by manually copying an older manuscript, a scribe could commit several forms of reading mistakes. A scribe might skip a word or a line (called "haplography"), write a word or a line twice (called "dittography"), misspell a word, reverse the order of letters within a single word, or reverse the order of words within a sentence. Sometimes a scribe would see a note made in the margin of an early text and, thinking it was part of the text, decide to incorporate this marginal gloss into his new copy. These are only some of the ways unintentional errors might occur.

Intentional changes in the wording in the text could occur for a variety of reasons. A scribe might feel compelled to correct the spelling or improve the grammar of a manuscript being copied. Whether the scribe's "correction" was right or wrong, this would introduce yet another variation into the textual tradition. The scribe might also choose to rearrange the order of words, sentences, or even paragraphs, and on occasion add material if he felt the need to do so. This may have been done to produce a more coherent or a more logically sequential account. In any event, such changes, transpositions, and glosses were made by scribes, even when they were copying sacred texts. Although we may now be able to determine that their "correction" was "wrong," they probably thought they were improving the text.

Scribes also changed texts intentionally for theological or doctrinal reasons. If the text being copied contained a statement with which the scribe disagreed, it was sometimes changed or expanded to make it conform to what the scribe regarded as a more orthodox position. Ancient Hebrew scribes, for example, noted at least eighteen cases in the Hebrew Bible in which the text had been changed for theological reasons. In some cases, the scribe might simply omit the offensive verse or passage. Whenever intentional changes were made in the text—and they were made for other reasons as well—they were made in order to improve the text or its content.

Manuscript Families

Ancient biblical writings were copied frequently and became widespread throughout the Mediterranean world. As one might expect, certain centers, usually major cities such as Jerusalem, Babylon, Alexandria, and Rome, became the home of certain biblical texts. This occurred either because early copies might have been preserved in one of these centers or because the names of revered biblical personalities or scribes came to be associated with such cities.

We can easily imagine how a distinctive textual tradition might develop within one geographical locale. By examining the many remaining copies of the biblical writings, especially the NT and the Greek versions of the OT, scholars have assigned them to families or recensions. These groupings are based on linguistic similarities among manuscripts as well as the association of certain manuscripts with single geographical locales. Not every surviving biblical manuscript easily fits into one of these families, but grouping manuscripts according to geographical location, such as Alexandrian, Caesarean, or Western (Rome), is a convenient form of classification. This is especially true of NT manuscripts, which have been typically grouped in families based on their genealogical relationship.

Such groupings are based on linguistic, grammatical, or even theological tendencies that textual critics detect in manuscripts. For example, a particular textual variant may have been introduced in the fourth century CE and then show up later in an entire group of manuscripts.

If this single variant, or if a pattern based upon several variants, occurs repeatedly in a group of manuscripts, these scribal tendencies enable textual critics to group the manuscripts displaying such characteristics into the same family. Since they possess the same genealogical relationship, they are said to belong to the same text type.

As scholars have studied the various tendencies within families of manuscripts, they have noted certain characteristics. Some manuscript families tend to be expansionist, because they contain variant readings that are consistently longer than those in other groupings. Other manuscript families, by contrast, may be more conservative, because they exhibit reluctance to include any changes, either expansions or reductions in wording.

Knowing these tendencies helps us in assessing the relative merits of particular variants. For example, if we encounter a variant reading in a particular passage and we discover that it is supported only by a single manuscript, or a group of manuscripts, with an expansionist tendency, we would have good reason to reject it, all other things being equal.

Critical Editions of the Bible

As the study of textual criticism has developed over the centuries, our knowledge of the process by which early manuscripts have been transmitted and preserved has increased dramatically. In addition, detailed knowledge of particular manuscripts, such as their date and place of origin, peculiarities of style, and how they relate to other manuscripts, has been accumulated. Archaeological discoveries, such as the Qumran writings or the Dead Sea Scrolls, have also provided valuable information for textual criticism. The results of these scholarly activities continue to be available in books and periodicals, but they come to fruition most visibly in the production of critical editions of the biblical writings and in the modern translations produced by committees of scholars using such critical editions.

A critical edition of any ancient writing, including the OT and the NT, contains a text in the original language in which the writing was produced, along with an extensive set of footnotes—the critical apparatus—that lists textual variants and the different ancient sources in which the various readings have been preserved. Typically these witnesses are listed in the following order: ancient manuscripts (including papyri and parchment manuscripts), versions (translations into other languages), and patristic citations (the works of early commentators and scholars).

Some critical editions provide only a selection of all the textual variants, while others attempt to include every variation within the text. Although modern committee translations do not reproduce the text in the original language, these modern translations have been produced by scholars who have given close attention to text-critical matters. None of the modern committee translations contains an extensive critical apparatus; they rather provide footnotes that report the most important variations in wording and describe the nature of those variations. In a tightly compact form these footnotes typically describe the type of variation, whether it is an addition, omission, alteration, or transposition. They also give some indication of the ancient manuscript evidence that supports the reading adopted in the main text and the variant readings listed in the footnote.

The latest critical editions of the Hebrew and Greek texts, and the latest committee translations of the Bible, both OT and NT, provide the most up-to-date accumulation of the scholarship produced by textual critics working with biblical texts. These editions are the most compact final form into which the work of textual critics is cast.

Evaluating Textual Variants

When we encounter variations within the text, our primary task is to examine the variants, assess their relative importance, and decide how they affect the passage to be interpreted. Naturally, the beginning student must rely on the work of experts, since textual criticism is a highly developed, complex field of study. Even so, it is important to understand what textual criticism seeks to achieve and how it works.

Textual criticism has a threefold aim: (a) to determine how textual variants arose as ancient biblical writings were transmitted and preserved; (b) to establish the original wording, when this is judged to be possible or feasible; and (c) to determine the best form and wording of the text that the modern reader should use.

Textual critics have developed various criteria for assessing variant readings. In spite of their complexity, they are often based on common sense and ingenuity. These scholars have identified the kinds of changes that occurred when ancient texts were composed, copied, preserved, and transmitted. They have also established the reasons why such changes occur. Criteria for judging these changes often consist in working back from the variants toward the more original form of the text.

One of the most fundamental axioms with which textual critics work is this: the more difficult reading is to be preferred. This rule is based on the observation that scribes tended to smooth out difficulties rather than create them. Consequently, given two variations of wording, the more difficult reading is more likely to have given rise to the simpler reading, rather than vice versa.

An example occurs in Mark's account of the healing of the demoniac (Mark 5:1–20). Verse 1 reports that Jesus and the disciples, after crossing the Sea of Galilee, came to "the country of the Gerasenes." Since this region was located several miles away from the seacoast, some ancient scribes substituted more probable locations, including "Gergesenes" and "Gadarenes." Since "Gerasenes" is the more difficult reading, it is preferred (see textual note on "Gerasenes" in Mark 5:1 in the NRSV).

Another general rule is that the shorter reading is to be preferred. Because copyists tended to expand the text rather than shorten it, textual critics generally give priority to a shorter reading rather than a longer one. They have discovered that scribes, as a general rule, tended to make additions to the text rather than delete elements from it.

In Acts 19:9, for example, Luke reports that Paul, after meeting resistance from synagogue leaders in Ephesus, began teaching "daily in the lecture hall of Tyrannus." Some ancient manuscripts read "[the lecture hall] *of a certain Tyrannus, from eleven o'clock in the morning to four in the afternoon.*" Knowing that this variant reading occurs in an ancient manuscript that tends to be expansionistic, that is, that tends to add words and phrases to the text, textual critics prefer the shorter reading (see textual note on "Tyrannus" in Acts 19:9 in the NRSV).

Yet another general rule is this: a reading that helps explain the origin of the other readings is probably more original. In 1 Corinthians 13:3, Paul writes, "and if I hand over my body so that I may boast," but some ancient manuscripts read "body to be burned." Other forms of "burn" are found in other ancient manuscripts. Confusion probably resulted from similar sounding verbs: *kauchēsōmai* ("I may boast") and *kauthēsomai* ("I may be burned"). Several considerations have convinced textual critics that "I may boast" is the preferred reading, among them that it is probably the reading from which the various alternate readings originated (see textual note on "boast" in 1 Cor. 13:3 in the NRSV).

Scribes also tended to harmonize divergent readings rather than create them. For this reason, a variant reading that looks harmonistic tends to be discounted in favor of one that creates a problem of some sort.

In addition to these scribal tendencies, textual critics also take into account matters of style, vocabulary, and literary context. For example, if a variant reading tends to diverge from the author's vocabulary and style found elsewhere in the same document, it is less likely to be original. A variant reading that does not easily fit into the larger literary context of the document because it introduces a new theme or motif is usually suspicious.

All of these considerations are regarded as internal evidence, because they pertain to statements or characteristics inherent within the text itself. External evidence includes observations that are outside the text, such as the date and character of the manuscript witnesses, the geographical distribution of the manuscript witnesses, and the genealogical relationship among the various families of texts.

As noted earlier, textual critics have classified most of the manuscript witnesses into types or families. They have also established both dates and geographical locales for the manuscripts. In some instances, the manuscripts contain this information; in other instances, it has to be deduced from other considerations, such as the style of writing or the type of material on which the manuscript was written. Lists of the relevant manuscripts, with their assigned dates and locations, are contained in critical editions and are easily available in standard works, such as Aland and Aland, *The Text of the New Testament*.

As we evaluate textual variants, we inevitably raise questions of chronology: When did the variant enter the manuscript tradition? Was it original or not? If not, was it an early or late change? Generally speaking, the earlier a reading, the more likely it is to be authentic. And yet, this is not invariably the case, because of what we know about the process of manuscript transmission. For example, a corrupt reading might be attested in a fourth-century manuscript, while an eighth-century manuscript preserves a reading that is possibly much earlier, thus better. In this case, the reading in the later, or younger, manuscript is to be preferred.

Similarly, if a corrupt reading is attested in several extant manuscripts, whereas a clearly authentic reading is attested in only one extant manuscript, the latter would be preferred, although supported by only one manuscript witness. Because poor readings may be supported by many manuscripts and good readings may be attested in only one or a few manuscripts, textual critics have also formulated another principle: manuscripts should not only be counted, but also weighed.

As we try to decide among variant readings, we soon discover that no single criterion will work in every case. Some criteria apply in certain cases, some do not. In some cases, one criterion tends to cancel another criterion. By reading the scholarly discussions of textual critics or commentators who employ the work of textual critics, we can observe how they proceed. Typically, they begin with a particular instance—a problem text—accumulate all the evidence possible, both internal and external, and try to evaluate the options on their individual merits. Textual critics will consider various criteria that relate to a specific case, but their final decision is based on their own informed judgment and creative insight.

Beginning students are sometimes put off by text-critical analysis because it is a complicated, technical process. But the more we work with ancient texts, the more familiar we become with text-critical criteria and how they work. It also helps if we try to understand the logic of text-critical analysis and remember that widely accepted text-critical principles are based on common sense. In many ways, text-critical analysis resembles detective work. We often find ourselves looking for clues to explain how a particular reading arose and to develop hypotheses that account for the evidence before us. As we develop deeper understanding of the origin and transmission of texts, we can make better sense of what we find in the critical apparatuses of modern editions of the Bible and in the textual footnotes of modern committee translations.

How to Proceed

But how should the beginning student actually proceed in addressing text-critical problems?

First, consult the text and the footnotes in a modern committee translation of the Bible. Even better, consult several such translations. These notes are usually located at the bottom of the page, near the actual text. In annotated study Bibles, these notes are typically separated from the notes that serve as a short commentary on the text. Because of limited space, these notes generally report only the most important textual problems. Text-critical notes are usually introduced with such phrases as "Other ancient manuscripts read . . ." or "Other ancient authorities lack . . ." This text-critical information should be distinguished from other notes located in the same place that indicate alternate forms of translation or other explanatory information. Alternate translations of a particular Hebrew or Greek word are not textual variants or variant readings in a text-critical sense. The latter set of terms refers to variations of wording within the ancient manuscript tradition.

Second, determine the type of problem involved. Any abbreviations or symbols used in the text-critical notes will be explained in the preface of the edition being used. By consulting these explanatory notes, you can determine more precisely the nature of the problem.

Third, after looking at the evidence reported in the textual notes of a committee translation, you should consult a biblical commentary on the passage. A critical commentary, as opposed to a more general, expository commentary, will discuss all of the important text-critical problems. Even though critical commentaries will employ Hebrew and Greek terms, students who do not know these original languages can usually determine the gist of the problem. If the translators of a particular edition have produced a handbook explaining their choice of various readings, these should also be consulted. After making these preliminary moves and examining one or more critical commentaries, you are then ready to move to the next step.

Fourth, identify the variant reading or readings and list them alongside the reading adopted in the translation or edition that you are using. Beside each variant, list the supporting witnesses, that is, which ancient manuscripts, versions (translations), or patristic authors support each variant. Once this is done, apply the external criteria. Determine the date of the witnesses that support the different readings and evaluate how much stock to place in them. Then consider the internal criteria, asking whether a particular reading conforms to the general expectations of the document based on what is known about it internally. For example, is it consistent with the style, vocabulary, context, and theology of the rest of the document? Is it a simpler reading or a more difficult reading? Is it shorter or longer?

Quite often, valuable discussions of important passages are contained in books devoted to textual criticism. You should check the index of biblical references in some of the standard text-critical works to see if the passage under consideration is discussed.

If you have some facility with Hebrew or Greek, your ability to pursue text-critical questions is increased considerably. In this case, you should first consult one of the standard critical editions of the Bible.

This will enable you to identify the alternative readings, determine the exact nature of the problem, and then proceed to collect and assess the evidence. For external criteria, lists of the manuscripts and their characteristics are readily available. These should be consulted as you itemize the manuscript witnesses supporting each variant. In close conjunction with your own listing of the external evidence, you should consult critical commentaries to get a more informed understanding of the problem.

For OT texts, you can compare the text under consideration with the reading of the Aramaic Targums in English translation by consulting the so-called Aramaic Bible. It may also be profitable to compare the text with the Greek translation (for example, in Brenton's *The Septuagint with Apocrypha: Greek and English*) as well as the Dead Sea Scrolls readings in English translation in the *Dead Sea Scrolls Bible* (translated by Abegg, Flint, and Ulrich).

Regardless of the level of technical proficiency at which you are working, your aim should be to determine the exact nature of the text-critical problem, identify and evaluate the main options, and decide how these relate to your overall understanding of the passage.

BIBLIOGRAPHY

Critical Editions of the Old Testament

Brooke, Alan E., Norman McLean, and Henry St J. Thackeray, eds. *The Old Testament in Greek*. 3 vols. Cambridge: Cambridge University Press, 1906–40. Incomplete.

Goshen-Gottstein, Moshe H., et al., eds. Hebrew Bible Critical Edition. Hebrew University Bible Project. Jerusalem: Magnes, 1975–.

Kittel, Rudolf, Karl Elliger, Wilhelm Rudolph, Hans P. Rüger, and Gérard E. Weil, eds. *Biblia Hebraica Stuttgartensia*. Stuttgart: Deutsche Bibelgesellschaft, 1997 (1967).

Rahlfs, Alfred, and R. Hanhart, eds. *Septuaginta*. 2nd rev. ed. Stuttgart: Deutsche Bibelgesellschaft, 2006.

Rahlfs, Alfred, Joseph Ziegler, et al., eds. *Septuaginta: Vetus Testamentum Graecum, auctoritate Societatis Litterarum Gottingensis editum*. Göttingen: Vandenhoeck & Ruprecht, 1926–.

Schenker, Adrian, Yohanan A. P. Goldman, Arie van der Kooij, Gerard J. Norton, Stephen Pisano, Jan de Waard, and Richard D. Weis, eds. *Biblia Hebraica: Quinta editione cum apparatus criticus novis curis elaborato*. Stuttgart: Deutsche Bibelgesellschaft, 2004–.

Critical Editions of the New Testament

Aland, Kurt, ed. *Synopsis Quattuor Evangeliorum: Locis parallelis evangeliorum apoc-ryphorum et Patrum adhibitis.* 15th ed. Stuttgart: Deutsche Bibelgesellschaft, 1997.

———, ed. *Synopsis of the Four Gospels: Greek-English Edition of the Synopsis Quattuor Evangeliorum . . . the English text is the second edition of the Revised Standard Edition.* 12th ed. Stuttgart: German Bible Society, 2001.

Aland, Kurt, and Barbara Aland, eds. *The Greek New Testament.* 4th rev. ed. Stuttgart: Deutsche Bibelgesellschaft; New York and London: United Bible Societies, 2002.

Burer, Michael H., W. Hall Harris, Daniel B. Wallace, Eberhard Nestle, Erwin Nestle, Kurt Aland, and Barbara Aland. *New Testament: New English Translation, Novum Testamentum Graece.* Stuttgart: Deutsche Bibelgesellschaft; Dallas: NET Bible Press, 2004.

Funk, Robert W. *New Gospel Parallels.* 2 vols. Philadelphia: Fortress, 1985–1987.

Huck, Albert, ed. *Synopsis of the First Three Gospels.* 9th ed., rev. by Hans Lietzmann; Tübingen: J. C. B. Mohr (Paul Siebeck), 1950; English ed. by F. L. Cross; Oxford: Basil Blackwell, 1976.

Huck, Albert, and Heinrich Greeven, eds. *Synopse der drei ersten Evangelien: mit Beigabe der johanneischen Parallelstellen = Synopsis of the First Three Gospels with the Addition of the Johannine Parallels.* 13th ed. Tübingen: J. C. B. Mohr (Paul Siebeck), 1981.

Nestle, Eberhard, Erwin Nestle, Barbara Aland, and Kurt Aland, eds. *Novum Testamentum Graece.* 27th ed. Stuttgart: Deutsche Bibelgesellschaft, 2004.

Nestle, Eberhard, Erwin Nestle, and George D. Kilpatrick, eds. *Hē Kainē Diathēkē.* 2nd ed. London: British and Foreign Bible Society, 1964.

Throckmorton, Burton H., Jr., ed. *Gospel Parallels: A Comparison of the Synoptic Gospels.* 5th ed. Nashville: Thomas Nelson, 1992.

Textual Criticism—General

*Wegner, Paul D. *A Student's Guide to Textual Criticism of the Bible: Its History, Methods, and Results.* Downers Grove, IL: IVP Academic/InterVarsity Press, 2006.

Old Testament Textual Criticism

*Ap-Thomas, Dafydd R. *A Primer of Old Testament Text Criticism.* 2nd rev. ed. Philadelphia: Fortress, 1971.

Barthélemy, Dominique, Adrian Schenker, and John A. Thompson. *Preliminary and Interim Report on the Hebrew Old Testament Text Project.* 5 vols. 2nd rev. ed. New York: United Bible Societies, 1979–1980.

Cross, Frank M., and Shemaryahu Talmon, eds. *Qumran and the History of the Biblical Text.* Cambridge, MA: Harvard University Press, 1976.

Jellicoe, Sidney. *The Septuagint and Modern Study.* Winona Lake, IN: Eisenbrauns, 1993 (1968).

————, ed. *Studies in the Septuagint: Origins, Recensions, and Interpretations: Selected Essays with a Prolegomenon.* New York: Ktav, 1974.

Klein, Ralph W. *Textual Criticism of the Old Testament: The Septuagint after Qumran.* Philadelphia: Fortress, 1974.

Leiman, Shnayer Z., ed. *The Canon and Masorah of the Hebrew Bible.* New York: Ktav, 1974.

*McCarter, P. Kyle. *Textual Criticism: Recovering the Text of the Hebrew Bible.* Philadelphia: Fortress, 1986.

Roberts, Bleddyn J. *The Old Testament Text and Versions: The Hebrew Text in Transmission and the History of the Ancient Versions.* Cardiff: University of Wales Press, 1977.

Tov, Emanuel. *The Text-Critical Use of the Septuagint in Biblical Research.* 2nd ed., rev. and enl. Jerusalem: Simor, 1997.

————. *Textual Criticism of the Hebrew Bible.* 2nd rev. ed. Minneapolis: Fortress; Assen: Royal Van Gorcum, 2001.

*Weingreen, Jacob. *Introduction to the Critical Study of the Text of the Hebrew Bible.* Oxford: Clarendon Press; New York: Oxford University Press, 1982.

Wonneberger, Reinhard. *Understanding BHS: A Manual for the Users of Biblia Hebraica Stuttgartensia.* 3rd rev. ed. Rome: Editrice pontificio istituto biblico, 2001.

*Würthwein, Ernst. *The Text of the Old Testament: An Introduction to the Biblia Hebraica.* 2nd ed., rev. and enl. Grand Rapids: Eerdmans, 1995.

New Testament Textual Criticism

*Aland, Kurt, and Barbara Aland. *The Text of the New Testament: An Introduction to the Critical Editions and to the Theory and Practice of Modern Textual Criticism.* 2nd ed., rev. and enl. Grand Rapids: Eerdmans, 1995.

*Black, David A., ed. *Rethinking Textual Criticism.* Grand Rapids: Baker Academic, 2002.

Ehrman, Bart D. *Misquoting Jesus: The Story behind Who Changed the Bible and Why.* New York: HarperSanFrancisco, 2005. Reprinted as *Whose Word Is It? The Story behind Who Changed the New Testament and Why.* London and New York: Continuum, 2006.

————. *The Orthodox Corruption of Scripture: The Effect of Early Christological Controversies on the Text of the New Testament.* New York: Oxford University Press, 1993.

————. *Studies in the Textual Criticism of the New Testament.* Leiden: Brill, 2006.

Ehrman, Bart D., and Michael W. Holmes, eds. *The Text of the New Testament in Contemporary Research: Essays on the Status Quaestionis.* Grand Rapids: Eerdmans, 1995.

Epp, Eldon J. *Perspectives on New Testament Textual Criticism: Collected Essays, 1962–2004.* Leiden and Boston: Brill, 2005.

Epp, Eldon J., and Gordon D. Fee, eds. *New Testament Textual Criticism: Its Significance for Exegesis.* Oxford: Clarendon Press; New York: Oxford University Press, 1981.

————, eds. *Studies in the Theory and Method of New Testament Textual Criticism.* Grand Rapids: Eerdmans, 1993.

Fee, Gordon D. *New Testament Exegesis: A Handbook for Students and Pastors.* 3rd ed. Louisville, KY: Westminster John Knox, 2002.

Finegan, Jack. *Encountering New Testament Manuscripts: A Working Introduction to Textual Criticism.* Grand Rapids: Eerdmans, 1980; London: SPCK, 1975.

Greenlee, J. Harold. *Introduction to New Testament Textual Criticism.* Rev. ed. Peabody, MA: Hendrickson, 1995.

Hatch, William H. P. *Facsimiles and Descriptions of Minuscule Manuscripts of the New Testament.* Cambridge, MA: Harvard University Press, 1951.

————. *The Principal Uncial Manuscripts of the New Testament.* Chicago: University of Chicago Press, 1939.

Kenyon, Frederic G. *The Text of the Greek Bible.* 3rd ed., rev. and augmented by Arthur W. Adams. London: Duckworth, 1975.

Metzger, Bruce M. *The Early Versions of the New Testament: Their Origin, Transmission, and Limitations.* Oxford: Clarendon Press, 1977.

————. *A Textual Commentary on the Greek New Testament.* 2nd ed. Stuttgart: Deutsche Bibelgesellschaft; New York: United Bible Societies, 2002.

*Metzger, Bruce M., and Bart D. Ehrman. *The Text of the New Testament: Its Transmission, Corruption, and Restoration.* 4th ed. New York: Oxford University Press, 2005.

Moulton, Harold K. *Papyrus, Parchment and Print: The Story of How the New Testament Text Has Reached Us.* London: United Society for Christian Literature and Lutterworth, 1967.

Parker, David C. *The Living Text of the Gospels.* Cambridge and New York: Cambridge University Press, 1997.

Tasker, Randolph V. G., ed. *The Greek New Testament: Being the Text Translated in the New English Bible, 1961.* London: Oxford University Press, 1964.

Taylor, Vincent. *The Text of the New Testament: A Short Introduction.* 2nd ed. London: Macmillan; New York: St. Martin's, 1963.

Vaganay, Léon, Christian-Bernard Amphoux, and Jenny Read-Heimerdinger. *An Introduction to New Testament Textual Criticism.* 2nd ed. revised and updated. Cambridge and New York: Cambridge University Press, 1991.

Discussions of English Translations of the Bible

*Bailey, Lloyd R., ed. *The Word of God: A Guide to English Versions of the Bible.* Atlanta: John Knox, 1982.

Brockington, Leonard H., ed. *The Hebrew Text of the Old Testament: The Readings Adopted by the Translators of the New English Bible.* London: Oxford University Press and Cambridge University Press, 1973.

Bruce, Frederick F. *The Books and the Parchments: Some Chapters on the Transmission of the Bible.* Rev. ed. London: Pickering, 1991.

*————. *History of the Bible in English: From the Earliest Versions.* 3rd ed. London: Lutterworth Press, 1979.

Daniell, David. *The Bible in English: Its History and Influence.* New Haven, CT: Yale University Press, 2005.

Kenyon, Frederic G. *Our Bible and the Ancient Manuscripts: Being a History of the Text and Its Translations.* Columbus, OH: Lazarus Ministry, 1998 (1895).

*Kubo, Sakae, and Walter F. Specht. *So Many Versions? Twentieth-Century English Versions of the Bible.* Rev. and enl. ed. Grand Rapids: Zondervan, 1983.

Lewis, Jack P. *The English Bible. From KJV to NIV: A History and Evaluation.* 2nd ed. Grand Rapids: Baker, 1992.

Metzger, Bruce M. *The Bible in Translation: Ancient and English Versions.* Grand Rapids: Baker Academic, 2001.

Nineham, Dennis E., ed. *The New English Bible Reviewed.* London: Epworth, 1965.

Orlinsky, Harry M. *Notes on the New Translation of the Torah.* Skokie, IL: Varda, 2000 (1969).

Pope, Hugh, and Sebastian Bullough. *English Versions of the Bible.* Westport, CT: Greenwood, 1972.

Robinson, H. Wheeler, ed. *The Bible in Its Ancient and English Versions.* Westport, CT: Greenwood, 1970.

Sheeley, Steven M., and Robert N. Nash. *The Bible in English Translation: An Essential Guide.* Nashville: Abingdon, 1997.

————. *Choosing a Bible: A Guide to Modern English Translations and Editions.* Nashville: Abingdon, 1999.

Textual Notes on the New American Bible. Paterson, NJ: St. Anthony's Guild, 1974.

Parallel Bibles

The Catholic Comparative New Testament: Douay-Rheims, New American Bible, Revised Standard Version, New Revised Standard Version, Jerusalem Bible, New Jerusalem Bible, Good News Translation, and Christian Community Bible. New York: Oxford University Press, 2006.

The CBD Parallel Bible: King James Version, New King James Version, New International Version, New Living Translation. Peabody, MA: Prince (Christian Book Distributors), 2003.

The Complete Parallel Bible: Containing the Old and New Testaments with the Apocryphal/Deuterocanonical Books: New Revised Standard Version, Revised English Bible, New American Bible, New Jerusalem Bible. New York: Oxford University Press, 1993.

The Hendrickson Parallel Bible: King James Version, New King James Version, New International Version, New Living Translation. Peabody, MA: Hendrickson, 2005.

Kohlenberger, John R., III, ed. *The Contemporary Parallel Bible: New King James Version, New International Version.* Oxford and New York: Oxford University Press, 2004.

————, ed. *The Essential Evangelical Parallel Bible: New King James Version, English Standard Version, New Living Translation, The Message.* New York: Oxford University Press, 2004.

————, ed. *The Evangelical Parallel New Testament: New King James Version, New International Version, Today's New International Version, New Living Translation, English Standard Version, Holman Christian Standard Bible, New Century Version, The Message.* New York: Oxford University Press, 2003.

————, ed. *The Parallel Apocrypha: Greek Text, King James Version, Douay Old Testament, the Holy Bible by Ronald Knox, Today's English Version, New Revised Standard Version, New American Bible, New Jerusalem Bible.* New York: Oxford University Press, 1997.

The NIV/KJV Parallel Bible: New International Version, King James Version. Grand Rapids: Zondervan, 2002.

Weigle, Luther A. *The New Testament Octapla: Eight English Versions of the New Testament in the Tyndale–King James Tradition.* New York: Thomas Nelson, 1962.

Zondervan Today's Parallel Bible (King James Version, New International Version, New Living Translation, and New American Standard Bible). Grand Rapids: Zondervan, 2000.

Translations of Ancient Versions

Abegg, Martin G., Peter W. Flint, and Eugene C. Ulrich. *The Dead Sea Scrolls Bible: The Oldest Known Bible.* San Francisco: HarperSanFrancisco, 1999.

Brenton, Lancelot C. L., ed. *The Septuagint with Apocrypha: Greek and English.* Peabody, MA: Hendrickson, 1986 (1851).

The Holy Bible Translated from the Latin Vulgate (Douay Version). New York: Benziger, 1914 (1609–10).

McNamara, Martin, et al., eds. The Aramaic Bible: The Targums. 22 vols. Collegeville, MN: Michael Glazier/Liturgical Press, 1987–.

3

Historical Criticism

The Setting in Time and Place

Historical criticism of documents assumes that a text is historical in at least two senses: it may relate history as well as have its own history. For this reason, we can distinguish between the "history *in* the text" and the "history *of* the text."

History and the Text

The "history *in* the text" refers to what the text itself narrates or relates about history, whether persons, events, social conditions, or even ideas. In this sense, a text may serve as a window through which we can peer into a historical period. From a critical reading of what the text says, we can draw conclusions about political, social, or religious conditions of the period(s) during which the text was produced.

The "history *of* the text" refers to something different, for it is not concerned with what the text itself says or describes—the story it tells—but with the story of the text, or what one writer calls the "career of the text"—its own history: how, why, when, where, and in what circumstances it originated; by whom and for whom it was written, composed, edited, produced, and preserved; why it was produced and the various influences that affected its origin, formation, development, preservation, and transmission.

If one does a historical-critical analysis of *The Histories* of Herodotus (fifth century BCE), for example, both of these aspects come into play. In investigating the historical and cultural descriptions in the work itself, the critic asks such questions as: Whose history is being described? What events are seen as important? Who and what are talked about in the text? What information and perspectives gained from sources outside Herodotus's work can be brought to bear on his work to aid in understanding? Are there special emphases of the author that dominate and color the presentation? How reliably does Herodotus describe matters and events?

In addition to what Herodotus relates in *The Histories*—the history *in* the text—the critic also investigates the situation of the author himself and the context in which the history was written—the history *of* the text. Here the following types of questions are addressed: What is known biographically about the author and the place of this work in his or her life's activity? What cultural factors of the day may explain the production of the work? What tendencies and interests of the writer and his or her time influenced the work, its shape, and its contents? What goals did the writer have in mind for his or her work?

Historical criticism of the biblical writings is based on assumptions similar to those used in working with other ancient texts. The biblical critic is concerned with what is depicted in the text and the situation in which the text was written. The first of these is more relevant when the biblical books are concerned directly with historical matters, such as Genesis through 2 Kings, 1–2 Chronicles, Ezra, Nehemiah, the Gospels, and Acts. Even in nonhistorical books, such as Proverbs and Psalms, the cultural situations and conditions reflected in the texts are of concern to the interpreter. For all the biblical materials, the historical and cultural conditions out of which they came are of interest to the interpreter as an aid to understanding. This is the case even though interpreters frequently know nothing about the actual authors or collectors of various books.

Ancient Approaches to Historical Criticism

These two aspects of historical criticism were applied in a limited fashion to biblical writings by ancient Jewish and Christian interpreters as well as by others. Jewish interpreters tried to assign the various OT books to particular authors and even debated such issues as whether

Moses could have written the account of his own death found in Deuteronomy 34. Tradition sought, for example, to depict the life situation within which David supposedly wrote many of the Psalms. These attributions appear even in the biblical text itself (see Psalms 3; 7; 18; 34; 51; 52; 54; 56; 57; 59; 60; 63; and 142).

Chronological problems and discrepancies in the text were also recognized. The Christian writer Julius Africanus (ca. 160–240) produced a world history and major encyclopedia in which he analyzed the historical reliability of some biblical texts. Jerome (ca. 342–420) reports that he once received a letter from Hedibia, a woman living in Gaul, inquiring about the discrepancies in the accounts of Jesus' resurrection and appearances in the four Gospels. Two pagan writers, Celsus (second cent. CE) and Porphyry (ca. 232–303 CE), wrote volumes in which they addressed both of these historical dimensions. They challenged not only the reliability of what was reported in some biblical texts on the basis of internal evidence but also what was taught about some texts, for example, the traditional authorship of some books.

Ancient interpreters, however, sought to defend what was written in, and what was reported about, the text. They attempted to resolve problems within the text by defending traditional views about authorship. They often tried to harmonize discrepancies in the text at all costs. A rabbinic axiom held that in Scripture "there is no before or after." This interpretive attitude enabled rabbis to deal with chronological problems more easily or ignore them entirely.

Little did ancient Jewish and Christian interpreters recognize that discrepancies in the text might be the result of two different texts having been woven or edited together, each reflecting a different viewpoint or stemming from a different historical setting. Nor was there a clear recognition that two conflicting texts, perhaps from different books, might stem from different historical periods, with one reflecting an earlier, the other a later outlook. We might say that ancient interpreters overlooked, minimized, or ignored the history of the text and tended to read the Bible "on the flat." Exegesis based on such a view of the text failed to appreciate that the Bible is an anthology of writings, deriving from different historical contexts and cultural situations, produced and collected over centuries.

Since the development of modern historical consciousness and the methodologies that have resulted, the historical aspects of the biblical materials have received extensive attention in exegesis. Given the impact of these developments over the last few centuries, historical dimensions of the Bible cannot be ignored. Instead we must ask: How does the exegete utilize and benefit from historical criticism? What are the tools that can be used to facilitate this endeavor?

History *in* the Text

First, let us consider the history *in* the text, or the situation the text describes. Quite obviously, if the text contains references to persons, places, and customs strange to the reader, we must become acquainted sufficiently with the historical period or cultural setting described in the text to understand what is being said at the most elementary level. The tools most useful for obtaining this type of information will normally be the standard Bible dictionaries and encyclopedias. Equally useful, however, will be histories, sociological descriptions, and handbooks of the period being described. Histories of Israel and of early Christianity are the most useful sources to consult on matters of history, chronology, names, and events. In addition to these, individual books on the culture, sociological context, and social life of biblical times may provide well-organized information on different facets of daily life presupposed or referred to by the text. This type of information is often included in Bible atlases and geographies, although these works are usually consulted primarily to locate place names and find other geographical information related to the text.

Another source that can often illuminate the situation depicted in the text itself is comparative nonbiblical literature. Other writings of antiquity may reflect a similar outlook, derive from roughly the same period, discuss the same topic, or provide valuable background information. Although the importance of these parallel references has been recognized for centuries, they have received even greater prominence since the beginning of the twentieth century, often by scholars interested in studying the history of ancient religious traditions other than Judaism and early Christianity. This "history-of-religion" approach uncovered and collected vast amounts of materials from the ancient world that have shed light and provided new insights on the biblical writings.

By reading the creation stories of Genesis 1–3 alongside other creation stories from the ancient Near East, we can see more clearly their respective similarities and differences. This comparative reading enables us to understand the biblical text even better. Archaeological discoveries have also unearthed hundreds of letters and other ordinary documents from daily life, especially from the Hellenistic-Roman period. This rich trove of writings has contributed greatly to our understanding of NT letters.

Historical scholarship in the last two centuries has greatly affected every aspect of our biblical understanding. Not only has our understanding of particular passages been increased, but also our knowledge of the history and language of the biblical text itself. This has led to an increased awareness that the biblical writings reflect the historical situation out of which they arose. Recognizing this historical dimension of biblical writings is now regarded as an essential feature of any informed exegesis of a biblical text. For this reason, most biblical commentaries, especially those produced within the past century, provide numerous references to such parallel texts and normally incorporate into their interpretation insights gained from studying such documents.

In order to locate such parallel texts, the student should consult two kinds of sources: (a) critical commentaries, which usually provide references in footnotes, and (b) anthologies of writings from the ancient world, usually arranged by literary genre, such as "creation stories," "legal texts," "historical documents," "birth stories," "letters," and "apocalypses."

History *of* the Text

The second historical dimension exegetes must explore is the history *of* the text. This includes the situation out of which the text arose—both that of the author and the audience. It is now well known that many of the biblical books are anonymous, even though later tradition assigned authors to them. None of the four Gospels, for example, contains an explicit reference to who wrote it, even though in the second and third centuries they were assigned to Matthew, Mark, Luke, and John.

It is now widely recognized that many of the writings of the Bible were edited rather than written by single individuals and that many persons and groups engaged in this editing process, which often extended over decades or even centuries. Especially is this the case with the Pentateuch, but with other parts of the Bible as well.

This has required a shift in the way interpreters understand the relationship between the biblical writings and the original senders and receivers of these writings. In very few instances does it appear that a single author penned a writing, from start to finish, in one sitting. Even in those cases where this appears to have happened, there is strong evidence suggesting that these writings frequently continued to be edited, either by the author, or by the author's successors.

In some instances, the situation described in the text and the situation out of which the text arose may reflect the same historical setting. On the other hand, these two situations may represent different historical settings, separated by long periods of time. The situation described in Paul's letters to the Corinthians is contemporary with Paul's own situation. Handbooks describing the mid-fifties of the first century CE will be useful in illuminating both. The Pentateuch, on the other hand, was written centuries after the events that it purports to describe. Similarly, the Gospels were written decades after the events they describe. In such cases, the exegete should seek to determine as much as possible about the situation out of which the passage or its source arose, as well as the historical situation it describes.

One of the best illustrations of this point occurs in the OT book of Daniel, in which the events depicted in the text extend from the sixth to the second century BCE. The time of the book's final composition, however, has been established as the mid-second century BCE. To understand a passage from the book of Daniel, we must become familiar with the sixth century, the period it describes, and the second century, the period in which it was written.

Similarly, in interpreting the Gospels, we must know about historical developments in Judaism and Christianity within the last quarter of the first century CE, the time of their probable composition. But we must also be familiar with the early part of the first century in which Jesus' ministry occurred. Because Jesus' polemic against the Pharisees in Matthew 23 reflects severely strained Jewish-Christian relations after the destruction of Jerusalem in 70 CE, to understand this passage we must know the historical situation in Palestine both before and after this pivotal event.

Authorship

An important part of the history *of* the text is who produced it. This introduces two further considerations: (a) multiple authorship and (b) pseudonymous authorship. These may be considered in turn.

Although biblical books are often attributed to a single author, such as Isaiah, David, Solomon, Matthew, or Paul, we cannot always assume direct authorship of the works bearing their name. We may find it difficult, if not impossible, to determine who actually wrote the book, or even who is responsible for its final editing. These considerations often require us to modify our interpretations by making more modest claims about the text than what we assumed at the outset.

The standard handbooks on the OT provide detailed descriptions of the best known instance of this: the multiple authorship of the Pentateuch and the various historical contexts in which its different parts arose.

We noted earlier the common practice in antiquity of collecting writings under the name of a revered individual of the past or of assigning writings to such an individual. Apocalyptic writings, such as the book of Daniel mentioned above, provide numerous instances of pseudonymous authorship, but this practice also occurs elsewhere in the biblical writings. The canonical book of Isaiah, though constituting a single book within the OT, is now widely recognized as the work of at least two separate "authors," one addressing an eighth-century BCE setting, the other writing in the sixth century BCE. In the NT, thirteen writings are attributed to the apostle Paul, but his direct authorship of six of these letters is widely disputed. Although attributed to Paul, they may have been compiled in their final form after his death.

Such questions of authorship and context are dealt with extensively in introductions to the OT and NT, as well as in the introductory sections of commentaries on biblical books. On any particular passage, the student may check either of these sources for help in determining whether the passage is thought to be the result of pseudonymous or multiple authorship and whether it reflects a period of time much later than that described in the passage itself.

Literary Composition of the Text

Yet another aspect of this "external history" involves the literary composition of the text itself. This will be treated more fully in a later chapter on literary criticism, but it is mentioned here as part of the history *of* the text. Because the final form of the biblical text has often resulted from extensive editing, a single book may contain units whose relationship to each other is not altogether clear. Such sections may have been inserted, or interpolated, into the writing. The interpreter must determine, if possible, why and how this was done.

Many of the prophetic books of the OT are not uniform literary compositions but contain sections consisting of narratives and oracles whose relationship to each other may be unclear. Some of the Pauline letters are probably composite documents in which smaller letters or fragments of letters have been combined into a single document. In such cases, we must be open to a variety of possibilities in explaining how such writings originated.

Reusing Older Traditions

A third aspect of the external history of a passage relates to the way in which certain parts of the Bible have incorporated older biblical traditions and presented them in a new, modified form. In the OT books of Chronicles, we find material from the books of Samuel and Kings presented in a new way and written from a different viewpoint. Similarly, the book of Daniel appropriates and reinterprets older biblical traditions. In Daniel 9, the interpretation of the seventy years of desolation draws on Jeremiah (25:11–12; 29:10), which itself is based on an earlier ancient Near Eastern formulaic tradition. In the NT, Matthew and Luke depend directly on Mark, even though they expand Mark's story, changing it in many respects.

Throughout the Bible, we often find that earlier materials have been incorporated and re-presented in later materials. Recognizing that the same biblical material has often been "reprocessed" or "recycled" allows us to see how it has undergone historical development. This provides a valuable perspective for us as interpreters. Knowing that Matthew has used Mark, for example, gives us a distinct perspective in interpreting a passage that occurs in both Gospels. We can see how an event in the life of Jesus or one of his sayings is understood by two different biblical authors in their respective settings. This historical perspective exposes several interpretive moments or situations for understanding a passage: What did the event or teaching mean in Jesus' situation? What did it mean in the evangelists' situations?

This becomes especially important as we interpret the OT and NT together. Since NT writers frequently draw on OT stories and traditions, even citing OT passages directly, we are introduced to "recycling" over a much longer period of time. We often find that an OT theme or motif, such as the new covenant, has been interpreted and reinterpreted many times between the period of its original composition and its incorporation into a NT text. The "career" of an OT text becomes vitally important when we find it quoted and reinterpreted in the NT text.

We can state this another way. The authors of the biblical writings were not only composing new texts but also often transmitting and interpreting older texts and traditions as well. Seen this way, much of the Bible may be said to have originated as a series of interpretations in which authors took older traditions and reinterpreted them in light of their own situation.

Using the Reception History of a Text in Interpretation

This chain of interpretation did not end when the biblical writings ceased to be written, or even when the biblical documents were collected into their final canonical form. Long after the OT and NT writings were recognized as canonical, Jewish and Christian authors continued to quote and interpret them. These later interpretations can be extremely helpful to the contemporary interpreter as well. By paying attention to this "reception history of the text," we can often see a passage of Scripture in a new light and develop new levels of understanding otherwise missed if we jump from our own time to the time of original composition and reception.

An illuminating example is the well-known reference to the conception of a child by a "virgin," first mentioned in Isaiah 7:14 and later quoted in both Matthew and Luke. In developing an interpretation of Matthew 1:21, we can note, first, the differences between the context of Isaiah and that of Matthew. After examining the passage in its original literary setting, we can trace how this passage was interpreted during the centuries prior to the Christian era. By following the "historical career" of Isaiah 7:14, we gain a better sense of how subsequent readers understood the "virgin-conceived child." When we turn to the NT, we are then in a better position to evaluate the birth and infancy stories of Jesus in both Matthew and Luke. Even then, it is useful to see how later Christian writers understood the same passage through the centuries. Because the history of interpretation of a text may be long and continuous, it may provide us a broader framework in which to develop our own interpretation.

BIBLIOGRAPHY

Dictionaries and Encyclopedias

Achtemeier, Paul J., Roger S. Boraas, Michael Fishbane, Pheme Perkins, William O. Walker Jr., with the Society of Biblical Literature, eds. *The HarperCollins Bible Dictionary.* Rev. ed. San Francisco: HarperSanFrancisco, 1997.

Alexander, T. Desmond, and David W. Baker, eds. *Dictionary of the Old Testament: Pentateuch.* Downers Grove, IL: InterVarsity, 2003.

Bromiley, Geoffrey W., Everett F. Harrison, and Edgar W. Smith Jr., eds. *International Standard Bible Encyclopedia.* Rev. ed. 4 vols. Grand Rapids: Eerdmans, 1980–88.

Coggins, R. J., and J. L. Houlden, eds. *Dictionary of Biblical Interpretation.* London: SCM, 2003 (1990).

Ford, John T. *Saint Mary's Press Glossary of Theological Terms.* Winona, MN: Saint Mary's Press, 2006.

*Freedman, David N., ed. *Anchor Bible Dictionary.* 6 vols. New York: Doubleday, 1992.

*Freedman, David N., Allen C. Myers, and Astrid Beck, eds. *Eerdmans Dictionary of the Bible.* Grand Rapids: Eerdmans, 2000.

Green, Joel B., Scot McKnight, and I. Howard Marshall, eds. *Dictionary of Jesus and the Gospels.* Downers Grove, IL: InterVarsity, 1992.

Harvey, Van A. *A Handbook of Theological Terms.* New York: Simon & Schuster, 1964.

Hawthorne, Gerald F., Ralph P. Martin, and David G. Reid, eds. *Dictionary of Paul and His Letters.* Downers Grove, IL: InterVarsity, 1993.

Jeffrey, David L., ed. *A Dictionary of Biblical Tradition in English Literature.* Grand Rapids: Eerdmans, 1992.

Lemche, Niels P. *Historical Dictionary of Ancient Israel.* Lanham, MD: Scarecrow, 2004.

Martin, Ralph P., and Peter H. Davids, eds. *Dictionary of the Later New Testament and Its Developments.* Downers Grove, IL: InterVarsity, 1997.

McKim, Donald K. *Westminster Dictionary of Theological Terms.* Louisville, KY: Westminster John Knox, 1996.

Roth, Cecil, Geoffrey Wigoder, and Raphael Posner, eds. *Encyclopaedia Judaica.* 16 vols. Jerusalem: Keter, 1974.

Ryken, Leland, James C. Wilhoit, and Tremper Longman, III, eds. *Dictionary of Biblical Imagery.* Downers Grove, IL, and Leicester, UK: InterVarsity, 1998.

Sakenfeld, Katharine D., et al., eds. *New Interpreter's Dictionary of the Bible.* 5 vols. Nashville: Abingdon, 2006–.

Tenney, Merrill C., James D. Douglas, and Frederick F. Bruce, eds. *The New International Bible Dictionary.* Grand Rapids: Zondervan, 1999 (1987).

Toorn, Karel van der, Bob Becking, and Pieter W. van der Horst, eds. *Dictionary of Deities and Demons in the Bible.* 2nd rev. ed. Leiden: Brill, 1999.

Vanhoozer, Kevin J., Craig G. Bartholomew, Daniel J. Treier, and N. T. Wright, eds. *Dictionary for Theological Interpretation of the Bible.* Grand Rapids: Baker; London: SPCK, 2005.

Histories of Israel and Judah

Ahlström, Gösta W. *The History of Ancient Palestine.* 2nd ed. Sheffield, UK: JSOT, 1993; Minneapolis: Fortress, 1994.

Bright, John. *A History of Israel*. 4th ed. with introduction and appendix by William P. Brown. Louisville, KY: Westminster John Knox, 2000.

Coogan, Michael, ed. *The Oxford History of the Biblical World*. New York: Oxford University Press, 1998.

Finkelstein, Israel, and Neil A. Silberman. *The Bible Unearthed: Archaeology's New Vision of Ancient Israel and the Origin of Its Sacred Texts*. New York: Simon & Schuster, 2002.

Isserlin, B. S. J. *The Israelites*. London: Thames & Hudson, 1998; Minneapolis: Augsburg Fortress, 2001.

Kaiser, Walter C. *A History of Israel: From the Bronze Age through the Jewish Wars*. Nashville: Broadman & Holman, 1998.

Kitchen, Kenneth A. *On the Reliability of the Old Testament*. Grand Rapids: Eerdmans, 2003.

Liverani, Mario. *Israel's History and the History of Israel*. London: Equinox, 2005.

*Matthews, Victor. *A Brief History of Israel*. Louisville, KY: Westminster John Knox, 2002.

*Miller, J. Maxwell, and John H. Hayes. *A History of Ancient Israel and Judah*. 2nd ed. Louisville, KY: Westminster John Knox, 2006.

Provan, Iain W., V. Philips Long, and Tremper Longman III. *A Biblical History of Israel*. Louisville, KY: Westminster John Knox, 2003.

Redford, Donald B. *Egypt, Canaan, and Israel in Ancient Times*. Princeton, NJ: Princeton University Press, 1992.

Soggin, J. Alberto. *An Introduction to the History of Israel and Judah*. 3rd ed. London: SCM, 1999.

History and Literature of Intertestamental Judaism

*Cohen, Shaye J. D. *From the Maccabees to the Mishnah*. 2nd ed. Louisville, KY: Westminster John Knox, 2006.

Collins, John J. *Between Athens and Jerusalem: Jewish Identity in the Hellenistic Diaspora*. New York: Crossroad, 1983.

Grabbe, Lester L. *A History of the Jews and Judaism in the Second Temple Period*. London and New York: T. & T. Clark, 2004–.

———. *An Introduction to First Century Judaism: Jewish History and Religion in the Second Temple Period*. Edinburgh: T. & T. Clark, 1996.

Hayes, John H., and Sara Mandell. *The Jewish People in Classical Antiquity: From Alexander to Bar Kochba*. Louisville, KY: Westminster John Knox, 1998.

Hengel, Martin. *Judaism and Hellenism: Studies in Their Encounter in Palestine during the Early Hellenistic Period*. 2 vols. Philadelphia: Fortress, 1974.

Mulder, M. J., and Harry Sysling, eds. *The Literature of the Jewish People in the Period of the Second Temple and Talmud*. 3 vols. Assen: Van Gorcum; Philadelphia: Fortress, 1990.

*Nickelsburg, George W. E. *Jewish Literature between the Bible and the Mishnah: A Historical and Literary Introduction.* 2nd ed. Minneapolis: Fortress, 2005.

Sanders, E. P. *Judaism: Practice and Belief, 65 B.C.E.–66 C.E.* Eugene, OR: Wipf & Stock, 2004 (1992).

Schäfer, Peter. *The History of the Jews in the Graeco-Roman World.* London: Routledge, 2003.

*Schürer, Emil, Géza Vermès, and Fergus Millar, eds. *The History of the Jewish People in the Age of Jesus Christ (175 B.C.–A.D. 135): A New English Version Revised and Edited.* 3 vols. in 4. Edinburgh: T. & T. Clark, 1973–86.

Histories of Early Christianity

Barnett, Paul. *The Birth of Christianity: The First Twenty Years.* Grand Rapids: Eerdmans, 2005.

———. *Jesus and the Rise of Early Christianity: A History of New Testament Times.* Downers Grove, IL: InterVarsity, 1999.

Brown, Raymond E., and John P. Meier. *Antioch and Rome: New Testament Cradles of Catholic Christianity.* New York: Paulist, 1983.

Bruce, Frederick F. *New Testament History.* Garden City, NY: Doubleday, 1971.

*Chadwick, Henry. *The Early Church.* Rev. ed. London and New York: Penguin, 1993.

*Conzelmann, Hans. *History of Primitive Christianity.* Nashville: Abingdon, 1973.

Ehrman, Bart D. *Lost Christianities: The Battles for Scripture and the Faiths We Never Knew.* New York: Oxford University Press, 2003.

Goppelt, Leonard. *Apostolic and Post-Apostolic Times.* London: A. & C. Black, 1970; repr. Grand Rapids: Baker, 1977.

*Leaney, Alfred R. C. *The Jewish and Christian World 200 B.C. to A.D. 200.* Cambridge and New York: Cambridge University Press, 1984.

Lietzmann, Hans. *A History of the Early Church.* 4 vols. in 2. Cambridge: J. Clarke, 1993 (1953).

Niswonger, Richard L. *New Testament History.* Grand Rapids: Academie, 1988.

Pfeiffer, Robert H. *History of New Testament Times with an Introduction to the Apocrypha.* Westport, CT: Greenwood, 1976; repr. London: A. & C. Black, 1989 (1949).

Reicke, Bo. *The New Testament Era: The World of the Bible from 500 B.C. to A.D. 100.* London: A. & C. Black, 1978 (1968); repr. Philadelphia: Fortress, 1975.

Weiss, Johannes. *Earliest Christianity: A History of the Period A.D. 30–150.* 2 vols. Gloucester, MA: Peter Smith, 1970 (1959).

Witherington, Ben. *New Testament History: A Narrative Account.* Grand Rapids: Baker; Carlisle, UK: Paternoster, 2001.

Atlases and Geographies

Aharoni, Yohanan. *The Land of the Bible: A Historical Geography.* 2nd ed. rev. and emended. Philadelphia: Westminster; London: Burns & Oates, 1979.

*Aharoni, Yohanan, and Michael Avi-Yonah, Anson F. Rainey, and ZeTev Safrai. *The Macmillan Bible Atlas.* 3rd ed., completely rev. New York: Macmillan; Oxford: Maxwell Macmillan, 1993.

Avi-Yonah, Michael. *The Holy Land: A Historical Geography from the Persian to the Arab Conquests (536 B.C. to A.D. 640).* Jerusalem: Carta, 2002 (1977).

Baly, Denis. *Geographical Companion to the Bible.* New York: McGraw-Hill; London: Lutterworth, 1963.

―――. *The Geography of the Bible.* 2nd ed. New York: Harper & Row; Guildford, UK: Lutterworth, 1979.

Beitzel, Barry J. *The Moody Atlas of Bible Lands.* Chicago: Moody, 1985.

Grollenberg, Lucas H. *The Penguin Shorter Atlas of the Bible.* Harmondsworth, UK: Penguin, 1984 (1959).

Lawrence, Paul, Alan R. Millard, Heinrich von Siebenthal, and John Walton, eds. *The IVP Atlas of Bible History.* Downers Grove, IL: InterVarsity, 2006.

*May, Herbert G., G. N. S. Hunt, R. W. Hamilton, and John Day. *Oxford Bible Atlas.* 3rd ed. New York and London: Oxford University Press, 1984.

*Mittmann, Siegfried, and Götz Schmitt. *Tübingen Bible Atlas.* Stuttgart: Deutsche Bibelgesellschaft, 2001.

Negenman, Jan H., and Harold H. Rowley, eds. *New Atlas of the Bible.* Garden City, NY: Doubleday; London: Collins, 1969.

Pritchard, James B., ed. *The Harper/Times Atlas of the Bible.* New York: Harper & Row/Time Books, 1996 (1987).

*Rainey, Anson F., and R. Steven Notley. *The Sacred Bridge: Carta's Atlas of the Biblical World.* Jerusalem: Carta, 2006.

Rasmussen, Carl. *Zondervan NIV Atlas of the Bible.* Grand Rapids: Regency Reference Library/Zondervan, 1989.

Rogerson, John W. *Atlas of the Bible.* London: Phaidon; New York: Facts on File, 1985.

*Smith, George A. *The Historical Geography of the Holy Land.* 19th ed. London: Hodder & Stoughton, 1993 (1896).

Archaeology

Bartlett, John R. *Archaeology and Biblical Interpretation.* London and New York: Routledge, 1997.

Ben-Tor, Amnon, ed. *The Archaeology of Ancient Israel.* New Haven, CT: Yale University Press; Tel Aviv: Open University of Israel, 1992.

Blaiklock, Edward M., and Roland K. Harrison, eds. *The New International Dictionary of Biblical Archaeology.* Grand Rapids: Zondervan, 1983.

Charlesworth, James H., ed. *Jesus and Archaeology.* Grand Rapids: Eerdmans, 2006.

Finegan, Jack. *The Archaeology of the New Testament: The Life of Jesus and the Beginning of the Early Church.* Princeton, NJ: Princeton University Press, 1969.

―――. *The Archaeology of the New Testament: The Mediterranean World of the Early Christian Apostles.* Boulder, CO: Westview; London: Croom Helm, 1981.

Hoffmeier, James K., and Alan Millard, eds. *The Future of Biblical Archaeology: Reassessing Methodologies and Assumptions.* Grand Rapids: Eerdmans, 2004.

Levy, Thomas E., ed. *The Archaeology of Society in the Holy Land.* London: Continuum, 2003 (1995).

*Mazar, Amihai. *Archaeology of the Land of the Bible, 10,000–586 B.C.E.* New York: Doubleday; Cambridge: Lutterworth, 1990.

Meyers, Eric M., ed. *The Oxford Encyclopedia of Archaeology in the Near East.* 5 vols. London and New York: Oxford University Press, 1997.

*Stern, Ephraim. *Archaeology of the Land of the Bible: The Assyrian, Babylonian, and Persian Periods, 732–332 B.C.E.: Volume II.* New York: Doubleday, 2001.

*Stern, Ephraim, Ayelet Levinzon-Gilboa, and Joseph Aviram, eds. *The New Encyclopedia of Archaeological Excavations in the Holy Land.* 4 vols. Jerusalem: Israel Exploration Society and Carta; New York: Simon & Schuster, 1993.

Biblical Backgrounds: Culture and Daily Life

Aune, David E. *The New Testament in Its Literary Environment.* Philadelphia: Westminster, 1989.

Bickerman, Elias J. *Chronology of the Ancient World.* 2nd ed. London: Thames & Hudson; Ithaca, NY: Cornell University Press, 1980.

Borowski, Oded. *Daily Life in Biblical Times.* Atlanta: Society of Biblical Literature (Scholars), 2003.

———. *Every Living Thing: Daily Use of Animals in Ancient Israel.* Walnut Creek, CA: AltaMira, 1998.

Campbell, Ken M. *Marriage and Family in the Biblical World.* Downers Grove, IL: InterVarsity, 2003.

Carter, Charles E., and Carol L. Meyers, eds. *Community, Identity, and Ideology: Social Science Approaches to the Hebrew Bible.* Winona Lake, IN: Eisenbrauns, 1996.

Cary, Max, and Theodore J. Haarhoff. *Life and Thought in the Greek and Roman World.* Westport, CT: Greenwood, 1985 (1940).

Charlesworth, James H., ed. *The Bible and the Dead Sea Scrolls.* 3 vols. Waco, TX: Baylor University Press, 2006.

De Vaux, Roland. *Ancient Israel: Its Life and Institutions.* Grand Rapids: Eerdmans, 1997 (1961).

Esler, Philip F., ed. *Ancient Israel: The Old Testament in Its Social Context.* Minneapolis: Fortress, 2005.

Evans, Craig A., and Stanley E. Porter, eds. *Dictionary of New Testament Background.* Downers Grove, IL: InterVarsity, 2000.

*Ferguson, Everett. *Backgrounds of Early Christianity.* 3rd ed. Grand Rapids: Eerdmans; Northam: Roundhouse, 2004.

Finegan, Jack. *Handbook of Biblical Chronology: Principles of Time Reckoning in the Ancient World and Problems of Chronology in the Bible.* Rev. ed. Peabody, MA: Hendrickson, 1998.

Gager, John G. *Kingdom and Community: The Social World of Early Christianity.* Englewood Cliffs, NJ: Prentice-Hall, 1975.

Grant, Michael, and Rachel Kitzinger, eds. *Civilization of the Ancient Mediterranean: Greece and Rome.* 3 vols. New York: Scribner's, 1988.

Harrison, Roland K. *Old Testament Times: A Social, Political, and Cultural Context.* Grand Rapids: Baker, 2005 (1970).

Hoerth, Alfred J., Gerald L. Mattingly, and Edwin M. Yamauchi. *Peoples of the Old Testament World.* Grand Rapids: Baker; Cambridge: Lutterworth, 1994.

Jeremias, Joachim. *Jerusalem in the Time of Jesus: An Investigation into Economic and Social Conditions during the New Testament Period.* Philadelphia: Fortress, 1975.

*King, Philip J., and Lawrence E. Stager. *Life in Biblical Israel.* Louisville, KY: Westminster John Knox, 2001.

*Klauck, Hans-Josef. *The Religious Context of Early Christianity: A Guide to Graeco-Roman Religions.* Minneapolis: Fortress; Edinburgh: T. & T. Clark, 2003.

*Koester, Helmut. *Introduction to the New Testament, Vol. 1: History, Culture, and Religion of the Hellenistic Age.* 2nd ed. New York: de Gruyter, 2000.

*Lohse, Eduard. *The New Testament Environment.* Nashville: Abingdon; London: SCM, 1976.

Malherbe, Abraham J. *Social Aspects of Early Christianity.* 2nd ed. enl. Eugene, OR: Wipf & Stock, 2001 (1983).

Malina, Bruce J. *The New Testament World: Insights from Cultural Anthropology.* 3rd ed. rev. and exp. Louisville, KY: Westminster John Knox, 2001 (1981).

—. *Christian Origins and Cultural Anthropology.* Atlanta: John Knox, 1986.

Matthews, Victor H. *Manners and Customs in the Bible.* 3rd ed. Peabody, MA: Hendrickson, 2006.

Matthews, Victor H., and Don C. Benjamin. *Social World of Ancient Israel, 1250–587 B.C.E.* Peabody, MA: Hendrickson, 1993.

McNutt, Paula M. *Reconstructing the Society of Ancient Israel.* Louisville, KY: Westminster John Knox, 1999.

Meeks, Wayne A. *The First Urban Christians: The Social World of the Apostle Paul.* 2nd ed. New Haven, CT: Yale University Press, 2003.

—. *The Moral World of the First Christians.* Philadelphia: Westminster, 1986; London: SPCK, 1987.

Perdue, Leo G., Joseph Blenkinsopp, John J. Collins, and Carol Meyers, eds. *Families in Ancient Israel.* Louisville, KY: Westminster John Knox, 1997.

*Roetzel, Calvin J. *The World That Shaped the New Testament.* Rev. ed. Louisville, KY: Westminster John Knox, 2002.

Safrai, S., and M. Stern, eds. *The Jewish People in the First Christian Century.* 2 vols. Assen, Netherlands: Van Gorcum; Philadelphia: Fortress, 1974–76.

Schuller, Eileen M. *The Dead Sea Scrolls: What Have We Learned?* Louisville, KY: Westminster John Knox, 2006.

Stambaugh, John E., and David L. Balch. *The New Testament in Its Social Environment.* Philadelphia: Westminster, 1986.

Theissen, Gerd. *The First Followers of Jesus: A Sociological Analysis of the Earliest Christianity*. London: SCM, 1978.

———. *The Social Setting of Pauline Christianity: Essays on Corinth*. Eugene, OR: Wipf & Stock, 2004 (1982).

VanderKam, James C., and Peter W. Flint. *The Meaning of the Dead Sea Scrolls: Their Significance for Understanding the Bible, Judaism, Jesus, and Christianity*. Edinburgh: T. & T. Clark, 2005.

Van der Toorn, Karel. *Family Religion in Babylonia, Syria, and Israel: Continuity and Changes in the Forms of Religious Life*. Leiden: Brill, 1996.

Van der Toorn, Karel, and Sara J. Denning-Bolle. *From Her Cradle to Her Grave: The Role of Religion in the Life of the Israelite and the Babylonian Woman*. Sheffield, UK: JSOT, 1994.

*van der Woude, A. S., ed. *The World of the Bible*. Grand Rapids: Eerdmans, 1986.

Guides for Using Nonbiblical Comparative Materials

Evans, Craig A. *Ancient Texts for New Testament Studies: A Guide to the Background Literature*. Peabody, MA: Hendrickson, 2005.

Sparks, Kenton L. *Ancient Texts for the Study of the Hebrew Bible: A Guide to the Background Literature*. Peabody, MA: Hendrickson, 2005.

Collections of Nonbiblical Comparative Materials

*Arnold, Bill T., and Bryan Beyer. *Readings from the Ancient Near East: Primary Sources for Old Testament Study*. Grand Rapids: Baker Academic, 2002.

Barnstone, Willis, ed. *The Other Bible: Jewish Pseudepigrapha, Christian Apocrypha, Gnostic Scriptures, Kabbalah, Dead Sea Scrolls*. Rev. ed. San Francisco: HarperSanFrancisco, 2005.

Barrett, Charles K. *The New Testament Background: Writings from Ancient Greece and the Roman Empire That Illuminate Christian Origins*. Rev. ed. San Francisco: HarperSanFrancisco, 1995 (1987).

Beyerlin, Walter, ed. *Near Eastern Religious Texts Relating to the Old Testament*. London: SCM; Philadelphia: Westminster, 1978.

Cartlidge, David R., and David L. Dungan, eds. *Documents for the Study of the Gospels*. Rev. and enl. ed. Minneapolis: Fortress, 1994.

Charles, R. H., ed. *The Apocrypha and Pseudepigrapha of the Old Testament in English: With Introductions and Critical and Explanatory Notes*. 2 vols. Berkeley, CA: Apocryphile, 2004 (1913, 1917).

*Charlesworth, James H., ed. *The Old Testament Pseudepigrapha*. 2 vols. Garden City, NY: Doubleday; London: Darton, Longman & Todd, 1983–85.

Chavalas, Mark W., ed. *The Ancient Near East: Historical Sources in Translation*. Oxford: Blackwell, 2005.

Crossan, John D. *Sayings Parallels: A Workbook for the Jesus Tradition*. Philadelphia: Fortress, 1986.

Ehrman, Bart D. *The New Testament and Other Early Christian Writings: A Reader.* 2nd ed. New York: Oxford University Press, 2003.

*Elliott, J. Keith. *The Apocryphal New Testament: A Collection of Apocryphal Christian Literature in an English Translation.* New ed. Oxford: Clarendon Press; New York: Oxford University Press, 2005 (1993).

*Feldman, Louis, and Meyer Reinhold. *Jewish Life and Thought among Greeks and Romans: Primary Readings.* Minneapolis: Fortress, 1996.

Foster, Benjamin R. *Before the Muses: An Anthology of Akkadian Literature.* 3rd ed. Bethesda, MD: CDL Press, 2005.

*Hallo, William W., and K. Lawson Younger Jr., eds. *The Context of Scripture: Canonical Compositions, Monumental Inscriptions, and Archival Documents from the Biblical World.* 3 vols. Leiden: Brill, 1997–2002.

Hennecke, Edgar, Wilhelm Schneemelcher, and Robert M. Wilson, eds. *New Testament Apocrypha.* Rev. ed. 2 vols. Cambridge: J. Clarke, 1992; Louisville, KY: Westminster John Knox, 2003.

Kee, Howard C. *The Origins of Christianity: Sources and Documents.* London: SPCK, 1980 (1973).

Lewis, Naphtali, and Meyer Reinhold, eds. *Roman Civilization: Selected Readings.* 3rd ed. 2 vols. New York: Columbia University Press, 1990.

Malherbe, Abraham J. *Moral Exhortation: A Greco-Roman Sourcebook.* Louisville, KY: Westminster/John Knox, 1989 (1986).

Martinez, Florentino Garcia, and Eibert J. C. Tigchelaar. *The Dead Sea Scrolls Study Edition.* 2nd ed. 2 vols. Leiden: Brill; Grand Rapids: Eerdmans, 2000.

Matthews, Victor H., and Don C. Benjamin. *Old Testament Parallels: Laws and Stories from the Ancient Near East.* 3rd ed. Mahwah, NJ: Paulist, 2006.

Meyer, Marvin W. *The Ancient Mysteries: A Sourcebook.* Philadelphia: University of Pennsylvania Press, 1999 (1987).

Montefiore, Claude G., and Herbert M. J. Loewe. *A Rabbinic Anthology.* New York: Schocken, 1974 (1938).

Nickelsburg, George W. E., and Michael E. Stone. *Faith and Piety in Early Judaism: Texts and Documents.* Philadelphia: Trinity, 1991 (1983).

Pritchard, James B., ed. *The Ancient Near East in Pictures Relating to the Old Testament.* 2nd ed. Princeton, NJ: Princeton University Press, 1969.

*————, ed. *Ancient Near Eastern Texts Relating to the Old Testament.* 3rd ed. Princeton, NJ: Princeton University Press, 1969.

Robinson, James M., ed. *The Coptic Gnostic Library: A Complete Edition of the Nag Hammadi Codices.* 5 vols. Leiden: Brill, 2000 (1975).

Robinson, James M., and Richard Smith, eds. *The Nag Hammadi Library in English.* 4th rev. ed. Leiden: Brill, 1996.

Schiffman, Lawrence H. *Texts and Traditions: A Source Reader for the Study of Second Temple and Rabbinic Judaism.* Hoboken, NJ: Ktav, 1998.

*Sparks, Hedley F. D., ed. *The Apocryphal Old Testament.* Oxford: Clarendon Press; New York: Oxford University Press, 1985.

Vermes, Géza. *The Complete Dead Sea Scrolls in English*. Rev. ed. London: Penguin, 2004.

*Whittaker, Molly. *Jews and Christians: Graeco-Roman Views*. Cambridge and New York: Cambridge University Press, 1984.

Introductions to the Old Testament

Anderson, Bernhard W., Steven Bishop, and Judith H. Newman. *Understanding the Old Testament*. 5th ed. Upper Saddle River, NJ: Pearson Prentice Hall, 2007.

Birch, Bruce C., Walter Brueggemann, Terence E. Fretheim, and David L. Petersen, eds. *A Theological Introduction to the Old Testament*. 2nd ed. Nashville: Abingdon, 2005.

Brueggemann, Walter. *An Introduction to the Old Testament: The Canon and Christian Imagination*. Louisville, KY: Westminster John Knox, 2003.

Carvalho, Corrine L. *Encountering Ancient Voices: A Guide to Reading the Old Testament*. Winona, MN: Saint Mary's Press, 2006.

Childs, Brevard S. *Introduction to the Old Testament as Scripture*. Philadelphia: Fortress, 1979; London: SCM, 1983.

*Collins, John J. *Introduction to the Hebrew Bible*. Minneapolis: Fortress; Edinburgh: Alban, 2004.

*Coogan, Michael D. *The Old Testament: A Historical and Literary Introduction to the Hebrew Scriptures*. New York: Oxford University Press, 2006.

*Eissfeldt, O. *The Old Testament: An Introduction Including the Apocrypha and Pseudepigrapha and Also the Works of a Similar Type from Qumran: The History of the Formation of the Old Testament*. New York: Harper, 1976 (1965).

Fohrer, Georg. *Introduction to the Old Testament*. Nashville: Abingdon, 1968; London: SPCK, 1976.

Gottwald, Norman K. *The Hebrew Bible—A Socio-literary Introduction*. Philadelphia: Fortress, 2003 (1985).

Harrison, Roland K. *Introduction to the Old Testament: Including a Comprehensive Review of Old Testament Studies and a Special Supplement on the Apocrypha*. Peabody, MA: Hendrickson, 2004 (1969).

*Hayes, John H. *Introduction to Old Testament Study*. Nashville: Abingdon, 1979; London: SCM, 1982.

Matthews, Victor H., and James C. Moyer. *The Old Testament: Text and Context*. 2nd ed. Peabody, MA: Hendrickson, 2005.

Rendtorff, Rolf. *The Old Testament: An Introduction*. Philadelphia: Fortress, 1991 (1983).

Schmidt, Werner H. *Old Testament Introduction*. 2nd ed. Louisville, KY: Westminster John Knox; New York: de Gruyter, 1999.

Soggin, J. Alberto. *Introduction to the Old Testament: From Its Origins to the Closing of the Alexandrian Canon*. 3rd ed. Louisville, KY: Westminster/John Knox, 1989.

Varughese, Alex, Robert Branson, Jim Edlin, and Timothy Mark Green, eds. *Discovering the Old Testament: Story and Faith*. Kansas City: Beacon Hill, 2003.

Introductions to the New Testament

*Brown, Raymond E. *An Introduction to the New Testament*. New York: Doubleday, 1997.

Carson, Donald A., and Douglas J. Moo. *An Introduction to the New Testament*. 2nd ed. Grand Rapids: Zondervan, 2005.

Childs, Brevard S. *The New Testament as Canon: An Introduction*. Valley Forge, PA: Trinity, 1994 (1985).

Cousar, Charles B. *An Introduction to the New Testament: Witnesses to God's New Work*. Louisville, KY: Westminster John Knox, 2006.

*Ehrman, Bart D. *The New Testament: A Historical Introduction to the Early Christian Writings*. 3rd ed. New York: Oxford University Press, 2004.

Guthrie, Donald. *New Testament Introduction*. 4th rev. ed. Downers Grove, IL: InterVarsity, 1990.

*Holladay, Carl R. *A Critical Introduction to the New Testament: Interpreting the Message and Meaning of Jesus Christ*. With expanded CD-ROM version. Nashville: Abingdon, 2005.

*Johnson, Luke T., with Todd C. Penner. Rev. ed. *The Writings of the New Testament: An Interpretation*. Philadelphia: Fortress, 2002.

*Koester, Helmut. *Introduction to the New Testament*. 2nd ed. 2 vols. New York: de Gruyter, 1995–2000.

Kümmel, Werner G. *Introduction to the New Testament*. Rev. and enl. ed. Nashville: Abingdon, 1986.

Marxsen, Willi. *Introduction to the New Testament: An Approach to Its Problems*. Oxford: Blackwell, 1968; Philadelphia: Fortress, 1974.

Perrin, Norman, Dennis C. Duling, and Robert L. Ferm. *The New Testament, An Introduction: Proclamation and Parenesis, Myth and History*. 2nd ed. New York: Harcourt Brace Jovanovich, 1982.

Schnelle, Udo. *The History and Theology of the New Testament Writings*. Minneapolis: Fortress, 1998.

Wikenhauser, Alfred. *New Testament Introduction*. New York: Herder & Herder, 1967 (1958).

Reception History

Carasik, Michael, ed. *The Commentators' Bible: The JPS Miqra'ot Gedolot*. Philadelphia: Jewish Publication Society, 2005–.

Oden, Thomas C., gen. ed. Ancient Christian Commentary on Scripture. Downers Grove, IL: InterVarsity, 1998–.

Sawyer, John F. A., Christopher Rowland, and Judith Kovacs, eds. *Blackwell Bible Commentaries*. Oxford: Blackwell, 2004–.

Seow, C. L., and Hermann Spieckermann, eds. *Encyclopedia of the Bible and Its Reception*. Berlin and New York: de Gruyter, 2007–.

4
Grammatical Criticism
The Language of the Text

If textual criticism is concerned with establishing the wording of the text, and historical criticism with investigating the history *in* and *of* the text, grammatical criticism analyzes a text through its language.

An idea may be conveyed through a single word, but ideas are usually expressed through words arranged in various combinations with each other. Grammatical criticism is concerned not only with how individual words function as carriers of meaning but also with how those words are arranged in phrases and sentences to form meaningful sense units. Using analytical skills related to the study of meanings (semantics), language (philology and linguistics), word origins (etymology), rules of usage (grammar and syntax), dictionaries and lexicons (lexicography), and similar disciplines, grammatical criticism enables us to enter, even re-create, an author's thought world. It assumes that the language we use gives others access to our thoughts.

Analyzing the Language of the Text

We may begin by looking at the way in which we analyze the most fundamental unit of communication—the word. Even though meaning can be conveyed through complex patterns of word arrangement, interpretation often focuses on a single word or phrase. Cracking the code of an important term or expression often provides the key to interpreting a much larger passage. When we read biblical texts, we frequently encounter unfamiliar words or phrases. This often results from the cultural gap modern readers experience when interpreting ancient texts. We may run across a term or expression that means one thing to us as modern interpreters but had a special meaning within ancient Israel or the early church.

Some unfamiliar words or phrases, such as the names of persons and places, are treated as part of historical criticism. But others are not. Such terms as "remnant," "covenant," "repentance," and "justification" receive special treatment in Bible dictionaries and encyclopedias because of their specialized usage by biblical writers. Definitions of such terms in standard English dictionaries are often inadequate, even misleading. Not only are these modern definitions usually brief, but their perspective is also limited to English-language usage. Seldom do these general dictionaries give nuanced treatment to the perspectives of the ancient world that inform the usage of key theological terms in biblical texts.

Quite often we can begin our analysis of a biblical text by isolating prominent words or expressions that we suspect are important but whose meaning we may find unclear. In Jeremiah 31:31–34, the well-known passage proclaiming the coming of a "new covenant," we immediately recognize that the term "covenant" is so central to the passage that we must investigate it thoroughly in order to understand the passage. By concentrating on this single term and its frequent use throughout the Bible, we can learn more about the Israelite understanding of "covenant." As we do so, other aspects of the passage will come into much sharper focus.

In Matthew 16:28, when Jesus asserts that some of those in his audience would not die before they saw "the Son of Man coming in his kingdom," we can easily see that the phrases "Son of Man" and "kingdom" must be investigated before we can understand the passage. By focusing on these key expressions, we can examine how they are used elsewhere in the Gospel of Matthew, in other NT writings, and in other writings of the first century CE. As we learn more about first-century usage of these expressions, we can make better sense of their use in Matthew 16:28.

Language Tools

Bible Dictionaries and Encylopedias

In dealing with individual words or phrases, three kinds of exegetical tools are valuable. First is Bible dictionaries and encyclopedias, which contain articles treating important biblical ideas and concepts. Such articles are usually comprehensive in scope, yet sufficiently specific to provide the exegete with a general grasp of the issues relating to a particular passage. They will also provide useful bibliography for further study.

Wordbooks and Lexicons

A second major resource is biblical wordbooks and lexicons, which usually focus on specific terms or groups of related terms—semantic fields—that are typically used to express certain concepts. Rather than providing information about biblical history and culture, the articles in these books are usually oriented toward the origin and development of biblical language. Single-volume wordbooks contain useful word studies of important biblical terms as well as broader concepts to which a whole cluster of biblical terms may relate. Multivolume wordbooks on both the OT and the NT are also available. Although these are based on the original languages, they are useful to students who know neither Hebrew nor Greek. These multivolume wordbooks contain lengthy articles on individual words, arranged in word families, in which the usage of terms is treated historically, from the time of their earliest usage until the time of their occurrence in the biblical texts, and even after. While these articles are heavily philological in orientation, they also contain valuable theological, historical, cultural, and bibliographical information.

Biblical Concordances

A third resource for investigating the language of the text is the biblical concordance. This tool provides little or no explanatory information comparable to that found in a Bible dictionary, encyclopedia, wordbook, or lexicon. Its primary purpose is to list the various biblical verses in which a word occurs. Ordinarily, a concordance gives the line of the passage in which the word or phrase occurs in order to assist us in discerning the context. The concordance is frequently used to locate a verse in the Bible when we can remember only a word or phrase from the verse. But the concordance does more than help us find a verse we have forgotten. It is a sophisticated tool that gives us access to patterns of language usage within a particular author or biblical writing. In the hands of a technically trained scholar, a concordance is probably the single most useful resource available for doing exegesis. The beginning exegete should aspire to developing similar expertise in using the concordance.

Using Concordances

There are various types of concordances. First, some concordances, such as the popular *Cruden's Concordance*, a work originally published in the eighteenth century, are organized simply. In such works, all the words of the Bible, in this case the KJV, are listed in alphabetical order, and the biblical passages in which the word occurs are listed in canonical order. If, for example, we want to know all the places in the Bible where the word "covenant" occurs, rather than having to read through the entire Bible, find them on our own, and list them by hand, we can turn in the concordance to "covenant" and find that the concordance has already listed them for us. In this type of concordance, however, all the passages from Genesis through Revelation are listed, with no attempt made to differentiate or classify the various meanings or usages of the word.

Second, some concordances are "analytical." These works classify all the passages in which a term occurs into subcategories based on (1) the different Hebrew or Greek words that are translated by a single English word, (2) general themes or topics under which several different words may be included, and (3) the different senses or uses of a single word or expression. We look at these in turn.

1. The first type of analytical concordance (such as Young, Strong, and Morrison) enables us to determine which Hebrew or Greek word the English term translates. This becomes a useful step for doing further word study, and a necessary one, if we want to use the various tools that are based on the original language.

2. The second type of analytical concordance (such as Darton), recognizing that several different words may all relate to the same theme or topic, treats thematically related words as a single group. Since this type of concordance is more topical in its organization, it can be useful in investigating broader concepts that may encompass several different biblical words.

3. A third type of analytical concordance (such as Lisowsky, Moulton and Geden, and Aland) employs a principle of classification which recognizes that even the same Hebrew or Greek word or expression may be used in various senses throughout the biblical writings. Accordingly,

it groups together all those passages in which a term is used in a similar sense. This may be shown by key indicators listed at the beginning of the entry or by arranging the passages in separate groups. In either case, this type of arrangement greatly assists the exegete because it provides a natural place to begin the investigation without having to examine every single biblical verse in which the word occurs.

As we noted earlier, comparing how language is used in related literature, often designated "apocryphal" or "deuterocanonical," can help us understand the meaning and use of terminology found in other biblical texts. Where concordances exist for this literature, such as biblical concordances that include the apocryphal and deuterocanonical writings (for example, the *NRSV Concordance Unabridged* or Hatch and Redpath's *Concordance to the Septuagint*) or those devoted explicitly to these writings (such as Metzger's *Concordance to the Apocryphal/Deuterocanonical Books of the Revised Standard Version*), the same process of investigation can be pursued. Frequently, by examining how a term or expression is used in these writings, we discover information that may be relevant to our understanding of a usage in a particular text or author.

Once we have looked up an important term in the concordance and located the relevant passages in which it occurs, we can develop interpretive questions that enable us to understand the significance of what we have found: Is the term used in the same sense in the different passages? Does it have a technical meaning? Are there different nuances in its various usages? If so, why? In what type of literature does the term occur? Is it always used in the same type of literature or the same historical setting? Does it have a literal or metaphorical meaning? Does it tend to be used by one author, or in one section of biblical writings, to the exclusion of others? If so, why? Do these patterns of usage provide clues to understanding an individual verse, a section, or even an entire writing?

By asking such questions—and many others that occur to us as we work with the material—we gradually broaden our understanding of the term, the passage itself, and the other biblical writings in which it occurs. By formulating such questions and analyzing what we find, we are able to reconstruct the thought world of the text or author.

An Example from the New Testament: Matthew 16:28

We can see how this is done by looking at the example we mentioned earlier, the use of "Son of Man" in Matthew 16:28. If we look up this expression in an analytical concordance (such as Young, Strong, or Moulton and Geden), we immediately notice several things.

First, the expression tends to cluster in certain biblical writings. It is used most frequently in the NT, especially in the Synoptic Gospels. As we scan its occurrences in the NT as a whole, we notice that it occurs less frequently in writings attributed to John and Paul. This suggests that it was relatively unimportant, or even inconsequential, in these writings. This negative observation can be useful because it provides a point of contrast with the Matthean usage.

Second, the expression occurs in the OT in several places and in several senses. We should note these different senses (which are already classified for us in an analytical concordance) and ask which of these, if any, bears on the usage in our passage. As it turns out, a crucial exegetical question discussed in commentaries is whether the term used by Jesus in the Gospels has a general sense, as it does in Ezekiel, or a more technical sense, as it does in Daniel.

Third, if we examine the usages of the term in Matthew alone, we discover that it is used in at least three ways: (a) in a general sense, almost as a synonym for "man" or "human being"; (b) in an eschatological sense to refer to a figure who will appear at the end of time as judge; and (c) in a specifically christological sense, especially when the suffering of the Messiah is discussed. Next, we try to determine how the expression is used in Matthew 16:28. We may even ask whether its usage in Matthew 16:28 relates to one or more of its three senses. Does it have one or several senses? Do the three senses tend to merge with each other?

After examining patterns of usage in Matthew, we can do the same with Mark and Luke. As we broaden the scope of our investigation, we try to relate what we find in these parallel accounts to Matthew. Here we are trying to determine how Matthew's use of the expression relates to Mark's and Luke's understanding. By examining significant similarities and differences among the Synoptic Gospels, we can sometimes get a better sense of distinctive features of one of the Gospels, in this case, Matthew.

Fourth, we can expand our investigation by examining the use of the expression in other writings from roughly the same historical period, especially the OT Apocrypha and Pseudepigrapha (or deuterocanonical writings), asking similar questions.

Entering the "Semantic World" of the Text

This short exercise illustrates the importance of examining key terms and concepts as they are used in the biblical writings. By locating the various passages in which key expressions occur and formulating questions relevant to these occurrences, we can expand our understanding of the "semantic world" in which these expressions were used.

Using concordances in this way assumes that the various texts in which an expression occurs provide a valuable context in which it should be understood. Wordbooks, lexicons, and other studies focusing on single terms or phrases are prepared using the concordance as the basic tool. To save time, we may consult such works first, but we should not bypass concordance work that requires us to consult the texts directly. Not only do we gain better control of the data by examining them for ourselves, but we also often see things that the standard wordbooks or lexicons miss. If we defer too quickly to experts, we may miss valuable new discoveries that come only through our own firsthand examination of relevant data. If we skip this all-important primary level of investigation, our exegesis tends to be derivative rather than original. It is much better for us to do the primary investigative work first, formulate our own hypotheses and interpretive explanations based on these observations, and then use the wordbooks and similar tools to check our own insights and findings.

Our remarks have been suggestive rather than comprehensive. To list all of the ways in which a concordance can be used in exegesis would require a lengthy discussion. But we hope to have shown that the concordance is the single most valuable resource for the exegete who wishes to do original work on a passage.

Moving from English to Hebrew or Greek

Knowing the original biblical languages is obviously an advantage to the exegete, but students without such knowledge can still use most of these grammatical and linguistic tools. This requires us to be aware of special problems that arise when our investigation moves beyond the English language to the original Hebrew or Greek. Some suggestions and observations are in order.

First, as noted earlier, some concordances are designed to accommodate students without knowledge of Hebrew or Greek. Along with the English words, these concordances list their equivalent Hebrew and Greek terms. They usually supply the definition of each Hebrew or Greek word and transliterate them into English (write the word using equivalent English letters). In this way, students without knowledge of Hebrew or Greek can determine the transliterated form of the original word, which also provides a clue to pronunciation.

Second, since a single Hebrew or Greek word is usually rendered by several English words, the analytical concordances provide appendices containing comprehensive indexes of these terms and their various English renderings. The terms in the concordances are coded for making reference to the appendices.

Third, in recent editions of concordances, words are keyed to their corresponding entries in standard lexicons and wordbooks. This allows the student to (1) identify a word in the English translation, (2) locate it in a concordance, and (3) use the code number to find the related entry in a lexicon or wordbook. Without knowing the Hebrew or Greek alphabet, a student can move from an English word used in translation to its counterpart in a Hebrew or Greek lexicon.

Fourth, a student may determine the original Hebrew or Greek word by consulting an interlinear, an edition of the Bible that provides the original text of the Bible on one line and an English translation on an adjacent line.

Moving from an English translation to the original Hebrew or Greek is not an easy process. Nor is it obvious in every case. But the diligent student who has access to basic tools for biblical exegesis can make this transition. By careful use of such resources, and by consulting with those who know the original languages, beginning students can draw on this body of information for gaining deeper understanding of the language of the text.

Some Cautions about Wordbooks and Word Studies

While word studies are often illuminating, they can be misleading. As we use biblical wordbooks, lexicons, and dictionaries, we should be aware that they are sometimes based on faulty conceptions of language. Scholarly critique of well-known biblical wordbooks and lexicons has identified several principles that we should keep in mind when using such tools.

1. Words in Hebrew, Aramaic, and Greek, like words in any other language, frequently possess a wide variety of meanings. Dictionaries based on more sophisticated principles of linguistics tend to offer several meanings for words—a range of meanings—rather than give a single meaning from which all others are assumed to derive. But some biblical wordbooks give the impression that biblical terms had a single basic meaning that was "carried" in the root form of the word. This

assumption is known as the "root fallacy." Even though this conception of root meanings informs many wordbooks or word studies, it should be avoided.

2. Biblical writers and characters were no more aware of the history of the words and expressions they used than are modern writers and speakers. Most of us are unaware of the history of the words we use. Before using a word, we rarely try to determine its "original meaning." Unless we are historical philologists, such matters are seldom more than a curiosity. What matters is whether the words we are using communicate what we want to say. As exegetes, we should not assume that an "original meaning" exists for each biblical word. Nor should we assume that ancient speakers or authors were especially concerned with the "original meaning" of words they used. In analyzing biblical language, nothing requires us to ascertain the "original meaning" of a particular word or phrase within a given passage.

3. Generally speaking, individual words or phrases are not in themselves the bearers of special theological meaning. When a term, even a technical term, occurs in a biblical text, we should not assume that the original reader would automatically associate it with various theological concepts, much less a theological system. The term "covenant," for example, was used in many different contexts in ancient Israel. Its appearance in a text should not be understood automatically as a reference to a special divine-human relationship. Similarly, the NT word for love, *agapē*, does not necessarily refer to some special form of self-giving affection (see Luke 11:43).

4. An idea or theological concept can be expressed in one way with one set of terms in one text. But the same idea or a similar concept can be expressed in another way with a different set of terms in another text. We should not assume that ideas or concepts can be expressed with only one set of terms.

5. The best guide to the meaning of a word is the context in which it is used. This means, first of all, the immediate context of the passage in which it occurs. If a word has several meanings, we should explore the range of meanings and see how they fit or do not fit in the context. A broader context is the whole document in which the term appears. This requires us to explore how a term is used elsewhere in the writing. A further context is the biblical and nonbiblical documents that are contemporary with the document being studied. Since the meaning and usage of words change through history, we should not conclude that an expression found in one historical context necessarily denotes

the same thing in another time and place. Some of the terms used in the KJV, for example, now mean something totally different.

Grammar and Syntax

As noted earlier, the language of the text consists not only of words, but also of words arranged in meaningful combinations. Consequently, grammatical criticism also includes questions of syntax and grammar. Here the exegete deals with the words of the text as they are combined with each other to form phrases, sentences, and paragraphs, as well as the special problems this creates.

A sound knowledge of English grammar makes it easier to engage in this aspect of interpretation. But many beginning exegetes experience difficulty at this point because in recent years schools at every level have de-emphasized explicit aspects of English grammar. While students may speak or write acceptable English, they may not have enough formal knowledge of the language and its rules of usage to analyze and discuss the grammar of the English Bible. The beginning exegete may need to consult a standard English composition or grammar book before other exegetical tools will be of much use. We must know the parts of speech and possess some elementary knowledge about them, along with basic grammatical terms, before we can analyze the syntax of a biblical passage.

Questions of syntax and grammar often arise when we try to discern the meaning of a sense unit. Such questions can surface when we compare two or more English translations and notice the various ways in which the passage is rendered into English. Translators' footnotes may also provide indications of such questions. Two examples may be noted.

In 2 Corinthians 5:19, the New Revised Standard Version reads "in Christ God was reconciling the world to himself." An alternative translation is provided in the note: "God was in Christ reconciling the world to himself." Consulting other translations, such as the Revised English Bible, points up the exegetical difficulty even further. The exegetical significance is far-reaching. The NRSV lays greater stress on the act of reconciliation as initiated by God while the NRSV note lays greater stress on Christ as the locus and agent of reconciliation. The exegete must decide whether the passage is fundamentally a statement about salvation as an act of grace initiated by God—a soteriological claim— or a christological statement about the incarnation. In this case, the meaning of the words themselves poses little difficulty. It is rather their combination with each other—their syntax—that is the problem.

A similar exegetical problem is presented in Genesis 1:1, which the New Revised Standard Version renders "In the beginning when God created the heavens and the earth." The alternative translations, "When God began to create . . ." and "In the beginning God created . . . ," are possible because the grammatical evidence is evaluated differently. As before, the other translations point to the same exegetical problem.

To resolve such questions, we must deal with the grammar and syntax of the passage. This becomes evident when one consults critical commentaries on the passage where the various options are outlined and discussed. Eventually, it may be necessary to consult standard grammars of the Hebrew and Greek languages.

It may be useful to diagram the passage. Older methods of diagraming sentences, which were used in English composition courses, may prove useful in this regard. The system of diagraming need not be conventional or even highly structured. What is often needed, more than anything else, is for the student to rewrite the passage, diagraming it in a series of sense units, in order to see how the various parts relate to each other. In this way, it often becomes clear that certain phrases can be located in one or more places, each location altering the interpretation of the sentence. This is a worthwhile practice if the text is poetic, for we may discover parallel structures not otherwise obvious, especially if the text is printed as straight prose in the English edition of the Bible we are using.

Analyzing the syntax of the passage and assessing grammatical rules as they apply to the passage should be done only when the text requires it. Some texts require little or no grammatical analysis of this sort, while others—some Pauline passages, for example—will be difficult to understand without it.

This aspect of exegesis deals with the author's world of thought as it is expressed through written words. The language of the text provides the skeletal structure of the author's thought. Grammatical criticism enables us to enter the author's thought world through a particular passage. As we relate the patterns of language usage in one passage to other relevant passages by the same author, we gain a better sense of the author's larger thought world. As we extend our grammatical search to other biblical writings, we are able to place our particular passage within the broader framework of biblical thought.

BIBLIOGRAPHY

Old Testament Lexicons and Aids

*Armstrong, Terry A., Douglas L. Busby, and Cyril F. Carr. *A Reader's Hebrew-English Lexicon of the Old Testament: Four Volumes in One.* Grand Rapids: Regency Reference Library, 1989.

Brown, Francis, Samuel R. Driver, and Charles A. Briggs. *The Brown-Driver-Briggs Hebrew and English Lexicon, with an Appendix Containing the Biblical Aramaic, Coded with the Numbering System from Strong's Exhaustive Concordance of the Bible.* Peabody, MA: Hendrickson, 2005 (1906).

Clines, David J. A. *The Dictionary of Classical Hebrew.* 8 vols. Sheffield, UK: Sheffield Academic Press, 1993–.

Davidson, Benjamin. *The Analytical Hebrew and Chaldee Lexicon.* Peabody, MA: Hendrickson, 1995 (1850).

Einspahr, Bruce. *Index to Brown, Driver and Briggs Hebrew Lexicon.* Chicago: Moody, 1976.

Gesenius, Wilhelm. *Gesenius' Hebrew-Chaldee Lexicon to the Old Testament Scriptures: Numerically Coded to Strong's Exhaustive Concordance.* Grand Rapids: Baker, 1979.

*Holladay, William L., ed. *A Concise Hebrew and Aramaic Lexicon of the Old Testament, Based upon the Lexical Work of Ludwig Köhler and Walter Baumgartner.* Leiden: Brill; Grand Rapids: Eerdmans, 1988.

Jastrow, Marcus. *A Dictionary of the Targumim, the Talmud Babli and Yerushalmi, and the Midrashic Literature.* Peabody, MA: Hendrickson, 2005 (1943).

Kochler, Ludwig, Walter Baumgartner, Mervyn E. J. Richardson, and Johann J. Stamm. *The Hebrew and Aramaic Lexicon of the Old Testament.* 5 vols. Leiden: Brill, 1994–2000. Study ed. 2 vols. Leiden: Brill, 2001.

Lust, Johan, Erik Eynikel, K. Hauspie, and G. Chamberlain, eds. *A Greek-English Lexicon of the Septuagint.* Stuttgart: Deutsche Bibelgesellschaft, 1992–.

Robinson, Maurice A. *Indexes to All Editions of Brown-Driver-Briggs Hebrew Lexicon and Thayer's Greek Lexicon.* Grand Rapids: Baker, 1981.

New Testament Lexicons and Aids

Abbott-Smith, George. *A Manual Greek Lexicon of the New Testament.* 3rd ed. Edinburgh: T. & T. Clark, 1936.

Alsop, John R. *An Index to the Revised Bauer-Arndt-Gingrich Greek Lexicon.* 2nd ed. Grand Rapids: Zondervan, 1982.

Bullinger, Ethelbert W. *A Critical Lexicon and Concordance to the English and Greek New Testament.* Grand Rapids: Kregel, 1999 (1877).

*Danker, Frederick W., ed. *A Greek-English Lexicon of the New Testament and Other Early Christian Literature.* 3rd ed. Chicago: University of Chicago Press, 2000.

Friberg, Timothy, Barbara Friberg, and Neva F. Miller. *Analytical Lexicon of the Greek New Testament.* Victoria, BC: Trafford, 2005.

*Kubo, Sakae. *A Reader's Greek-English Lexicon of the New Testament*. Grand Rapids: Zondervan, 1975.

Liddell, Henry G., Robert Scott, Henry S. Jones, and Roderick McKenzie. *A Greek-English Lexicon*. Rev. and augmented. Oxford: Clarendon Press; New York: Oxford University Press, 1996.

*Louw, J. P., and Eugene A. Nida. *Greek-English Lexicon of the New Testament, Based on Semantic Domains*. 2nd ed. 2 vols. New York: United Bible Societies, 1989.

Moulton, Harold K. *The Analytical Greek Lexicon Revised*. Grand Rapids: Zondervan (Harper Collins), 1991 (1852).

Moulton, James H., and George Milligan. *The Vocabulary of the Greek Testament, Illustrated from the Papyri and Other Non-Literary Sources*. Peabody, MA: Hendrickson, 1997 (1930).

Rogers, Cleon L., Jr., Cleon L. Rogers III, and Fritz Rienecker. *The New Linguistic and Exegetical Key to the Greek New Testament*. Grand Rapids: Zondervan, 1998.

Thayer, Joseph H. *Thayer's Greek-English Lexicon of the New Testament: Coded with the Numbering System from Strong's Exhaustive Concordance of the Bible*. Peabody, MA: Hendrickson, 1996.

Zerwick, Max, and Mary Grosvenor. *A Grammatical Analysis of the Greek New Testament*. Unabridged 5th rev. ed. Rome: Pontificio Istituto Biblico, 1996.

Hebrew and Aramaic Grammars

Arnold, Bill T., and John H. Choi. *A Guide to Biblical Hebrew Syntax*. New York and Cambridge: Cambridge University Press, 2003.

Ben Zvi, Ehud, Maxine Hancock, and Richard Beinert. *Readings in Biblical Hebrew: An Intermediate Textbook*. New Haven, CT: Yale University Press, 1993.

Gesenius, Wilhelm, Emil Kautzsch, and Arthur E. Cowley. *Gesenius' Hebrew Grammar*. Mineola, NY: Dover, 2006 (1910).

Green, Jennifer S., G. Brooke Lester, Joseph F. Scrivner, and C. L. Seow. *Handbook for a Grammar to Biblical Hebrew*. Nashville: Abingdon, 2005.

Greenberg, Moshe. *Introduction to Hebrew*. Eugene, OR: Wipf & Stock, 2005 (1965).

Greenspahn, Frederick E. *An Introduction to Aramaic*. 2nd ed. Atlanta: Society of Biblical Literature, 2003.

Johns, Alger F. *A Short Grammar of Biblical Aramaic*. Rev. ed. Berrien Springs, MI: Andrews University Press, 1972.

Joüon, Paul, and T. Muraoka. *A Grammar of Biblical Hebrew*. 2 vols. Rome: Pontifical Institute, 1991.

Kelley, Page H., Daniel S. Mynatt, and Timothy G. Crawford. *The Masorah of Biblia Hebraica Stuttgartensia: Introduction and Annotated Glossary*. Grand Rapids: Eerdmans, 1998.

Kittel, Bonnie P., Vicki Hoffer, and Rebecca A. Wright. *Biblical Hebrew: A Text and Workbook*. 2nd ed. New Haven, CT: Yale University Press, 2005.

*Lambdin, Thomas O. *Introduction to Biblical Hebrew.* New York: Scribner, 1971; London: Darton, Longman & Todd, 1973.

Rosenthal, Franz. *A Grammar of Biblical Aramaic.* 7th exp. ed. Wiesbaden: Harrassowitz, 2006.

*Seow, Choon Leong. *A Grammar for Biblical Hebrew.* Rev. ed. Nashville: Abingdon, 1995.

Waltke, Bruce K., and Michael P. O'Connor. *An Introduction to Biblical Hebrew Syntax.* 9th corrected printing. Winona Lake, IN: Eisenbrauns, 2004 (1990).

Weingreen, Jacob, and Hannah C. Jaffe. *Practical Grammar for Classical Hebrew.* 2nd ed. Oxford: Oxford University Press, 1959.

Greek Grammars

Blass, Friedrich, A. Debrunner, and Robert W. Funk. *A Greek Grammar of the New Testament and Other Early Christian Literature.* Chicago: University of Chicago Press, 1973.

Countryman, L. William. *Read It in Greek: An Introduction to New Testament Greek.* Grand Rapids: Eerdmans, 1993.

*Croy, N. Clayton. *A Primer of Biblical Greek.* Grand Rapids: Eerdmans, 1999.

Duff, Jeremy, and John W. Wenham. *The Elements of New Testament Greek.* 3rd ed. Cambridge and New York: Cambridge University Press, 2005.

Funk, Robert W. *A Beginning-Intermediate Grammar of Hellenistic Greek.* 2nd ed. 3 vols. Missoula, MT: Scholars Press for the Society of Biblical Literature, 1977.

Kubo, Sakae. *A Beginner's New Testament Greek Grammar.* New rev. ed. Lanham, MD: University Press of America, 1979.

*Machen, J. Gresham, and Dan McCartney. *New Testament Greek for Beginners.* 2nd ed. Upper Saddle River, NJ: Pearson and Prentice Hall, 2004 (1951).

Moule, Charles F. D. *An Idiom Book of New Testament Greek.* 2nd ed. Cambridge: Cambridge University Press, 1959.

Moulton, James H., Wilbert F. Howard, and Nigel Turner. *A Grammar of New Testament Greek.* 4 vols. Edinburgh: T. & T. Clark, 1929–76.

*Mounce, William D. *Basics of Biblical Greek Grammar.* 2nd ed. Grand Rapids: Zondervan, 2003.

Owings, Timothy. *A Cumulative Index to New Testament Greek Grammars.* Grand Rapids: Baker, 1983.

Robertson, A. T. *A Grammar of the Greek New Testament in the Light of Historical Research.* 4th ed. Nashville: Broadman, 1934.

―――. *A New Short Grammar of the Greek New Testament for Students Familiar with the Greek New Testament. Parts I, III, and IV.* New York: Harper, 1935.

*Smyth, Herbert W. *Greek Grammar.* Rev. ed. Cambridge, MA: Harvard University Press, 1984.

Swetnam, James. *An Introduction to the Study of New Testament Greek.* Rome: Editrice Pontificio Istituto Biblico, 1998–.

Thackeray, Henry St J. *A Grammar of the Old Testament in Greek according to the Septuagint.* Hildesheim and New York: Georg Olms, 1987 (1909).

Voelz, James W. *Fundamental Greek Grammar.* St. Louis: Concordia, 1986.

Wallace, Daniel B. *The Basics of New Testament Syntax: An Intermediate Greek Grammar.* Grand Rapids: Zondervan, 2000.

*———. *Greek Grammar beyond the Basics: An Exegetical Syntax of the New Testament with Scripture, Subject, and Greek Word Indexes.* Grand Rapids: Zondervan, 1996.

Concordances

Aland, Kurt. *Vollständige Konkordanz zum griechischen Neuen Testament: Unter Zugrundelegung aller modernen kritischen Textausgaben und des Textus Receptus.* 2 vols. Berlin and New York: de Gruyter, 1983.

Bachmann, Horst, and Wolfgang A. Slaby, eds. *Computer Concordance to the Novum Testamentum Graece of Nestle-Aland, 26th Edition, and to the Greek New Testament, 3rd Edition.* 2nd ed. Berlin and New York: de Gruyter, 1985.

Cruden, Alexander. *Cruden's Concordance.* Rev. ed. Cambridge: Lutterworth, 2002 (1737).

Darton, Michael. *Modern Concordance to the New Testament.* London: Darton, Longman & Todd; Garden City, NY: Doubleday, 1976.

Davidson, Benjamin. *A Concordance of the Hebrew and Chaldee Scriptures.* London: Bagster, 1876.

Ellison, John W. *Nelson's Complete Concordance of the Revised Standard Version Bible.* 2nd ed. Nashville: Nelson, 1984.

Even-Soshan, Avraham, and John Sailhamer. *A New Concordance of the Bible: Thesaurus of the Language of the Bible.* 2nd ed. Jerusalem: Kiryat Sefer, 1990.

Goodrick, Edward W., and John R. Kohlenberger. *New International Bible Concordance.* Grand Rapids: Zondervan, 1981.

Goodrick, Edward W., John R. Kohlenberger, and James A. Swanson. *Zondervan NIV Exhaustive Concordance.* 2nd ed. Grand Rapids: Zondervan, 1990.

Hartdegen, Stephen J. *Nelson's Complete Concordance of the New American Bible.* Nashville: Nelson; Collegeville, MN: Liturgical Press; Toronto: Welch, 1977.

Hatch, Edwin, and Henry A. Redpath. *A Concordance to the Septuagint and the Other Greek Versions of the Old Testament Including the Apocryphal Books.* 2nd ed. 3 vols. Grand Rapids: Baker, 1998 (1954). See also Elmar Camilo Dos Santos, *An Expanded Hebrew Index for the Hatch-Redpath Concordance to the Septuagint* (Jerusalem: Dugith, 1987).

*Kohlenberger, John R. *The Concise Concordance to the New Revised Standard Version.* New York: Oxford University Press, 1994.

———. *The New American Bible Concise Concordance.* New York: Oxford University Press, 2003.

*———. *The NRSV Concordance Unabridged: Including the Apocryphal/Deuterocanonical Books.* Grand Rapids: Zondervan, 1991.

Köstenberger, Andreas, and Raymond Bouchoc, eds. *The Book Study Concordance of the Greek New Testament.* Nashville: Broadman & Holman, 2003.

Lisowsky, Gerhard, and Hans P. Rüger. *Konkordanz zum hebräischen Alten Testament.* 3rd ed. Stuttgart: Deutsche Bibelgesellschaft, 1993.

Mandelkern, Solomon, Moshe H. Goshen-Gottstein, and F. Margolin. *Veteris Testamenti concordantiae hebraicae atque chaldaicae.* Tel Aviv: Schocken, 1978.

Metzger, Bruce M. *Concordance to the Apocryphal/Deuterocanonical Books of the Revised Standard Version.* Grand Rapids: Eerdmans; London: Collins, 1983.

Morgenthaler, Robert. *Statistik des neutestamentlicher Wortschatzes.* 4th ed. Zurich: Gotthelf, 1992.

Morrish, George. *Concordance of the Septuagint.* London: Bagster, 1970; Grand Rapids: Zondervan, 1976.

*Morrison, Clinton. *An Analytical Concordance to the Revised Standard Version of the New Testament.* Philadelphia: Westminster, 1979.

Moulton, William F., Alfred S. Geden, and Harold K. Moulton. *A Concordance to the Greek Testament according to the Texts of Westcott and Hort, Tischendorf and the English Revisers.* 5th ed. Edinburgh: T. & T. Clark, 1978.

*Moulton, William F., Alfred S. Geden, and I. Howard Marshall. *A Concordance to the Greek Testament.* 6th ed. London and New York: T. & T. Clark, 2002.

Schmoller, Alfred. *Handkonkordanz zum griechischen Neuen Testament.* 8th ed. Stuttgart: Deutsche Bibelgesellschaft, 1989 (1938).

Strong, James, John R. Kohlenberger, and James A. Swanson. *The Strongest Strong's Exhaustive Concordance of the Bible.* Grand Rapids: Zondervan, 2001 (1890).

Wigram, George V. *The Englishman's Greek Concordance of the New Testament: Coded with the Numbering System from Strong's Exhaustive Concordance of the Bible.* Peabody, MA: Hendrickson, 1999 (1903).

———. *The Englishman's Hebrew and Chaldee Concordance of the Old Testament Numerically Coded to Strong's Exhaustive Concordance.* Grand Rapids: Baker, 1980.

Wigram, George V., and Ralph D. Winter. *The Word Study Concordance.* Pasadena, CA: William Carey Library; Wheaton, IL: Wheaton, 1978.

*Young, Robert. *Young's Analytical Concordance to the Bible.* Peabody, MA: Hendrickson, 1992 (1879).

Wordbooks

Bauer, Johannes B., ed. *Encyclopedia of Biblical Theology: The Complete Sacramentum Verbi.* New York: Crossroad, 1970.

*Botterweck, G. Johannes, Helmer Ringgren, and Heinz-Josef Fabry, eds. *Theological Dictionary of the Old Testament.* Grand Rapids: Eerdmans, 1974–.

Brown, Colin, ed. *The New International Dictionary of New Testament Theology.* 4 vols. Grand Rapids: Zondervan, 1986. CD-ROM: Version 5.1. Grand Rapids: Zondervan, 2004.

Gowan, Donald E., ed. *The Westminster Theological Wordbook of the Bible*. Louisville, KY: Westminster John Knox, 2003.

*Jenni, Ernst, and Claus Westermann, eds. *Theological Lexicon of the Old Testament*. 3 vols. Peabody, MA: Hendrickson, 1997.

*Kittel, Gerhard, Gerhard Friedrich, and Geoffrey W. Bromiley, eds. *Theological Dictionary of the New Testament*. 10 vols. Grand Rapids: Eerdmans, 1964–99. 1-vol. abridged ed., 1985.

Léon-Dufour, Xavier, P. Joseph Cahill, and E. M. Stewart. *Dictionary of Biblical Theology*. 2nd ed. London: Burns & Oates, 1988.

*Richardson, Alan, ed. *A Theological Word Book of the Bible*. London: SCM; New York: Macmillan, 1950.

Robertson, A. T. *Word Pictures in the New Testament*. 6 vols. Nashville: Broadman, 1985 (1930).

Turner, Nigel. *Grammatical Insights into the New Testament*. London and New York: T. & T. Clark, 2004.

———. *Christian Words*. Edinburgh: T. & T. Clark, 1980; Nashville: Nelson, 1982.

Van Gemeren, Willem A., ed. *New International Dictionary of Old Testament Theology and Exegesis*. 5 vols. Grand Rapids: Zondervan, 1997.

Vincent, Marvin R. *Word Studies in the New Testament*. 4 vols. Peabody, MA: Hendrickson, 1991 (1887–1900).

Vine, William E. *Vine's Expository Dictionary of Old and New Testament Words*. Nashville: Nelson, 2003 (1939–41, 1981–84).

von Allmen, Jean-Jacques, and H. H. Rowley, eds. *The Vocabulary of the Bible: A Companion to the Bible*. Cambridge: James Clarke, 2002 (1958).

Interlinears

Berry, George R. *Interlinear Greek-English New Testament, with a Greek-English Lexicon and New Testament Synonyms*. Grand Rapids: Baker, 2003 (1897).

*Green, Jay P. *The Interlinear Bible, Coded with Strong's Concordance Numbers*. 2nd ed. Peabody, MA: Hendrickson, 2000 (1985).

Kohlenberger, John R. *The Interlinear NIV Hebrew-English Old Testament*. Grand Rapids: Zondervan, 1987.

*Marshall, Alfred. *The Interlinear KJV-NIV Parallel New Testament in Greek and English*. Grand Rapids: Zondervan, 1975.

———. *The Interlinear NIV Parallel New Testament in Greek and English*. Grand Rapids: Zondervan, 1999.

*———. *The Interlinear NRSV-NIV Parallel New Testament in Greek and English*. Grand Rapids: Zondervan, 1993.

———. *The RSV Interlinear Greek-English New Testament: The Nestle Greek Text with a Literal English Translation*. Grand Rapids: Zondervan, 1970.

Mounce, W. D. *Interlinears for the Rest of Us*. Grand Rapids: Zondervan, 2006.

Semantics and Linguistics

Barr, James. *Comparative Philology and the Text of the Old Testament.* Winona Lake, IN: Eisenbrauns, 1987.

*————. *The Semantics of Biblical Language.* Eugene, OR: Wipf & Stock, 2004 (1961).

Caird, George B. *The Language and Imagery of the Bible.* Grand Rapids: Eerdmans, 1980.

Gibson, Arthur. *Biblical Semantic Logic: A Preliminary Analysis.* London: Sheffield, 2001 (1981).

Louw, J. P. *Semantics of New Testament Greek.* Chico, CA: Scholars; Philadelphia: Fortress, 1982.

Nida, Eugene A., and Charles R. Taber. *The Theory and Practice of Translation.* Leiden: Brill, 2003 (1969).

5
Literary Criticism
The Composition and Rhetorical Style of the Text

Broadly speaking, literary criticism encompasses all questions pertaining to the composition of a text, including its authorship, historical setting, purpose for writing, and the overall structure, or form, that gives shape to the writing. These latter two elements are sometimes referred to as literary purpose and literary form or literary structure. Some of these questions we have treated in earlier chapters because they are discrete exegetical tasks.

What "Literary Criticism" Refers To

At an earlier period in biblical studies, literary criticism had a narrow focus. In the eighteenth century, it referred primarily to interpretation that focused on identifying sources, especially written documents, that had been used in composing biblical writings. At that time, interpreters became increasingly aware of certain difficulties posed by reading particular portions of the Bible as single, unified compositions. They observed literary clues within biblical texts, such as major thematic shifts or differences in writing style, that suggested compositions in which earlier literary sources, or strands of oral and literary material, had been woven together, or edited, into what we now know as "books" of the Bible.

This approach altered the way sections of the Bible, such as the Pentateuch, or individual books, such as 2 Corinthians, were understood.

Such writings were now seen as composites of various earlier works —secondary collections, as it were, of writings that were previously separate, even disparate. Because this interpretive approach sought to identify earlier literary sources that lay behind the final edited form of biblical writings, it was referred to as source criticism. Separating out these previous sources or layers of material, describing their content and characteristic features, and relating them to one another eventually also came to be designated as literary criticism. This was an appropriate label, since interpreters focused not only on earlier sources but also the entire process of literary composition. For them, identifying literary markers in the text, such as the author's use of language and style or editorial "seams" suggesting the stitching together of different documents, was literary criticism.

Among scholars who study the literature of different cultures or peoples, such as English or Russian literature, literary criticism encompasses a broad range of interests. These include

literary structure—how a text is arranged or organized;

literary style—techniques of language usage that distinguish an author or a text;

literary purpose—what a writing achieves either as an expression of the author's intent or as a function of the text itself;

literary mood—emotions associated with, or created by, a writing;

literary strategy—how various elements are deployed within a single genre to achieve a certain purpose;

literary imagination—the world reflected in a text (or the author's mind) and the world a text creates in the reader's mind.

While literary criticism in this broad sense informs the interpretation of many different literatures, its applicability to the Bible is evident. Each aspect of literary criticism mentioned above is relevant to biblical interpretation. To the extent that these perspectives inform biblical interpretation, the Bible is being read like any other body of literature. As with literature in general, we must read the Bible with some literary competence and discretion.

We all realize that different reading conventions are operative depending on the type of literature we are reading. We read prose with one set of expectations, poetry quite differently. Different forms of writing create different expectations of meaning and require appropriate strategies for meaningful interpretation. Readers discern "information" within a given writing in different ways, depending on how the writing is structured and how language is used. As we interpret texts, we must learn to ask different kinds of questions—questions that make sense for a particular form of writing. Some questions will yield meaningful answers; others will not. Our skill as interpreters—as literary critics—is directly related to our ability to ask intelligent questions of texts.

Rhetorical Criticism

Although rhetorical criticism is sometimes treated as a separate form of criticism, we include it with literary criticism. Rhetoric is one of the oldest academic disciplines. In the ancient world, especially in Greece and Rome, the study of rhetoric related primarily to oral discourse. But ancient rhetoricians, recognizing the close relationship between oral and written discourse, discussed strategies for composing written works. Aristotle, for example, gave extensive attention to the rules and conventions for composing narratives, such as history and drama, both tragedy and comedy, along with many other literary genres.

Because ancient rhetorical study encompassed both oral and written compositions, it dealt with many aspects of interpretation that we now include under literary criticism. So closely aligned are these two forms of criticism that we have chosen to treat them together.

Biblical writings are "purposeful" literature. Because the Bible seeks to persuade the reader about certain truths, positions, and courses of action, it is subject to rhetorical analysis. Biblical writings, for the most part, were produced for very particular situations. Paul, for example, wrote his letters to address special conditions in the life of early Christian communities. The ancient prophets delivered their speeches in particular historical and social contexts. Seen one way, the occasions and contexts that prompted such writings are rhetorical situations, because they presuppose an audience, a speaker or writer, an issue of mutual concern, and an occasion for communication. In a rhetorical situation, the communicator (speaker/writer) seeks to persuade the audience to accept an argument or point of view or adopt some course of action.

Ancient Greek Rhetoric

The study of rhetoric was highly developed among the ancient Greeks. Rhetorical skills were also valued in ancient Israel, even though we do not know how these were taught. According to Aristotle, rhetoric sought to discover the most effective means of persuasion. Students in ancient Greece learned that rhetoric included five essential elements:

1. invention—planning a discourse by deciding which arguments should be used and how supporting evidence should be deployed;
2. arrangement—deciding on the most effective way to organize the arguments and supporting evidence;
3. style—choosing effective language that fit the speaker's character, the content of the speech, and the occasion;
4. memory—preparing for the speech through study and practice;
5. delivery—using the voice and body gestures in presenting the speech.

In written discourse, only the first three steps were involved.

Three Types of Rhetorical Proofs

Ancient rhetoric paid particular attention to the nature of proof in developing persuasive discourse. Aristotle discussed three different modes of proof, depending upon whether they focused on the speaker, the audience, or the discourse: ethos, pathos, and logos.

Ethos relates to the character of speaker (or writer). Ethical proofs were seen as an extension of the speaker's personality. They were used to enhance the speaker's trustworthiness. The use of this form of ethical proof is found among biblical writers, for example, in Paul's frequent autobiographical references and in the prophets' reports of their experiences. Besides using personal references, biblical writers also reinforced their credibility in other ways. They quoted Scripture or appealed to tradition to align themselves with reliable authorities. The frequent use of lists in 1–2 Chronicles underscores the reliability of the author (or editor) who compiled these writings.

Pathos encompasses proofs or appeals that relate to human emotions, especially the feelings and reactions of the audience. A speaker was expected to consider how the speech could be composed and organized in order to appeal to the heart, which was considered the seat of human emotions in antiquity. Biblical imagery often appeals to the emotions and feelings of hearers (or readers). It is used to elicit certain responses and create certain moods among listeners.

Proofs relating to *logos* were concerned with whether a speech unfolded in a coherent and consistent manner. This determined whether a speech was compelling and convincing. Rather than focusing on the speaker or the audience, "logical proofs" dealt primarily with the speech itself. Ancient rhetoricians gave extensive attention to the kinds of arguments that were most effective. They also developed rules of logic that informed rhetorical compositions. They distinguished, for example, between inductive (reasoning from the particular to the general) and deductive (reasoning from the general to the particular) logic. These discussions were carried out among ancient rhetoricians in order to devise ways to compose purposeful, persuasive speeches and texts.

As exegetes, we must be alert to the literary and rhetorical dimensions of a text. Study of compositional techniques and rhetorical features aids in understanding how a writing has been developed, how its structure and style contribute to its presentation, and what objectives the writer may have had in mind.

Literary Context

Literary criticism of biblical texts recognizes that a single text, passage, or pericope (a short text or selection from a larger literary passage) generally forms a part of a larger whole—the document of which it is a part. The part not only contributes to the meaning of the whole but also derives meaning from the whole. A passage in Romans or a narrative in Genesis, for example, can be understood best when it is viewed as part of a larger literary whole—the entire letter of Romans or the book of Genesis.

When we refer to the literary context of a particular text or passage, we can mean several things. We sometimes refer to the immediate literary context, by which we mean what precedes and follows the text immediately. This may be the chapter in which the text is found or a slightly larger literary unit. Or we might think of the immediate literary context in broader terms—a larger subsection of a biblical book. Sometimes a single biblical book is part of a larger unit; it may be part of a multibook document, such as Luke–Acts or 1–2 Chronicles.

When we read a passage in its literary context, we are trying to understand how it relates to what surrounds it. Does it fit with the surrounding literary material, or does it interrupt the flow of the argument or the development of a theme? How does the surrounding material inform our particular passage? Are there characters, terms, or themes from the surrounding material that illuminate our text?

A helpful way to relate a passage to its larger literary context is to read through an entire document, construct an outline, and see where our passage fits within the outline. Consulting the outlines of biblical writings in commentaries and other works can help us see the overall structure and style of the writing and the compositional techniques employed in its production.

Literary Structure

Ancient authors and editors, like their modern counterparts, could use various compositional techniques to link smaller subunits and sections of material. Individual writings could be structured according to thematic interests (many Wisdom writings), chronological schemes (most historical books), plot or plot motifs (narratives), argumentative strategies (some Pauline letters), alphabetic lines in which the successive letters of the alphabet are used to give external arrangement to material (several of the Psalms, Lamentations), speeches and summations (Deuteronomy– 2 Kings, Matthew), geographical references (much of Exodus–Numbers), common subject matter (OT law codes), patterns dictated by use in rituals and worship (many of the Psalms), and series of visions (some OT prophetic books and Revelation). A single biblical book may be organized using several of these compositional techniques. A text may reflect standard forms, or genres, characteristic of the author's time, rather than being a special literary creation of the author or editor. (We will discuss this latter category in chapter 6, on form criticism.)

Structuring devices were used not only for single biblical books or groups of books but also for major sections and subsections within individual writings. Individual parts of a document might have their own distinctive structure. Prophetic books often contain a series of oracles, which constitute distinct literary forms in their own right. As exegetes, we must take into account major and minor literary structural units.

Because ancient authors and collectors often incorporated preexisting sources into their works, the structure of sections within a single work may reflect the structure of the earlier sources. We often find multilayered structures within the same document. In a heavily edited work like the Pentateuch, we can detect both the structure of the earlier sources and the structure of the final form of the text. When we interpret a particular text, we should try, at least ideally, to determine its place and function within each of the layers or sources of the text.

We can view a passage in the Pentateuch not only within the literary context of the final edited book but also within its context in the earlier

sources (the so-called J, E, D, and P documents). We find similar stratifi-
cation within the Synoptic Gospels. The earliest Gospel writer, probably
Mark, inherited cycles of tradition that were given new meaning when
they were included in his narrative. When these same materials from
Mark were later utilized by Matthew and Luke, they were often incorporated into these works using different organizing structures and compositional techniques. In this way, they acquired a new literary context.

As we analyze the literary structure of biblical writings, we can look
for several clues in order to detect the use and incorporation of earlier
sources. Among these are (1) changes in literary style, (2) shifts in
vocabulary, (3) breaks in continuity of thought, (4) connecting statements that suggest secondary linking, (5) changes in theological viewpoint, (6) duplications or repetition of material, (7) clearly defined and
isolatable subunits, and (8) chronological or factual inconsistencies.

Utilizing these indicators, we can often isolate earlier sources.
Nineteenth-century biblical criticism focused heavily on identifying
earlier sources that lay behind biblical writings, dating these sources,
and reconstructing their probable historical contexts.

Modern biblical scholarship has devoted enormous effort to establishing the overall literary structure of biblical writings and identifying
the underlying sources that have been incorporated into them. Scholars
frequently disagree about how individual works should be divided and
subdivided, but their discussion of these disagreements in critical introductions to the OT and NT and in other handbooks and encyclopedias
is often useful in identifying the main options. Introductory sections to
commentaries on individual books often provide information pertaining to literary markers within the text that indicate structural divisions
and structuring techniques. These markers may include such things as
the beginning and ending of sections or transitions within sections;
temporal, geographical, or spatial indicators; and technical or formulaic phrases.

Consulting reference works to ascertain the literary structure of biblical writings is valuable. But it is just as valuable, perhaps more so, for
us to do the structural analysis ourselves. It is often helpful to read a
particular text or literary unit several times, then read it within its larger
literary context—several times. Through these repeated readings, we
develop our own understanding of how the overall work is structured,
what constitutes the component parts, and how these parts relate to
each other. There is no substitute for this direct interaction with the
text itself.

Literary Form and Function: Some Examples

As we noted earlier, our ability to analyze literary structure often depends on our ability to ask relevant, useful questions about the text: How does the particular passage function within its immediate and larger context? Is it transitional—does it serve as a literary bridge from one section to another? Is it climactic—does it serve as the culmination of several paragraphs or sections immediately preceding it? Is it illustrative—does it provide an example of an earlier assertion? Is it extrinsic to the larger literary unit—does it intrude into the literary context?

By asking such questions, we are trying to relate the passage to its larger literary context by establishing internal textual connections. Doing so is an important aspect of exegesis because clues to interpreting the passage often lie outside the passage itself and are found in its larger literary setting.

If we are interpreting Luke's account of Jesus' sermon in Nazareth (see Luke 4:16–30), by viewing it in relation to the entire Gospel, we discover that the passage is not merely another event in the ministry of Jesus, but an inaugural event. Its placement at this point in Luke's account makes it crucial in the overall development of the story. Major literary and theological themes developed later in Luke–Acts are introduced at this point. Only by reading the entire Gospel can we recognize how many important Lukan themes are covered in this passage and how they are developed elsewhere in the narrative.

To cite another example, the middle section of Paul's letter to the Romans (chaps. 9–11) must be viewed in relation to the whole letter. How we understand the role of these three chapters within the larger letter directly affects our interpretation of the whole letter. If we read them as a digression, in which Paul addresses questions of marginal interest, we will interpret the letter one way. But if we read them as the culmination of a single argument that Paul has developed in chapters 1–8, we will interpret the letter another way. How we understand the literary function of a passage within its larger literary setting is a crucial interpretive decision.

Another way of formulating questions that help us determine the literary function of a particular passage is to ask, What if the passage were omitted from the document? Would it make a real difference? Would something critical be lost? Or would it have no effect?

We can also ask about how it functions at this location: What if the passage was relocated somewhere else in the document? How would this affect the overall structure and content of the document? Would the overall argument (or narrative) be affected?

Asking such questions about the literary placement and function of a passage often enables us to see certain things about the passage that we would miss otherwise. By looking at the immediate literary context, we may discover that the passage is one of a series of prophetic oracles, each of which has a particular function within a larger sequence (Amos 1–6). Or we may see that the passage is one of a series of miracle stories, each of which introduces some aspect of a messianic portrait (Mark 1–2; Matt. 8–9). If we place the passage in its larger literary context, we can develop a better understanding of the passage in its own right. We can identify the distinctive content and nuances of the passage itself but also characteristic features of the larger document. An individual passage not only shares in the meaning of the larger literary unit but also contributes to it.

Literary Devices and Rhetorical Techniques

By relating a passage to its larger literary context, we leave open the possibility that the author or editor composed the writing in order to achieve maximum effect. Ancient authors often employed rhetorical techniques or incorporated rhetorical devices within the text itself to help readers (and hearers) comprehend the message. These rhetorical strategies were also used to persuade the readers (and hearers) that the presentation was true. Since biblical writings were typically written to be read aloud, these rhetorical dimensions of the text figured prominently in the composition of texts. Ancient authors knew that messages had to address the ear. They had to construct compositions that hearers could listen to, follow, and respond to. As modern readers, who usually read silently, we often fail to recognize these rhetorical dimensions of the text. But they can be extremely valuable to us as exegetes in our interpretations of biblical writings.

The Gospel of Matthew has always been noted for its balance and symmetry. The author's fondness for organizing information in groups of threes and sevens is well known. Organizing the story of Jesus in this manner certainly makes it easier to remember the information. Catechetical considerations may have been one of the primary motivations in organizing the contents of this Gospel. As interpreters, we should consider that the group of seven parables found in chapter 13 represents the author's arrangement, rather than an actual historical situation. In this instance, giving attention to the rhetorical or compositional aspect of the text will bear directly on historical questions.

Similarly, because ancient authors were aware of the difficulty hearers and readers had in following an extended argument or narrative, they would often supply periodic summaries throughout the narrative to assist the reader in "catching up" with the story or argument. Numerous instances of this occur in the Gospel of Matthew and the book of Acts.

Various techniques were used for structuring not only individual units but also entire documents. One structural device that was frequently used is "chiasmus" or simply "chiasm," a designation formed on the basis of the Greek letter *Chi*, which was shaped like an *X*. In a chiastic structure, four (or more) elements were arranged in a symmetrical pattern corresponding to each of the four points of the *X*. In a four-part arrangement, the chiastic structure would follow an a-b-b-a pattern, in which "a" and "b" were placed on the top two prongs of the *X* and "b^1" and "a^1" on the bottom two. The first and fourth items corresponded to each other, as did the second and third items. Arranging a saying or literary section this way made it more memorable. The popular saying, "When (a) the going (b) gets tough, (b^1) the tough (a^1) get going," is catchy because it is arranged using a chiastic structure.

Another such device is "inclusio" or "inclusion." This refers to the literary practice of restating an opening idea at the conclusion of a passage in order to emphasize its importance. The term suggests that an argument or section returns to the point at which it originated.

Such rhetorical devices, which were used widely in antiquity, are found frequently in the biblical writings.

Knowing that ancient writers often employed rhetorical techniques often assists us in understanding how a document is structured. As modern readers, we may not grasp the overall structure of a biblical writing because it does not easily conform to how we understand logical sequence or coherent organization. But it may fit perfectly into ancient notions of arrangement. Once we understand the organizing principle and how this related to ancient rhetorical conventions, we may easily see the "logic" of how the material is presented.

Literary Mood

Another aspect of literary criticism should also be mentioned—literary mood. Language is often used as much to create effect as it is to convey information. As beginning exegetes, we sometimes concentrate on analyzing the words and phrases within a passage without being attentive to the more subtle ways in which the language is functioning. The phrase "You are rich!" (1 Cor. 4:8) read as a straight declarative sentence means one thing, but read as irony means quite the opposite. The Fourth Gospel is highly ironic in its use of language, even in the way the narrative is structured. As exegetes, we cannot ignore this dimension of the text, because it directly relates to literary mood. If the mood of a text—or the mood a text creates—is liturgical, we should read the language as poetic. It is probably intended to elicit certain emotions rather than convey theological propositions. How we understand a highly evocative passage from a liturgical setting differs radically from how we would read the same words within a fiercely polemical text. To read comedy as straightforward narrative is itself comic. As exegetes, we should be attentive to these unspoken dimensions of the text.

Conclusion

By focusing on the composition, structure, and style of a text, literary criticism enables us to see the "world of the text." Numerous studies are available to assist us in doing literary criticism. But nothing is more important than our ability to read a text closely and sympathetically, with both an eye and an ear to the internal dynamics of a text. Some messages come through loud and clear, others in a whisper. Still others are transmitted through pauses and silences. But they lie within the literary texture of a passage, waiting to be heard and read by attentive literary critics.

BIBLIOGRAPHY

General

*Alter, Robert. *The Art of Biblical Narrative*. New York: Basic Books; London: Allen & Unwin, 1981.

*————. *The Art of Biblical Poetry*. New York: Basic Books, 1985; Edinburgh: T. & T. Clark, 1990.

Bal, Mieke. *Narratology: Introduction to the Theory of Narrative*. 2nd ed. Toronto: University of Toronto Press, 1997.

Beardslee, William A. *Literary Criticism of the New Testament*. Philadelphia: Fortress, 1970.

Crossan, John D., and Loretta Dornisch, eds. *Paul Ricoeur on Biblical Hermeneutics*. Missoula, MT: Society of Biblical Literature (Scholars), 1975.

Exum, J. Cheryl, and David J. A. Clines, eds. *The New Literary Criticism and the Hebrew Bible*. Valley Forge, PA: Trinity; Sheffield, UK: JSOT, 1993.

Fishbane, Michael. *Biblical Text and Texture: A Literary Reading of Selected Texts*. Oxford: Oneworld, 1998.

————. *Text and Texture: Close Readings of Selected Biblical Texts*. New York: Schocken, 1979.

*Frye, Northrop, and Alvin A. Lee. *The Great Code: The Bible and Literature*. Toronto: University of Toronto Press, 2006 (1982).

Funk, Robert W. *Language, Hermeneutic, and Word of God*. New York: Harper & Row, 1966.

————, ed. *Literary Critical Studies of Biblical Texts*. Missoula, MT: Society of Biblical Literature (Scholars), 1977.

Gottcent, John H. *The Bible as Literature: A Selective Bibliography*. Boston: G. K. Hall, 1979.

*Gros Louis, Kenneth R. R., James S. Ackerman, and Thayer S. Warshaw. *Literary Interpretations of Biblical Narratives*. 2 vols. Nashville: Abingdon, 1974–82.

Gunn, David M., and Danna Nolan Fewell. *Narrative in the Hebrew Bible*. Oxford and New York: Oxford University Press, 1993.

Habel, Norman C. *Literary Criticism of the Old Testament*. Philadelphia: Fortress, 1971.

Jobling, David. *The Sense of Biblical Narrative: Structural Analyses in the Hebrew Bible*. 2nd ed. 2 vols. Sheffield, UK: JSOT, 1986.

Juel, Donald, James S. Ackerman, and Thayer S. Warshaw. *An Introduction to New Testament Literature*. Nashville: Abingdon, 1978.

Long, Burke O., ed. *Images of Man and God: Old Testament Short Stories in Literary Focus*. Sheffield, UK: JSOT Press (Almond), 1981.

*Malbon, Elizabeth S., and Edgar V. McKnight, eds. *The New Literary Criticism and the New Testament*. Valley Forge, PA: Trinity; Sheffield, UK: Sheffield Academic Press, 1994.

McKnight, Edgar V. *The Bible and the Reader: An Introduction to Literary Criticism*. Philadelphia: Fortress, 1985.

————. *Meaning in Texts: The Historical Shaping of a Narrative Hermeneutics*. Philadelphia: Fortress, 1978.

————. *Postmodern Use of the Bible: The Emergence of Reader-Oriented Criticism*. Nashville: Abingdon, 1988.

*Petersen, Norman. *Literary Criticism for New Testament Critics*. Philadelphia: Fortress, 1978.

Poland, Lynn M. *Literary Criticism and Biblical Hermeneutics: A Critique of Formalist Approaches*. Chico, CA: Society of Biblical Literature (Scholars), 1985.

Preminger, Alex, and Edward L. Greenstein, eds. *The Hebrew Bible in Literary Criticism*. New York: Ungar, 1986.

Quinn-Miscall, Peter D. *The Workings of Old Testament Narrative.* Chico, CA: Society of Biblical Literature (Scholars); Philadelphia: Fortress, 1983.

Resseguie, James L. *Narrative Criticism of the New Testament: An Introduction.* Grand Rapids: Baker, 2005.

Ricoeur, Paul. *The Conflict of Interpretations: Essays in Hermeneutics.* Evanston, IL: Northwestern University Press, 1974.

Ricoeur, Paul, and Lewis S. Mudge. *Essays on Biblical Interpretation.* Philadelphia: Fortress, 1980; London: SPCK, 1981.

Ringe, Sharon H., and Hyun C. P. Kim, eds. *Literary Encounters with the Reign of God.* New York: T. & T. Clark, 2004.

Robertson, David A. *The Old Testament and the Literary Critic.* Philadelphia: Fortress, 1977.

Ryken, Leland, ed. *The New Testament in Literary Criticism.* New York: Ungar, 1984.

Schwartz, Regina M. *The Book and the Text: The Bible and Literary Theory.* Cambridge, MA, and Oxford: Blackwell, 1990.

Sternberg, Meir. *The Poetics of Biblical Narrative: Ideological Literature and the Drama of Reading.* Bloomington: Indiana University Press, 1985.

Rhetorical Analysis

Classen, Carl Joachim. *Rhetorical Criticism of the New Testament.* Boston: Brill, 2002.

Clines, David J. A., David M. Gunn, and Alan J. Hauser, eds. *Art and Meaning: Rhetoric in Biblical Literature.* Sheffield, UK: JSOT Press, 1982.

Corbett, Edward P. J., and Robert J. Connors. *Classical Rhetoric for the Modern Student.* 4th ed. New York: Oxford University Press, 1999.

Gitay, Yehoshua. *Prophecy and Persuasion: A Study of Isaiah 40–48.* Bonn: Linguistica Biblica, 1981.

Jackson, Jared J., and Martin Kessler, eds. *Rhetorical Criticism: Essays in Honor of James Muilenburg.* Pittsburgh: Pickwick, 1974.

*Kennedy, George A. *New Testament Interpretation through Rhetorical Criticism.* Chapel Hill: University of North Carolina Press, 1984.

Kuypers, Jim A. *The Art of Rhetorical Criticism.* Boston: Pearson and Allyn & Bacon, 2005.

Meynet, Roland. *Rhetorical Analysis: An Introduction to Biblical Rhetoric.* Sheffield, UK: Sheffield Academic Press, 1998.

Porter, Stanley, Dennis L. Stamps, and Thomas H. Olbricht, eds. *Rhetorical Criticism and the Bible.* London and New York: Sheffield Academic Press, 2002.

Porter, Stanley, and Thomas H. Olbricht, eds. *Rhetoric and the New Testament: Essays from the 1992 Heidelberg Conference.* Sheffield, UK: JSOT Press, 1993.

———, eds. *Rhetoric, Scripture, and Theology: Essays from the 1994 Pretoria Conference.* Sheffield, UK: Sheffield Academic Press, 1996.

———, eds. *The Rhetorical Analysis of Scripture: Essays from the 1995 London Conference.* Sheffield, UK: Sheffield Academic Press, 1997.

Robbins, Vernon. *Exploring the Texture of Texts: A Guide to Socio-Rhetorical Interpretation*. Valley Forge, PA: Trinity, 1996.

————. *The Tapestry of Early Christian Discourse: Rhetoric, Society, and Ideology*. London and New York: Routledge, 1996.

Stamps, Dennis L., and Stanley E. Porter, eds. *The Rhetorical Interpretation of Scripture: Essays from the 1996 Malibu Conference*. Sheffield, UK: Sheffield Academic Press, 1999.

Tobin, Thomas H. *Paul's Rhetoric in Its Contexts: The Argument of Romans*. Peabody, MA: Hendrickson, 2004.

*Trible, Phyllis. *Rhetorical Criticism: Context, Method, and the Book of Jonah*. Minneapolis: Fortress, 1994.

Warner, Martin, ed. *The Bible as Rhetoric: Studies in Biblical Persuasion and Credibility*. London and New York: Routledge, 1990.

Watson, Duane F. *Persuasive Artistry: Studies in New Testament Rhetoric in Honor of George A. Kennedy*. Sheffield, UK: JSOT Press, 1991.

————. *Rhetorical Criticism of the New Testament: A Bibliographical Survey*. Leiderdorp: Deo; Norwich: SCM, 2005.

Wilder, Amos N. *Early Christian Rhetoric: The Language of the Gospel*. Cambridge, MA: Harvard University Press, 1971 (1964).

6

Form Criticism

The Genre and Life Setting of the Text

Literary criticism, as discussed in chapter 5, focuses on the "world of the text." In that chapter, we stressed the importance of seeing a text in relation to the larger literary composition in which it is located. Form criticism—or better, genre analysis—though not uninterested in the larger literary sections of material or even entire books, focuses more on the smaller literary units or pericopes.

Genres and Setting in Life (*Sitz im Leben*)

Genre analysis is criticism that examines the form, content, and function of a passage. Here we ask whether a literary unit exhibits certain features or conforms to a clearly identified structure that typify a well-defined genre. If language in the passage is used in a manner typical of a particular genre, or if it conforms to the pattern of that genre, we classify it accordingly. Assigning a passage to a literary genre enables us to ask appropriate interpretive questions.

Form criticism seeks to identify various literary genres and then to classify a passage within one of these genres. Form critics also recognize that literary classification is not enough. They also try to ascertain the "situation in life" (German: *Sitz im Leben*) in which genres originated and developed. The phrase "in life" reminds us that what we experience as literary forms—something we read—originally had a "life setting."

104

Imagining different situations in life, such as worship, teaching, preaching, and argument, enables us to appreciate the original oral form of literary genres. What we experience as formalized, written genres typically acquired their literary shape through oral repetition.

Through genre analysis, form critics have explored the close relationship between form, content, and meaning: the meaning of what is said is directly related to how it is said. As noted in an earlier chapter, in ordinary life we recognize that form and content are interconnected. A classified ad in a newspaper represents a well-defined literary genre with distinctive features that create predictable expectations. A description of property for sale in a classified ad is quite different from a description of the same property in a deed. One is an advertisement designed to sell a property; the other is a legal description designed to record accurately what has been sold. We all know that overstatement is allowed, even expected, in the former, but not in the latter. Consequently, we read the two literary descriptions with different expectations and interpret them accordingly. How we understand the description of the property—the "meaning" we attach to the description—is directly related to the literary genre in which the description occurs.

We also recognize, perhaps unconsciously, the importance of setting in life in interpreting a document. The newspaper advertisement has a life setting remarkably different from that of a legal document bound and shelved in a government building. When we advertise and sell property, we typically emphasize its positive features and de-emphasize or even ignore its negative features. When we listen to sales pitches or read advertisements, we expect exaggerated descriptions, inflated language, and other forms of overstatement. Experience teaches us that we should even expect misrepresentation and false statements. All of the dynamics related to advertising, selling, and buying comprise the life setting of marketing in which such descriptions originate. When we interpret an advertisement, we recognize instinctively the connections between what is said (content), how something is said (form), and in what setting it is said (setting in life). The more we know about a life setting, the better we can understand how form and content relate to that setting.

The Logic of Form Criticism: How It Works

This understanding of the relationship between various forms of speech and their social settings informs how form critics analyze biblical texts.

Form critics typically make distinct interpretive moves. As form critics try to understand what is said in a passage—its content—they observe how the content is stated. Noting its arrangement, they identify its literary genre or structure. For example, they tend to ask whether the passage can be classified as a prophetic oracle, a miracle story, or a parable. Does it belong to an easily identifiable literary category? As they seek to classify the passage according to its literary form, they also try to determine the life setting in which the text originated and developed. In this way, they try to ascertain how the text functioned in that setting. Efforts to identify both the literary form and setting in life have the same goal: to understand the content of the text.

These two dimensions of form criticism—literary classification of biblical material and sociological analysis of literary genres in the life of ancient Israel and the early church—have been increasingly recognized within the past century or so of biblical scholarship. In the nineteenth century, investigations of the biblical text tended to focus on historical and literary questions in a different sense. Historical criticism developed the awareness that many biblical writings grew out of certain historical contexts over a period of time. Literary and documentary criticism sought to detect various sources upon which the final form of the biblical texts was based.

These approaches, however, showed little interest in the individual literary units within a biblical writing and how they could be classified within specific genres. Nor were these approaches especially interested in the sociological aspects of literary analysis, such as identifying typical situations in human life in which certain forms of speech or writing originated. They were not interested in the sociological soil in which these literary units had taken root and grown. This sociological dimension of literary analysis acquired greater prominence as scholars went beyond historical and documentary analysis in order to understand how biblical texts had functioned in ancient cultures before they became fixed in writing.

Some Biblical Examples

The Old Testament Psalms

Form-critical analysis of the book of Psalms yielded fruitful results. One of form critics' most significant observations was that each main category of psalm displayed clear patterns of content, mood, and structure.

The psalms were classified into three primary and distinct genres: hymns that were sung during normal times; laments prayed in time of trouble (both individual and communal); and thanksgivings offered after the alleviation of trouble (both individual and communal). How these genres were used in worship services can be seen in the following diagram:

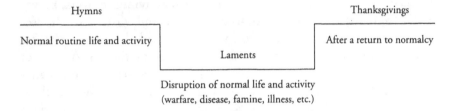

Scholars also identified other genres for classifying OT psalms.

Equally important was the recognition that the psalms, far from being a collection of hymns, poems, and odes written by a single figure, such as David, were produced within the community of Israel to address recurring needs. The majority of the psalms were now seen as liturgical texts used in Israelite worship. The Psalter began to be read as the song and prayer book of ancient Israel. As such, it reflected the richness and diversity of Israelite faith. The psalms could no longer be read as though they were part of a single genre, "the book of Psalms." They were now closely connected with life settings within Israel's life. The psalms not only gave expression to Israel's faith but also reflected the life supported by that faith. Form-critical analysis of the psalms made interpreters aware that the literary, historical, and sociological dimensions of these texts were interrelated.

The Book of Genesis and the Prophetic Writings

Just as the psalms "came to life" through form-critical investigations, so did other biblical texts. The narratives in Genesis were no longer explored merely to ascertain their documentary sources or their historical value, but were viewed as stories expressing the folk life of ancient Israel. Prophetic books were also read differently. Rather than being read as continuous prophetic discourses, they were now interpreted as smaller units that could be classified into different literary genres, such as discourses of judgment, promise, admonition, and exhortation. Interpreters could also relate these individual units to different life settings, thereby creating new possibilities of meaning and explanation.

The New Testament: Gospels

Form-critical analysis was also applied to NT writings, first to the Gospels and later to the letters. Investigations of the Gospels uncovered numerous smaller genres, such as miracle stories, pronouncement stories, parables, birth stories, to mention only a few. The epistles also revealed a wide variety of smaller genres, such as hymns, prayers, kerygmatic (sermon) summaries, exhortations, vice and virtue lists, household codes, and confessions. Form criticism had the same dramatic impact on our understanding of the NT as it had on the OT. Aspects of the early church's faith and life acquired richer texture as scholars analyzed NT literary forms and linked these to actual religious practices. The NT writings "came to life" as interpreters heard early Christians praying, singing, preaching, teaching, confessing, encouraging each other, and defending their faith.

Probing the Sociological Setting

If historical criticism allows us to see into "linear life" of biblical writings, form criticism opens up their "vertical life" by probing the sociological substructure of individual texts. We are able to see that biblical writings have not only historical breadth but also sociological depth. A given text can be one step or link within a continuous history, but it can also be the tip of a sociological iceberg, with a history and life of its own that lie hidden beneath the surface of a printed page.

Old Testament Psalms

When form critics analyze a royal enthronement psalm, such as Psalm 2, they focus as much on the life setting reflected within the psalm as they do on its content. The literary form of the psalm suggests that its probable setting was a coronation event within ancient Israel. In such a setting, the king was crowned and lavished with praise. So solemn was the setting and so elevated the language that the psalm could be repeated on successive occasions. An enthronement psalm composed for one king could be "recycled" in the celebration ceremony of a later king. This helps explain why the identity of certain persons mentioned in enthronement psalms, such as the "king" or "the Lord's anointed," remains ambiguous. These terms might have been applied to several different persons over time. But how we understand such terms and other features of the psalm depends on how we classify it and how we relate it to a life setting within ancient Israel. Here, again, we see how form, function, content, and life setting inform each other in form-critical interpretation.

A New Testament Example: The Healing of the Demoniac (Mark 5:1–20)

As an example from the NT, we can look at a well-known miracle story, the healing of the Gerasene demoniac (see Mark 5:1–20 and parallels). One way to examine this story is to explore the historical and social setting of Jesus' own ministry in which the story is reported. We might investigate demon possession within first-century Palestine, including how this phenomenon related to similar experiences in other cultures outside Palestine. We could also engage in literary analysis by looking at how Mark used the story in his narrative. We might ask: Why is the story located at this point? How does it relate to the other episodes immediately before and after? How does the story function literarily in the parallel accounts in Matthew and Luke? At this level, our interest is primarily trying to reconstruct the event reported in the story and explore how each evangelist used the story in his larger narrative.

Form-critical analysis takes a slightly different approach by asking other questions. A form critic would first identify the literary genre of the passage: a miracle story, more specifically an exorcism. By noting the formal elements in the story, we can observe its literary structure: (1) the description of the demon-possessed man (vv. 2–5); (2) his encounter with Jesus the miracle worker (vv. 6–10); (3) a description of the healing miracle itself (vv. 11–13); and the aftermath, including the impact on the crowds and a description of the healed man (vv. 14–20). By analyzing the formal structure of similar miracle stories, both biblical and nonbiblical, we see that the story exhibits a typical pattern seen in other ancient miracle stories. Once we determine this formal outline, we can see how the parallel accounts in Matthew (8:28–34) and Luke (8:26–39) have either expanded or compressed certain formal features.

Besides identifying the genre of the text and analyzing its formal structure, form-critical analysis also inquires into the so-called oral period, the time between the original occurrence of the episode within the life of Jesus and its inclusion into the final form of the written

Gospel. Form critics imagine that stories like this were probably told and retold, not only during Jesus' own ministry, but especially during the decades following his death. Rather than "floating in the air," as it were, such stories were repeated in specific contexts in which early followers of Jesus were preaching, teaching, worshiping, or arguing with their opponents. These stories may have been remembered and repeated orally, but they acquired a certain shape depending on the life setting in which they were told. Within these settings, such stories as Mark 5:1–20 acquired their present content and form. By the time Mark, the earliest evangelist, incorporated the story into his Gospel, the story had probably attained a definite form, although he may have altered it slightly to fit his narrative setting.

By giving special attention to the oral, preliterary period between the time of Jesus and the composition of the Gospels, form critics are able to explain variations within the same story as reported in two or more Gospels. As long as interpreters worked at the literary and historical levels exclusively, it was difficult to provide a satisfactory explanation of the differences in the content and arrangement of certain passages in the Gospels. The healing of the Gerasene demoniac exhibits intriguing variations in each of the Synoptic Gospels. In Matthew's account, there are *two* demoniacs, whereas in Mark and Luke there is only one. Mark records the number of swine as "about two thousand," whereas Matthew and Luke omit this fantastic detail. Such variations are easier to explain if the same story was told and retold on various occasions and in different settings. Form critics explain these variations by proposing that Matthew records one version of the story as it was told in the early church, whereas Mark and Luke preserve other versions of the same story that circulated in different churches or regions of the church.

Besides explaining how variations occur within a passage, form-critical analysis also allows us to see how a story or saying has been shaped, or edited, in the final stage of writing. Even in its final literary form, a text possesses another "life setting," that of the author/compiler. This setting—the setting of the evangelist—usually differs markedly from earlier settings in which the story or saying was used. This final setting in life includes the author's own historical, geographical, and social setting, but also his literary purposes and theological interests as well. This latter aspect will be discussed further in chapter 8, on redaction criticism, which focuses on the evangelist's literary and theological purposes as reflected in the final form of the text.

The Parables of Jesus

Form-critical analysis has been especially useful in interpreting the parables of Jesus. At one time, the parables were read as though they belonged to the single genre "allegory." Form-critical analysis has enabled us to see that there are different types of parables, such as parables of judgment, parables of growth, and parables of the kingdom. It has also explored the relationship between the content and formal structure of parables and how both relate to different life settings. When form critics read the parables, they use formal categories to reconstruct the probable settings in which the parables originated. They try to determine how different parables functioned within their respective settings.

Useful clues for interpreting parables are often indicated by where they are located with the Gospels. For example, the parable of the Lost Sheep occurs in different contexts in Matthew (18:12–14) and Luke (15:3–7). In Matthew, the context is concerned with proper behavior in the church. In this context, the parable reminds us to care for the "little ones," probably recent converts. In Luke, the same parable occurs in a context in which Jesus is disputing with Pharisees and scribes, who objected to his associating with social outcasts, the tax collectors and sinners. Joined with the parables of the Lost Coin and the Lost Son, the parable of the Lost Sheep in Luke underscores the inestimable worth of a single sinner. Matthew's catechetical setting provides practical instructions for church conduct. Luke's polemical setting creates a different framework for interpreting the parable of the Lost Sheep. These two *literary settings* may reflect the different *life settings* in which the parable circulated in the early church.

The Focus of Form Criticism: Stories and Small Units of Material

Form-critical perspectives on NT texts focus more on the stories as typical forms of expression rather than as narratives or reports about events in the life of Jesus. Form critics typically ask how texts were used in the life of the church and how they were shaped for specific purposes in different settings. Form criticism especially emphasizes the church's role in preserving and shaping stories about Jesus and sayings that were attributed to him.

Form criticism usually focuses on smaller literary units and subunits within larger biblical writings. It can also be employed usefully, however, in analyzing individual books of the Bible. Apocalypses, such as the books of Daniel and Revelation, belong to a distinct literary genre. Since they exhibit literary characteristics typical of this genre, we can interpret their content by exploring how they might have functioned within various settings in Israel and the early church. Most of the book of Deuteronomy can be classified within the literary genre of "farewell addresses." New Testament letters conform to widely used epistolary genres, although there were many different types of letters.

To classify a biblical writing as a particular genre does not necessarily mean that it contains no earlier materials or subgenres within it. Apocalyptic literature often contains such subgenres as "vision reports," which derived from earlier prophetic and historical literature. The book of Deuteronomy may conform to the genre of a farewell address, but it incorporates many other genres, including various forms of laws.

Not every biblical text lends itself to form-critical analysis. Some texts are fresh productions. They display no evidence of having incorporated earlier material. Since they were written for the literary setting in which they occur, they have no obvious prehistory. Their only life setting may be the document in which they are located and the situation of the author and audience in which it arose. By contrast, texts that display patterns of composition based on typical, recurrent literary forms and that appear to reflect prior stages of literary development yield themselves most readily to form-critical analysis.

Doing Form Criticism

Commentaries on biblical books usually classify individual passages according to their literary genres. More specialized studies often contain comprehensive lists of literary genres found in both the OT and the NT. Such lists provide us a range of possibilities for approaching a text: Is it a prophetic call narrative? A prophetic oracle? A proverb? A psalm of lament? A miracle story? A letter? A hymn? And so forth.

Even if this preliminary classification is provisional, we must begin by asking questions of literary form and life setting. If we classify a text as a psalm of communal lament, we can pose questions about its probable life setting: What circumstances could have prompted such a lament—a defeat in battle, a natural catastrophe, or a serious breach of trust within the community? How might the lament have been used in a worship setting? Was it connected to an annual event or celebration? Or was it an exceptional event?

By asking such questions, we usually get a better sense of how the content and form of the passage are related. This enables us to develop meaningful interpretations. A psalm may be incomprehensible to us until we discover that it is a communal lament sung by a community of worshipers in Israel. Then we understand that the parts of the psalm are stanzas that may have been sung antiphonally, first by the leader of worship, then by the community of worshipers. The "logic" of the psalm may escape us until we grasp its literary form; then the form provides the key to interpreting the content. Here again, we experience the interrelationship of form, content, and meaning.

BIBLIOGRAPHY

General

Dowd, Garin, Jeremy Strong, and Lesley Stevenson, eds. *Genre Matters: Essays in Theory and Criticism.* Bristol, UK, and Portland, OR: Intellect, 2006.

*Koch, Klaus. *The Growth of the Biblical Tradition: The Form-Critical Method.* New York: Macmillan, 1988 (1969).

*Lohfink, Gerhard. *The Bible: Now I Get It! A Form Criticism Handbook.* Garden City, NY: Doubleday, 1979.

Old Testament Form Criticism

*Buss, Martin. *Biblical Form Criticism in Its Context.* Sheffield, UK: Sheffield Academic Press, 1999.

———, ed. *Encounter with the Text: Form and History in the Hebrew Bible.* Philadelphia: Fortress, 1979.

Gunkel, Hermann. *The Psalms: A Form-Critical Introduction.* Philadelphia: Fortress, 1967.

Gunkel, Hermann, and Joachim Begrich. *Introduction to Psalms: The Genres of the Religious Lyric of Israel.* Macon, GA: Mercer University Press, 1998.

*Hayes, John H., ed. *Old Testament Form Criticism.* San Antonio, TX: Trinity University Press, 1974.

House, Paul R. *Beyond Form Criticism: Essays in Old Testament Literary Criticism.* Winona Lake, IN: Eisenbrauns, 1992.

Knierim, Rolf, Gene M. Tucker, and Marvin A. Sweeney, eds. *The Forms of the Old Testament Literature.* Grand Rapids: Eerdmans, 1981–.

Sandoval, Timothy, and Carleen Mandolfo, eds. *Relating to the Text: Interdisciplinary and Form-Critical Insights to the Bible.* London and New York: T. & T. Clark, 2003.

Sweeney, Marvin A. *Form and Intertextuality in Prophetic and Apocalyptic Literature.* Tübingen: Mohr Siebeck, 2005.

Sweeney, Marvin A., and Ehud Ben Zvi, eds. *The Changing Face of Form Criticism for the Twenty-First Century.* Grand Rapids: Eerdmans, 2003.

*Tucker, Gene M. *Form Criticism of the Old Testament.* Philadelphia: Fortress, 1988 (1971).

New Testament Form Criticism

*Bailey, James L., and Lyle D. Vander Broek. *Literary Forms in the New Testament: A Handbook.* Louisville, KY: Westminster/John Knox, 1992.

Bultmann, Rudolf, and John Marsh. *The History of the Synoptic Tradition.* Rev. ed. Peabody, MA: Hendrickson, 1994 (1968).

*Bultmann Rudolf, Karl Kundzins, and Frederick C. Grant. *Form Criticism: Two Essays on New Testament Research: The Synoptic Gospels.* New York: Harper, 1966.

Dibelius, Martin. *From Tradition to Gospel.* Greenwood, SC: Attic, 1982 (1971).

Güttgemanns, Erhardt. *Candid Questions concerning Gospel Form Criticism: A Methodological Sketch of the Fundamental Problematics of Form and Redaction Criticism.* Pittsburgh: Pickwick, 1979.

*McKnight, Edgar V. *What Is Form Criticism?* Eugene, OR: Wipf & Stock, 1997 (1969).

Riesenfeld, Harald. *The Gospel Tradition and Its Beginnings: A Study in the Limits of "Formgeschichte."* London: Mowbray, 1961.

Taylor, Vincent. *The Formation of the Gospel Tradition.* 2nd ed. London: Macmillan; New York: St. Martins, 1968 (1935).

7

Tradition Criticism

The Stages behind the Text

All cultures have traditions that are passed from one generation to the next. Such traditions give expression to peoples' self-understanding, their sense of their past, their systems of belief, and their codes of conduct. Subgroups within a society may even have their own special traditions. These traditions are passed down in many different forms, including stories, sayings, songs, poems, confessions, and creeds. Tradition criticism is concerned with the nature of these traditions and how they are used in a community's history.

Much of the Bible is composed of traditions that have crystallized at a particular stage in their formation. Within a single biblical writing, stages of the same tradition are sometimes visible at different places within the text. They may even function in different ways in the same writing. These shifts in perspective may reflect different chronological periods or theological perspectives, or both. (Within Judaism and Christianity, certain interpretations of biblical traditions have themselves become "traditions." In Judaism, the "oral Torah," the tradition about how a text was to be interpreted, became almost as authoritative as the "written Torah.")

Not every biblical text passed through stages of growth prior to its appearance in a biblical book, but many did. When this is clearly the case, tradition criticism offers a valuable perspective for looking at a biblical text. Using a distinctive set of methodological approaches, it illuminates features of the text that otherwise may be difficult to explain.

Recognizing the Origin and Growth of Biblical Traditions

Within the last two hundred years of biblical scholarship, we have learned that many parts of the Bible "grew" over long periods of time. In some cases, this growth occurred over a period of decades, in others, over centuries. The OT reflects this type of organic development in many of its parts, but the Pentateuch especially illustrates how one part of the Bible has been formed over a long period of time. Scholars now regard the Pentateuch as a work compiled by numerous editors working in different periods of time. By analyzing distinctive literary characteristics, such as language and style, and different theological perspectives noticeable within the text, scholars have identified different sources, or strata, within the Pentateuch. These layers have been designated J, E, D, and P.

Although the NT was composed over a much shorter span of time than the OT, it reflects a similar period of development prior to the actual writing of the documents themselves. This is especially the case with the Gospels.

In both the OT and the NT, therefore, a period prior to the final literary stage of the biblical documents can be recognized. This is usually called the oral period, because it is seen as a time in which stories and other traditions circulated in unwritten form. Before they were written down, these oral traditions were used and reused within the communities of Israel and the church respectively. As these oral stories and teachings were collected and transmitted, they acquired the status of sacred traditions. They were regarded as valuable enough, indeed sacred enough, to be passed on from generation to generation. In its simplest sense, the term "tradition" refers to customs or teachings that have been handed over, or passed along, from one generation to the next, regardless of whether they are regarded as sacred. But in the context of the OT or the NT, tradition refers to those stories and materials that Israel and the church regarded as sacred—and that eventually became normative—in defining their faith and practice.

Tradition criticism (in German, *traditionsgeschichtliche Studien* or *überlieferungsgeschichtliche Studien*) was a direct outgrowth of form criticism. Hermann Gunkel (1862–1932), the German scholar who pioneered the study of biblical materials according to their genres, was one of the first to trace the history of particular biblical themes and narratives. He noted that many elements in the Bible had ancient nonbiblical antecedents. In 1895, he published a work titled *Schöpfung und Chaos in Urzeit und Endzeit* (Creation and Chaos in Primordial Time and the End of Time), in which he traced the thematic and historical connections of the Babylonian account of creation, Genesis 1, and Revelation 12. As a member of the history-of-religion school (*religions-geschichtliche Schule*), he argued that often interpretations of biblical texts must pay attention to their prebiblical or nonbiblical antecedents.

In his commentary on Genesis (1903; 3rd ed. 1910; English translation of 1910 introduction, 1994), Gunkel analyzed the stories of Genesis, arguing that originally these were independent narratives often with nonbiblical prototypes. Many of the narratives about the patriarchs Abraham, Isaac, and Jacob were, according to Gunkel, originally independent stories about nameless characters, sometimes reflecting tribal and class history and relationships. Gradually traditions about these three figures grew into cycles and were assembled so that the patriarchs were depicted as father, son, and grandson.

Oral and Written Traditions

Since traditions may be oral or written, or even a combination of both, tradition criticism is not limited to the oral period. Even if a sacred story or tradition originally circulated in an oral form and was transmitted orally through several generations, it could still function as tradition after it was written down. Written traditions were also passed along from generation to generation. When we imagine the traditioning process, we should envision the transmission of oral and written traditions.

Whether tradition criticism focuses on oral or written traditions, its primary interest is biblical writings that grew over time. Some biblical texts have no prehistory. They appear to have been composed by a single individual at a single point in time for a specific situation. They did not exist prior to the time of composition in any prepackaged form. Such compositions reflect earlier traditions only to the extent that they draw, in a general way, on the ethos and atmosphere of their sacred communities. They always, however, use traditional themes, patterns, or plot motifs known within their communities.

Some biblical texts show clear signs of growth and development. They resemble geological formations in which earlier and later layers can be distinguished. In such cases, the interpreter's task is to identify the different strata of literary materials, then determine how and why the layering has occurred. The purpose of such analysis is to understand the final form of the text—what we read in the Bible itself.

Contemporary Example of Oral and Written Tradition: Hymns

Tradition criticism is not confined to ancient materials. Examples of the growth and development of traditions are all around us. We frequently find different versions of the same hymn in church hymnals. The hymn may have three verses in one hymnbook, five or six verses in another. The wording of the same verse may vary slightly in different hymnbooks.

If we are studying one version of a hymn, we might ask: Is this the original version of the hymn? Or even, was there *an* original version? Is this an earlier or later version? Was it written by the person to whom it is attributed? If so, in whole or in part? How does this version of the hymn compare with a shorter version in another hymnbook? Is the shorter version an earlier version that was expanded later, or is it a shortened form of a longer version?

When we find multiple versions of a hymn, we soon discover that it has gone through a traditioning process. It may have been composed by a hymn writer in a single, definitive form; or the original composer may have edited the hymn later, either lengthening or shortening it. Subsequent hymn writers or hymnbook editors may have modified it. Over time, the hymn has been transmitted and preserved in several forms.

Changes that occur in hymns often reveal significant shifts within the hymn tradition. Efforts to make the language of worship more inclusive by eliminating sexist language from many traditional hymns have resulted in numerous revisions. Such changes reflect historical, sociological, and theological interests. The new wording of some hymns may be difficult to comprehend unless we understand how changes in the tradition have arisen from specific life settings.

Another layer of tradition is added when a hymn is quoted in a sermon (or a journal article). Now the literary setting of the hymn has shifted from hymnbook to sermon. If the hymn is cited to make a theological point or to illustrate some moral lesson, its function has also changed. If we are interpreting the sermon in which the hymn is quoted, we recognize, first, the hymn itself. Knowing that the hymn was composed prior to the sermon, we deduce that it has a prehistory. Second, we notice that a particular version of the hymn is being cited. It may differ from other versions we know from memory or from ones that we could find in various hymnbooks. Third, we can gain a better understanding of the hymn quoted in the sermon if we have some sense of its prehistory: earlier versions of the hymn, their history of development, and changes that occurred in the hymn's tradition history.

Biblical Examples

The Sabbath Commandment

The biblical writings often reflect similar stages of growth that lie behind a particular text. Suppose, for example, we are interpreting the OT commandment to observe the Sabbath as recorded in Exodus 20:8–11. After examining the passage and noting its content and structure, we then discover another version of the commandment in Deuteronomy 5:12–15. We especially note some differences in these two versions of the Sabbath commandment. The Exodus version is shorter by several lines. The primary rationale for keeping the Sabbath is different in the two texts. In Deuteronomy, observance of the Sabbath is grounded in the exodus deliverance, while in Exodus it is related to the creation of the world. Further investigation would uncover other instances in the OT where brief, unelaborated injunctions to keep the Sabbath occur (Lev. 19:3).

Noting the differences in these two texts, we would ask several questions: How do the two versions of the same commandment in the supposedly identical Decalogue (Ten Commandments) relate to each other? Is the shorter form earlier than the longer, or is it an abbreviated later version? What accounts for the two different theological rationales that are given for keeping the Sabbath? Were there originally two versions of the Sabbath commandment, each preserved in an independent form? Or were there originally two different settings in which these two versions arose, each representing a different theological perspective? Was there an originally unelaborated form, and if so, how are these elaborated forms of the Sabbath ordinance related to the unelaborated form?

Interpreters interested in tradition criticism—tradition critics— would pose such questions as these, but they would go further. They would propose that the written forms of the same commandment in Exodus and Deuteronomy result from a long developmental process. Noting the content, formal structure, and setting reflected in each passage, tradition critics would try to reconstruct how the tradition of the Sabbath commandment originated and developed. After reconstructing the tradition history of the Sabbath commandment, they would return to the final form of the text in Exodus 20, since this was the original point of departure, and propose an explanation of it. They would probably also explain how this form of the commandment fits into its immediate literary context—the book of Exodus.

Pentateuchal Traditions about the Patriarchs

Many of the narratives of the Pentateuch have been analyzed through this history-of-tradition perspective. If we assume that these narratives originally existed as independent, self-contained units, we can imagine some of the stages of development through which they passed. An instructive example is the Jacob narrative (Gen. 25:19–36:43). The character Jacob initially appears to have been a trickster who succeeded by outmaneuvering other people (Esau and Laban). At this stage in the tradition, there were folktales in Israel that were common to many cultures at that time. The early stage of the Jacob saga probably drew on elements from this folktale tradition. When Jacob began to be identified in the stories with the community Israel, and his victims were identified with other groups (Esau = Edomites; Laban = Arameans), the tales acquired nationalistic overtones reflecting actual tensions that existed among different groups within Israel. (At a later period, the prophet Hosea reflects awareness of some of these traditions [Hos. 12]). When combined with comparable traditions about Abraham, Isaac, and the tribes of Israel, the Jacob stories moved toward being part of a large theological-historical portrait prefiguring the origin and history of the nation Israel.

The Exodus

One of the most widespread traditions in the OT concerns Israel's deliverance from Egypt. The exodus motif and the tradition of being led out of Egypt occur in OT narratives, psalms, and prophetical books. It was a tradition that could be used in various contexts. In Hosea, for example, the ruin of the nation is depicted as a return to Egypt (Hos. 8:13; 9:3), and Isaiah 40–55 presents Israel's return from exile as a new exodus.

The most fully expanded tradition of the exodus in the Pentateuch relates to the period in the wilderness. This section now extends from Exodus 15:22 through Deuteronomy 34. Sometimes, the wilderness goes unmentioned in creedal summaries of Israel's early tradition (see Deut. 26:5–11); at other times it is mentioned only incidentally (see Josh. 24:7b). The tradition of a wilderness wandering was developed in various ways in ancient Israel. It could be depicted as a time of trouble and wickedness (in most of Exodus–Numbers, Ezek. 20) or as a good time (Deut. 8; 29:2–6; Jer. 2:2–3; Hos. 2:14–15). We can see these two perspectives reflected in Psalms 105 and 106.

Other Old Testament Examples

Other important traditions surface elsewhere. Within many of the historical books, the traditions about the choice of David, his dynasty, and his city—Zion-Jerusalem—dominate (1–2 Sam.; 1–2 Chr.). These same traditions also figure prominently in many of the psalms (see especially Ps. 89). Depending on their location and use within a biblical writing, the traditions about David reflect different attitudes toward him and his dynasty.

Time and again, Israel expressed its self-understanding and hopes for the future by drawing on earlier traditions. Older traditions were reused as Israel engaged in dialogue with its past. By paying attention to this ongoing conversation between Israel and its past, the exegete can understand more fully various dimensions of the biblical writings. The German scholar Gerhard von Rad (1901–72), for example, used Israel's continuing reformulation of its traditions as the clue to understanding the theology of the OT.

The New Testament: 1 Corinthians 15:1–11

In the NT, one of the clearest examples of using earlier traditions occurs in 1 Corinthians 15:1–11. In this passage, Paul recites a summary of the message he had preached to the Corinthians on his founding visit. Scholars agree that verses 3–5 contain a pre-Pauline summary of Christian preaching, at least one version of it. Literary clues indicate this. Paul mentions that he "handed on" to the Corinthians what he "had received." These are technical phrases used by ancient writers to describe the transmission of a sacred tradition. Such phrases were even used to describe the passing on of nonreligious traditions, such as family or national history. This language tells us that the summary of early preaching quoted by Paul comes from an earlier period: it is a pre-Pauline tradition.

The summary has a four-part structure: Christ (a) died, (b) was buried, (c) was raised, and (d) appeared. This formal literary structure has a creedal quality. It echoes the language of early Christian worship in which believers confessed their faith. In this instance, Paul is not the author of the creedal formulation, only its transmitter. The person (or community) who transmits such traditions is sometimes called a traditor.

It is also interesting to ask where Paul stops quoting the earlier creedal tradition and begins amplifying it using his own words. Whether this transition occurs at verse 6 or verse 7 is uncertain, but by the end of the paragraph we hear Paul himself speaking, not the tradition.

Analyzing this passage as tradition critics, we can easily detect the layered quality of 1 Corinthians 15:1–11. The technical language alerts us to the presence of pre-Pauline traditional material. From the cadence of the fourfold structure, we can also sense that we are dealing with material that has been refined through repetition. Sifting through the layers of tradition, we can separate the portions of the text where Paul himself is speaking from those in which he is drawing on earlier traditional material.

Once we recognize that Paul is utilizing an earlier creedal tradition, we can examine other brief summaries elsewhere in the NT (e.g., 1 Thess. 1:9–10; Rom. 8:34). Or we could look at the more extensive sermon summaries in the speeches in the book of Acts (e.g., 2:14–36; 3:17–26). Finding other summaries of early Christian preaching helps us formulate questions that might illuminate the tradition history of 1 Corinthians 15:3–5. As before, when we looked at the two versions of the Sabbath commandment, we find a longer and shorter form of the text. In 1 Corinthians 15:3–5 we find a four-part summary, whereas Romans 8:34 presents a two-part summary: "It is Christ Jesus, who died, yes, who was raised." Does the latter represent an earlier form, which was later expanded into a four-part form? Or, is it an abbreviated version of a longer form? Or are the two forms independent of each other? How do these early summaries of the creed relate to more fully developed creedal statements, such as the Apostles' Creed? By answering these questions, we gain a better understanding of the tradition history of 1 Corinthians 15:3–5, which we can then incorporate into our discussion of the larger text, 1 Corinthians 15:1–11.

After examining the final form of the tradition, that is, Paul's quotation of the creedal summary in 1 Corinthians, we are prepared to interpret Paul's use of it. Here, we would try to decide where Paul's quotation of the tradition ceases and where his own remarks begin. Then we would try to explain how Paul uses this earlier tradition in addressing the Corinthians' questions about the resurrection. By identifying the creedal tradition, we can see that Paul is quoting a sacred text, which he then applies to the Corinthians' situation.

Here as elsewhere, efforts to understand the prehistory of a sacred tradition are made to illuminate the biblical text itself. The goal of exegesis, we should remember, is to understand the text before our eyes.

Using Tradition Criticism

Tradition criticism works best when we are dealing with biblical texts in which there has been cumulative growth. In these instances, biblical writers have drawn on earlier traditions, often recorded or alluded to elsewhere in the Bible. They have incorporated these older traditions into their new interpretations, which address new situations. As we noted earlier, these traditions are being recycled as they are being appropriated, reformulated, and reinterpreted.

In this sense, the biblical writings reflect the traditioning process. They also actually reveal how interpreters in every age, both ancient and modern, practice their art. What repeatedly occurs in both the OT and the NT is the following: an interpreter, whether an individual or a community, inherits a sacred tradition, oral or written ("receives the tradition," to use the technical term); repeats and interprets this tradition in light of the interpreter's own current situation; and then transmits this reinterpreted tradition to successors.

The biblical writings not only "received" and "handed on" earlier sacred traditions, but they also *became* sacred traditions, which were used by Israel and the Christian church and then transmitted to later generations. This traditioning process reveals various aspects of the faith and life of these related communities of faith. The communities' participation in the process of transmission is itself illuminating, because it helps us understand the final written text. Tradition criticism alerts us to these different dimensions of the biblical text.

Tradition criticism clearly depends on earlier methodologies and insights. In order to reconstruct the stages of development that led to the final form of a biblical text, tradition critics engage in form-critical analysis. They also have to examine historical and literary issues raised by the text. Textual criticism can also play a vital role in establishing the history of the tradition. Although tradition criticism works in close concert with other exegetical disciplines, it, nevertheless, constitutes a separate exegetical approach.

We should also note the hypothetical nature of tradition-critical work. Tradition critics are the first to admit the theoretical nature of their reconstructed history of particular texts or traditions. Isolating distinctive forms of the text, arranging them in chronological sequence, and assessing various aspects of the stages of development requires scholarly imagination. In some instances, this can be done confidently;

in other instances, the results may be only probable, or even only possible. Some reconstructions do not gain scholarly support at all. But all of these reconstructive efforts are made in order to interpret the final form of the biblical text, which becomes the ultimate control for all tradition-critical investigation.

BIBLIOGRAPHY

General

Jaffee, Martin S. *Torah in the Mouth: Writing and Oral Tradition in Palestinian Judaism, 200 B.C.E.–400 C.E.* New York: Oxford University Press, 2001.

Lord, Albert B., Stephen A. Mitchell, and Gregory Nagy. *The Singer of Tales.* 2nd ed. Cambridge, MA: Harvard University Press, 2000.

Pelikan, Jaroslav. *The Vindication of Tradition.* New Haven, CT: Yale University Press, 1984.

Shils, Edward. *Tradition.* Chicago: University of Chicago Press, 2005 (1981).

Vansina, Jan. *Oral Tradition: A Study in Historical Methodology.* New Brunswick, NJ: Aldine, 2005 (1965).

Vermès, Géza. *Scripture and Tradition in Judaism: Haggadic Studies.* 2nd rev. ed. Leiden: Brill, 1983.

Old Testament Tradition Criticism

Ackroyd, Peter R. *Studies in the Religious Tradition of the Old Testament.* London: SCM, 1987.

Brueggemann, Walter, and Hans W. Wolff. *The Vitality of Old Testament Traditions.* 2nd ed. Atlanta: John Knox, 1982.

Culley, Robert C., ed. *Oral Tradition and Old Testament Studies.* Missoula, MT: Society of Biblical Literature (Scholars), 1976.

Fishbane, Michael. *Biblical Interpretation in Ancient Israel.* Oxford: Clarendon Press; New York: Oxford University Press, 1985.

Gunkel, Hermann. *The Stories of Genesis.* Vallejo, CA: Bibal, 1994.

———. *Water for a Thirsty Land.* Minneapolis: Fortress, 2001.

Jeppesen, Knud, Benedikt Otzen, and Frederick H. Cryer, eds. *The Productions of Time: Tradition in Old Testament Scholarship.* Sheffield, UK: Almond, 1984.

*Knight, Douglas A. *Rediscovering the Traditions of Israel.* 3rd ed. Leiden: Brill, 2006.

———, ed. *Tradition and Theology in the Old Testament.* Sheffield, UK: JSOT, 1990 (1977).

Mowinckel, Sigmund. *The Spirit and the Word: Prophecy and Tradition in Ancient Israel.* Minneapolis: Fortress, 2002.

Niditch, Susan. *Oral World and Written Word: Ancient Israelite Literature.* Philadelphia: Westminster John Knox; London: SPCK, 1996.

Nielsen, Eduard. *Oral Tradition: A Modern Problem in Old Testament Interpretation.* London: SCM, 1954.

Noth, Martin. *A History of Pentateuchal Traditions.* Chico, CA: Society of Biblical Literature (Scholars), 1981 (1972).

Ohler, Annemarie. *Studying the Old Testament: From Tradition to Canon.* Edinburgh: T. & T. Clark, 1985.

Rast, Walter E. *Tradition History and the Old Testament.* Philadelphia: Fortress, 1972.

von Rad, Gerhard. *From Genesis to Chronicles: Explorations in Old Testament Theology.* Edited by K. C. Hanson. Minneapolis: Fortress, 2005.

———. *Old Testament Theology.* 2 vols. Louisville, KY: Westminster John Knox, 2001 (1962–65).

New Testament Tradition Criticism

*Barbour, Robert S. *Tradition-Historical Criticism of the Gospels: Some Comments on Current Methods.* London: SPCK, 1972.

Bornkamm, Günther, Gerhard Barth, and Heinz J. Held. *Tradition and Interpretation in Matthew.* London: SCM; Philadelphia: Westminster, 1963.

Byrskog, Samuel. *Jesus the Only Teacher: Didactic Authority and Transmission in Ancient Israel, Ancient Judaism and the Matthean Community.* Stockholm: Almqvist & Wiksell, 1994.

*———. *Story as History—History as Story: The Gospel Tradition in the Context of Ancient Oral History.* Tübingen: Mohr Siebeck; 2000; Boston: Brill, 2002.

Conzelmann, Hans. *The Theology of St. Luke.* London: Faber & Faber, 1960; New York: Harper & Row, 1961.

Davis, Casey Wayne. *Oral Biblical Criticism: The Influence of the Principles of Orality on the Literary Structure of Paul's Epistle to the Philippians.* Sheffield, UK: Sheffield Academic Press, 1999.

Dodd, C. H. *The Apostolic Preaching and Its Developments.* Grand Rapids: Baker, 1980 (1936).

Gerhardsson, Birger. *The Reliability of the Gospel Tradition.* Peabody, MA: Hendrickson, 2001.

Gerhardsson, Birger, and Eric J. Sharpe. *Memory and Manuscript: Oral Tradition and Written Transmission in Rabbinic Judaism and Early Christianity;* with *Tradition and Transmission in Early Christianity.* Grand Rapids: Eerdmans; Livonia, MI: Dove, 1998 (1961).

Hahn, Ferdinand. *The Titles of Jesus in Christology: Their History in Early Christianity.* London: Lutterworth; New York: World, 1969.

Horsley, Richard A., Jonathan A. Draper, John M. Foley, and Werner Kelber, eds. *Performing the Gospel: Orality, Memory, and Mark.* Minneapolis: Fortress, 2006.

Kelber, Werner. *The Oral and the Written Gospel: The Hermeneutics of Speaking and Writing in the Synoptic Tradition, Mark, Paul, and Q.* Bloomington: Indiana University Press, 1997 (1983).

Kirk, Allen, and Tom Thatcher, eds. *Memory, Tradition, and Text: Uses of the Past in Early Christianity.* Atlanta: Society of Biblical Literature, 2005.

Mournet, Terence C. *Oral Tradition and Literary Dependency: Variability and Stability in the Synoptic Tradition and Q.* Tübingen: Mohr Siebeck, 2005.

Perrin, Norman. *Rediscovering the Teaching of Jesus.* New York: Harper, 1976.

Wansbrough, Henry, ed. *Jesus and the Oral Gospel Tradition.* London and New York: T. & T. Clark, 2004 (1991).

8

Redaction Criticism

The Final Viewpoint and Theology

Redaction criticism is a type of biblical criticism that explores how an author's theology is reflected in changes that the author makes to previous material. Since these changes are usually made to literary materials, they are editorial in nature. "Redaction" and "redactional" are technical terms used to describe such editorial changes. In our discussion, we use "editorial" and "redactional" interchangeably. A redaction of a text is an editorial change made to that text.

How Redaction Critics Work

As used in biblical exegesis, redaction criticism refers to interpretation in which the primary focus is the editorial stage(s) that produced the final written form of a passage. This type of criticism draws on the insights and methods of tradition criticism and form criticism. It assumes that many biblical texts have a prehistory, which can be detected and reconstructed with relative certainty. Like tradition critics and form critics, redaction critics are interested in how a given story or tradition has undergone changes in its transmission history to reach its final stage.

Having noted changes in the form, content, and function of earlier materials, the redaction critic tries to account for them. The redaction critic's real focus, however, is the final form of the written text: to explain how editorial changes within the history of transmission relate to the final, edited form. Redaction critics also try to assess how these editorial changes, especially as reflected in the final written form, reflect the theological tendencies of the author or editor. Redaction critics view editorial changes as clues to the author's theological agenda.

Not all biblical texts readily lend themselves to redaction-critical analysis. Some texts are freshly composed. They show no signs that the author has drawn on earlier materials or traditions. Even if some texts employ conventional expressions or reflect cultural commonplaces, they are not suitable for redaction-critical analysis. If we cannot show that a text has incorporated previous traditions or is based on easily identifiable sources, we have no way of tracking editorial or redactional changes. In such cases, the most we can say is that the text has been written by an author. It does not contain earlier material that has been inherited, interpreted, and transmitted in a modified form.

When it is clear that a text incorporates previous traditions, texts, or stories, redaction criticism can be a valuable exegetical tool. The Gospels provide some of the best examples of such texts. The same event, episode, or saying is often reported in two, three, or even four different versions. Scholarly research on the Gospels over the last two centuries has enabled us to place these multiple versions of a passage in a probable chronological sequence. While there will never be universal agreement that Mark was the earliest Gospel, and that both Matthew and Luke used the Gospel of Mark as one of their sources, this theory (commonly called the Two Source Hypothesis) has strong support among scholars.

Even when scholars use other models to explain how the four Gospels are related to each other, they posit some form of literary dependence. If Matthew is seen as the earliest Gospel, which was used as a source by Luke, and if Mark wrote his Gospel utilizing Matthew and Luke as sources, an event or saying recorded in all three can still be analyzed redaction-critically. In this case, the redaction critic would try to track the editorial changes Luke made to Matthew, or that Mark made to Matthew and Luke. The technique of redaction criticism does not change, only the order in which the Gospels were written.

Using the Two Source Hypothesis, we can examine a story or saying of Jesus in Mark, then look at the same story in Matthew and Luke. By comparing the different Gospels, we can identify the ways in which Matthew and Luke have redacted Mark's version of the story.

Tools for Redaction Criticism: The Gospel Synopsis

A valuable resource for doing redaction criticism of the Gospels is the synopsis. Several good synopses are readily available, but they all have one thing in common: they arrange the accounts of the Synoptic Gospels—Matthew, Mark, and Luke—in parallel columns. Some synopses display all four Gospels in parallel columns. In some cases, they also include the second-century gnostic *Gospel of Thomas* for further comparison. Displaying the Gospels in this manner enables the reader to compare the various versions of a passage, noting both differences and similarities. (For a list of current synopses, see p. 48.)

The Gospels synopsis should not be confused with another exegetical tool, the harmony, even though both are arranged in similar fashion. Unlike a synopsis, a harmony of the Gospels seeks to harmonize the various stories into a single, coherent story. The attempt is to produce a single Gospel, as it were. A synopsis, by contrast, makes no conscious attempt to harmonize the Gospels or to underscore the differences, for that matter. It takes seriously the existence of four Gospels—not one Gospel—in the NT canon. Rather than weaving the different accounts into a single, coherent account, the synopsis isolates well-defined passages (pericopes) and presents them in parallel columns. In displaying each account, editors of synopses use spaces that help readers to spot similarities and differences more easily. The term "synopsis" itself means "seeing together." As a study tool for doing exegesis of passages in the Gospels, the synopsis allows students to "see together" the different accounts of the same passage.

A New Testament Example: The Passion Narrative in the Gospels

Within the four Gospels, the Passion Narrative—the account of the final days of Jesus—exhibits great uniformity. In this section of narrative, it becomes especially clear that Matthew and Luke have used Mark's account of Jesus' passion as their basic outline. This enables us to see at least two stages in the "tradition history" in almost every episode. First, we can look at the episode in Mark—stage 1—and then examine how it has been retold by either Matthew or Luke—stage 2. Once we have posited these two stages in the tradition history of an episode, we can interpret an episode in Matthew or Luke in light of how each has edited or redacted Mark. With such a convincing case that one text is literarily dependent on an earlier version of the same story, we can do redaction-critical analysis with some confidence.

The scene describing Jesus' death on the cross (Matt. 27:45–56; Mark 15:33–41; Luke 23:44–49; see John 19:17–37) may serve as an example. Reading the accounts carefully, we note that each one has its own distinctive profile. Matthew's account is longer than Mark's, while Luke's is shorter. Matthew has redacted Mark by expanding it, Luke by abbreviating it. Specific points are also different. In Matthew, the death of Jesus is followed by the tearing of the temple veil and an earthquake, which results in tombs being opened and saints being resurrected. Neither Mark nor Luke reports this sequence of events. Luke, in contrast to Matthew, omits certain features of Mark's account, most notably the cry of dereliction, "My God, my God, why have you forsaken me?" (Mark 15:34; also Matt. 27:46). Instead of this, Luke records Jesus' final words on the cross as follows: "Father, into your hands I commend my spirit!" (Luke 23:46). These last words of Jesus are recorded in none of the other Gospels (cf. John 19:30).

Another important difference is the words attributed to the Roman centurion standing guard at the crucifixion. Matthew follows Mark in recording his confession as "Truly this man was God's Son!" (Mark 15:39; Matt. 27:54). Luke's account of the confession is completely different: "Certainly this man was innocent" (Luke 23:47).

Redaction critics, rather than trying to harmonize these differences into a single story, try to let each account speak for itself. They also interpret the distinctive features of each account in light of two considerations: (a) how the later versions of Matthew and Luke compare with the earlier version of Mark and (b) how the distinctive features of each account relate to the theological perspective of the Gospel in which it occurs.

In addressing the first concern, a redaction critic would try to explain why Luke omitted Jesus' cry of dereliction. Perhaps Luke found this desperate utterance offensive theologically. It may have suggested a Christology that accented Jesus' suffering too heavily. By contrast, Jesus' words, "Father, into your hands I commend my spirit," may have been more compatible with Luke's view of Jesus as someone who died willingly, even obediently.

Similar questions would be posed to explain why Luke's version of the centurion's words differs from Matthew and Mark. Did Luke simply alter the form of the confession that he found in Mark? Did he have access to another tradition of the centurion's confession, which focused on Jesus' innocence rather than his divinity? If so, why did he record this alternative tradition?

What Is Being Said in and through the Story

At each point, the redaction critic who is interpreting Luke's account of the death of Jesus focuses on the final written form of Luke's text, but constantly compares it with the earlier account in Mark. Redaction critics distinguish between what is being said *in* the text and what is being said *through* the text.

What is being said *in* Luke is that Jesus died, uttering words of hope and confidence, not desperation, and that a Roman soldier, seeing this, declared him innocent.

What is being said *through* Luke's account? To answer this question, the redaction critic looks elsewhere in the Gospel. The point of this broader review is to determine whether Luke's handling of this episode is typical of how he tells the story of Jesus and the church as a whole.

What we discover is revealing. De-emphasizing the agony of the cross is consistent with Luke's Christology. Portraying Jesus as an obedient Son, who is responsive to his Father's will, is also a Lukan theme. Some scholars see in Luke's account an image of Jesus as the innocent martyr, who dies confidently, even triumphantly. Others see in Luke's account echoes of Plato's portrayal of Socrates' death: the religious teacher, unjustly convicted, who dies willingly.

The centurion's declaration of Jesus' innocence also reflects a broader Lukan theme. Throughout the Passion Narrative, Luke emphasizes Jesus' innocence. He consistently redacts Mark's account to make this point, either by additions, expansions, omissions, or abbreviations (see Luke 23:4, 14–15, 20, 22, 41; also Acts 3:13–14).

What is being said *through* the story is consistent with other features of Luke's Gospel: a serious miscarriage of justice was done to Jesus, the innocent prophet, who died confident that he would be vindicated as God's righteous prophet. By allowing the text to speak for itself, the redaction critic concentrates on what is being said *in the story*. But by listening to what is being said *through the story*, we gain insight into Luke's theological understanding of Jesus' death.

Some Cautions

When interpreting the Gospels, we may not always be confident that we can sketch the tradition history behind a text, but this is not an absolute prerequisite for doing redaction criticism. If we read a story in three or four different versions, we may not always be able to place them in a clear chronological sequence and show that one has depended on the other. But we can compare them in order to find distinctive features in each account. Such comparative study enables us to see each account in sharper profile. Once we identify these distinctive characteristics, we can try to correlate them with similar features elsewhere in the writing. Looking for recurrent themes in this manner may reveal important theological tendencies within the writing as a whole. Although redaction criticism depends heavily on the insights of tradition criticism and form criticism, this is not true in every case.

For beginning exegetes, it is important to remember that a text may exhibit editorial features that are clear and distinctive enough to develop a deeper understanding of the passage. Whether these features are uncovered by comparing the final version of a story with an earlier version on which it depends or they are detected by more general comparisons—either with other biblical versions of the same story or even with nonbiblical versions of a similar story or saying—matters little. What matters is to let the text speak its full message. We should not obscure the message of a text by reading other versions into it or by harmonizing other versions with it. This is an important caveat, because many readers of the Bible have inherited a single, homogenized version of the Gospel story. Christmas nativity scenes homogenize the birth and infancy stories of Luke and Matthew by placing the "three wise men," farm animals, and shepherds in the same scene. By fusing the Lukan and Matthean stories together, such "harmonies" effectively block each evangelist's message being conveyed *through the story*.

Discerning the Theology of the Evangelists

Redaction criticism has been a useful corrective in emphasizing the overall theological perspective conveyed within each Gospel. Interestingly enough, this same point was made when the early church in the second and third centuries ascribed titles to each Gospel. The "Gospel *according* to . . ." was their way of calling attention to the distinctive theological message of each Gospel. When we speak of the "theology" of Matthew, we are recognizing that the First Evangelist is doing more than collecting stories and traditions about Jesus and arranging them in a coherent narrative. Different traditions about Jesus have been collected, but they have been arranged to express a certain theological purpose. Matthew's theology is expressed through his arrangement of the stories and teachings of Jesus. Although the figure "Matthew" is now understood as a more shadowy figure than once thought, it is still possible to speak of Matthew's Gospel as a literary work that reflects a distinctive theological outlook. This emphasis on the evangelist's theology is one of the important legacies of redaction criticism.

Redaction criticism corrected the tendency within tradition criticism and form criticism to focus on small literary units and subunits. Instead, it viewed the Gospels as literary works composed to express a theological point of view. While redaction criticism can focus on individual pericopes and methodically analyze editorial changes made by an evangelist, it consistently tries to relate these individual findings to the larger perspective of the Gospel. Redaction critics may be interested in how editorial changes within a particular passage express an evangelist's theological outlook, but they are equally interested in relating these findings to the entire work. A single passage may provide clues to an evangelist's theology, but redaction critics are finally interested in understanding the evangelist's overall theology.

So far, we have concentrated on NT examples. This is only natural, since the term "redaction criticism" was coined by a NT scholar, Willi Marxsen, working on the Gospel of Mark in the 1950s. Other NT scholars, taking their cues from Marxsen, applied redaction-critical analysis to the other Gospels.

Old Testament Redaction Criticism

Although OT scholars were generally reluctant to speak of redaction criticism, at least initially, this language has become more prominent within OT scholarship in recent years. It would be a serious mistake to leave the impression that redaction criticism as an exegetical discipline began only in the 1950s. Scholars have long recognized that the various biblical writings exhibit distinctive theological "tendencies" or portray very clearly defined theological messages. Biblical scholars have also recognized that such theological tendencies must be taken into account when reading different texts.

It has long been noted that the various editors responsible for the final compilation of the Pentateuch displayed distinct theological outlooks that were consistent within certain sections of material.

Similarly, the theological outlook of the Chronicler (the assumed editor[s] of 1–2 Chronicles) has long been recognized. This distinctive viewpoint has been used to explain differences in how certain stories and traditions from 1–2 Samuel/1–2 Kings are interpreted in 1–2 Chronicles. David is portrayed in a more realistic fashion in 1–2 Samuel than in 1 Chronicles. Reinterpreting these earlier stories, the Chronicler reportrayed David and his time in a more idealistic light. The contrasting portraits of David in 1–2 Samuel/1–2 Kings and 1–2 Chronicles have been noted by scholars for well over two centuries.

Since OT scholars have long given attention to such theological tendencies and how they relate to editorial activity in compiling various biblical writings, redaction criticism should not be viewed as a completely new exegetical approach but as a self-conscious refinement of an older interest of biblical criticism.

We can illustrate some of the differences between the older type of "theology" criticism and the more recent redaction criticism by looking at 1 Samuel 8–12. In this section of biblical material, scholars have identified two basic attitudes (and probably sources) related to the origin of the monarchy. One is promonarchy (9:1–10:16; 11:1–15) and the other is antimonarchy (8:1–22; 10:17–27; 12:1–25). Most older interpreters were content to point out these differences, to work on their possible connections with other sources, and to correlate these different views with different historical periods or groups. Redaction critics, however, go further. They ask such questions as: Why have these materials been redacted in their final form? Why have the promonarchy materials been "enveloped" and interlaced with antimonarchy materials? From such questions, we can see that the antimonarchy materials are more dominant. The redactions in the final form of 1 Samuel 8–12 have placed qualifications on the monarchy as a historical institution.

Redaction critics would further note that 1 Samuel 8–12 is only one section within a larger work, 1–2 Samuel. They would also try to explain the significance of this editorial placement. In 1 Samuel 2:1–10 and 2 Samuel 22:1–23:7, we find that three poems on kingship have been redacted into the text. Again, in "envelope" fashion, these redactions tend to modify the restrictions placed on kingship in 1 Samuel 8–12 but do so in idealistic and "messianic" terms. In describing the theology of kingship found in 1–2 Samuel, redaction critics would have to take all of these texts into account. They would especially have to explain how the redactional activity relates to the overall theology of kingship in 1–2 Samuel.

Opportunities to apply redaction-critical analysis appear throughout the OT. For example, why does the Pentateuch (with its laws) end before the people enter the land? Was the Pentateuchal material redacted in this way to stress that Torah (the law) is the constitutive element of the society? Or was it done to address a community in "exile" away from the land? Or to emphasize that obedience to the law was a prerequisite to possession of the land? What is the significance of the redacted form of the prophetical books? Material from different chronological periods has been compiled to form the single book of Isaiah. How does this overall redactional activity affect our reading of Isaiah?

Concluding Remarks

From this discussion, we see that redaction criticism received special prominence in NT studies in the latter half of the twentieth century. But it built on earlier efforts within OT scholarship to identify theological tendencies within the biblical writings and even to correlate these with different strands of literary material. For NT studies, redaction criticism was received as a welcome change to the increasingly narrow focus of tradition and form criticism. By calling our attention to how individual redactional changes were related to the larger writing in which they occurred, redaction critics redefined the role of the evangelists. They were no longer seen as anonymous editors, who were "scissors-and-paste" figures collecting and arranging discrete bits of tradition; they were now seen as theologians—evangelists who operated with larger theological visions, far bolder in their outlook than editors sitting at a desk, wearing thick glasses and a sun visor, obsessing over minute scraps of papyri.

BIBLIOGRAPHY

Old Testament Redaction Criticism

Amit, Yaira. *The Book of Judges: The Art of Editing*. Leiden: Brill, 1999.
Biddle, Mark E. *A Redaction History of Jeremiah 2:1–4:2*. Zurich: Theologischer Verlag, 1990.
*Blenkinsopp, Joseph. *Prophecy and Canon: A Contribution to the Study of Jewish Origins*. Notre Dame, IN: University of Notre Dame Press, 1977.
Boorer, Suzanne. *The Promise of the Land as Oath: A Key to the Formation of the Pentateuch*. Berlin and New York: de Gruyter, 1992.
Collins, Terence. *The Mantle of Elijah: The Redaction Criticism of the Prophetical Books*. Sheffield, UK: JSOT Press, 1993.

*Coote, Robert B. *Amos among the Prophets: Composition and Theology.* Eugene, OR: Wipf & Stock, 2005 (1981).

Dozeman, Thomas B. *God on the Mountain: A Study of Redaction, Theology, and Canon in Exodus 19–24.* Atlanta: Society of Biblical Literature (Scholars), 1989.

Fox, Michael V. *The Redaction of the Books of Esther: On Reading Composite Texts.* Atlanta: Society of Biblical Literature (Scholars), 1991.

Keinänen, Jyrki. *Traditions in Collision: A Literary and Redaction-Critical Study on the Elijah Narratives 1 Kings 17–19.* Helsinki: Finnish Exegetical Society; Göttingen: Vandenhoeck & Ruprecht, 2001.

Marttila, Marko. *Collective Reinterpretation in the Psalms: A Study of the Redaction History of the Psalter.* Tübingen: Mohr Siebeck, 2006.

Mayes, Andrew D. H. *The Story of Israel between Settlement and Exile: A Redactional Study of the Deuteronomistic History.* London: SCM, 1983.

McKenzie, Steven L. *The Trouble with Kings: The Composition of the Book of Kings in the Deuteronomic History.* Leiden: Brill, 1991.

Morrow, William S. *Scribing the Center: Organization and Redaction in Deuteronomy 14:1–17:31.* Atlanta: Society of Biblical Literature (Scholars), 1995.

Nelson, Richard D. *The Double Redaction of the Deuteronomistic History.* Sheffield, UK: JSOT, 1981.

Nogalski, James. *Redactional Processes in the Book of the Twelve.* Berlin and New York: de Gruyter, 1993.

Noth, Martin. *The Deuteronomistic History.* Eugene, OR: Wipf & Stock, 2005 (1981).

Rendsburg, Gary A. *The Redaction of Genesis.* Winona Lake, IN: Eisenbrauns, 1986.

Seitz, Christopher R. *Zion's Final Destiny: The Development of the Book of Isaiah: A Reassessment of Isaiah 36–39.* Minneapolis: Fortress, 1991.

Van der Meer, Michaël N. *Formation and Reformulation: The Redaction of the Book of Joshua in the Light of the Oldest Textual Witnesses.* Leiden: Brill, 2004.

Van Seters, John. *The Edited Bible: The Curious History of the "Editor" in Biblical Criticism.* Winona Lake, IN: Eisenbrauns, 2006.

Vervenne, Marc, ed. *Studies in the Book of Exodus: Redaction, Reception, Interpretation.* Louvain: Leuven University Press, 1996.

Wagenaar, Jan A. *Judgement and Salvation: The Composition and Redaction of Micah 2–5.* Leiden: Brill, 2001.

Wénin, André, ed. *Studies in the Book of Genesis: Literature, Redaction, and History.* Louvain: Leuven University Press, 2001.

Wilson, Gerald H. *The Editing of the Hebrew Psalter.* Chico, CA: Society of Biblical Literature (Scholars), 1985.

Yee, Gale A. *Composition and Tradition in the Book of Hosea: A Redaction Critical Investigation.* Atlanta: Society of Biblical Literature (Scholars), 1987.

New Testament Redaction Criticism

Bornkamm, Günther, Gerhard Barth, and Heinz J. Held. *Tradition and Interpretation in Matthew.* London: SCM; Philadelphia: Westminster, 1963.

Conzelmann, Hans. *The Theology of St. Luke.* London: Faber & Faber; 1960; New York: Harper & Row, 1961.

Fortna, Robert. *The Fourth Gospel and Its Predecessor: From Narrative Source to Present Gospel.* London: T. & T. Clark, 2004 (1988).

Güttgemanns, Erhardt. *Candid Questions concerning Gospel Form Criticism: A Methodological Sketch of the Fundamental Problematics of Form and Redaction Criticism.* Pittsburgh: Pickwick, 1979.

Humphrey, Hugh. *From Q to 'Secret' Mark: A Composition History of the Earliest Narrative Theology.* London: T. & T. Clark, 2006.

Johnson, Sherman E. *The Griesbach Hypothesis and Redaction Criticism.* Atlanta: Society of Biblical Literature (Scholars), 1991.

Kingsbury, Jack D. *The Parables of Jesus in Matthew 13: A Study in Redaction-Criticism.* Richmond: John Knox, 1969.

Lightfoot, Robert H. *History and Interpretation in the Gospels.* London: Hodder & Stoughton; New York: Harper, 1935.

Marxsen, Willi. *Mark the Evangelist: Studies on the Redaction History of the Gospel.* Nashville: Abingdon, 1969.

Neyrey, Jerome. *The Passion according to Luke: A Redaction Study of Luke's Soteriology.* New York: Paulist, 1985.

Osborne, Grant. *The Resurrection Narratives: A Redactional Study.* Grand Rapids: Baker, 1984.

Peabody, David B. *Mark as Composer.* Macon, GA: Mercer University Press; Louvain: Peeters, 1987.

*Perrin, Norman. *What Is Redaction Criticism?* Philadelphia: Fortress, 1969; London: SPCK, 1970.

Repschinski, Boris. *The Controversy Stories in the Gospel of Matthew: Their Redaction, Form, and Relevance for the Relationship between the Matthean Community and Formative Judaism.* Göttingen: Vandenhoeck & Ruprecht, 2000.

*Rohde, Joachim. *Rediscovering the Teaching of the Evangelists.* London: SCM; Philadelphia: Westminster, 1968.

Selvidge, Marla J. *Woman, Cult, and Miracle Recital: A Redactional Critical Investigation on Mark 5:24–34.* Lewisburg, PA: Bucknell University Press; London: Associated University Presses, 1990.

Stein, Robert H. *Gospels and Tradition: Studies on Redaction Criticism of the Synoptic Gospels.* Grand Rapids: Baker, 1991.

Representative Biblical Theologies

Albertz, Rainer. *A History of Israelite Religion in the Old Testament Period.* 2 vols. Louisville, KY: Westminster John Knox, 1994.

Barr, James. *The Concept of Biblical Theology: An Old Testament Perspective.* Minneapolis: Fortress, 1999.

*Bultmann, Rudolf. *Theology of the New Testament.* 2 vols. New York: Charles Scribner's Sons, 1951–55; London: SCM, 1952–55.

*Caird, George B., and Lincoln D. Hurst. *New Testament Theology*. Oxford: Clarendon Press; New York: Oxford University Press, 1994.

Childs, Brevard S. *Old Testament Theology in a Canonical Context*. London: SCM,
1985; Philadelphia: Fortress, 1986.

Eichrodt, Walther. *Theology of the Old Testament*. 2 vols. Philadelphia: Westminster;
London: SCM, 1961–67.

Gerstenberger, Erhard. *Theologies in the Old Testament*. Minneapolis: Fortress, 2002.

*Goppelt, Leonhard, and Jürgen Roloff. *Theology of the New Testament*. 2 vols. Grand
Rapids: Eerdmans, 1981–82.

Kümmel, Werner G. *The Theology of the New Testament according to Its Major Witnesses: Jesus-Paul-John*. Nashville: Abingdon; London: SCM, 1973.

Ladd, George E. *A Theology of the New Testament*. Rev. ed. Cambridge: Lutterworth,
1994 (1974).

Levenson, Jon D. *The Hebrew Bible, the Old Testament, and Historical Criticism: Jews
and Christians in Biblical Studies*. Louisville, KY: Westminster/John Knox, 1993.

Ollenburger, Ben C., ed. *Old Testament Theology: Flowering and Future*. Rev. ed.
Winona Lake, IN: Eisenbrauns, 2004.

Perdue, Leo G. *The Collapse of History: Reconstructing Old Testament Theology*. Minneapolis: Fortress, 1994.

Rendtorff, Rolf. *The Canonical Hebrew Bible: A Theology of the Old Testament*. Leiden:
Deo, 2005.

Seitz, Christopher R. *Word Without End: The Old Testament as Abiding Theological
Witness*. Waco, TX: Baylor University Press, 2004.

*Strecker, Georg, and Friedrich W. Horn. *Theology of the New Testament*. Louisville,
KY: Westminster John Knox; New York: de Gruyter, 2000.

*Terrien, Samuel L. *The Elusive Presence: Toward a New Biblical Theology*. Eugene, OR:
Wipf & Stock, 2000 (1978).

*von Rad, Gerhard. *Old Testament Theology*. 2 vols. Louisville, KY: Westminster John
Knox, 2001 (1962–65).

9

Structuralist Criticism

The Universals in the Text

Most of the methods we have considered in the preceding chapters are primarily historical in orientation. Generally, they seek to understand an author's thought or intention within the original historical context. This is true even if a text has been produced by several "authors" over a long period of time. The goal remains the same: to understand the text in light of the circumstances that produced it.

In terms of our earlier diagrams on pages 22–24, historical methods of interpretation focus on (1) the originator of the text, (2) the original audience, and (3) their shared universe of ideas and events (their historical conditions and circumstances). Through exegesis, the interpreter reads, examines, and listens to the words of the text as a medium communicating the author's message. The text serves as a vehicle for expressing the author's thoughts. The exegete asks, "What did the author intend to say to the reader(s) through the text?" The text is the "signal" through which the author's thoughts are transmitted to the reader. The text may lie in the forefront, but ultimately the reader's task is to "get through" or "get behind" the text to the author's intended message. The text serves not as an end but as the means for understanding the author's intentions. The various methods of historical criticism use the text as a "window" through which the interpreter can view the author, the author's intention, the setting, and the context.

Within the last few decades, other methods of studying texts have de-emphasized, or even ignored, such historical considerations. In this sense, they are nonhistorical or ahistorical in their approach. We now look at these approaches under structuralist criticism. The name derives from methodologies used to analyze many types of human thought and behavior. Structuralism has been employed in academic fields as diverse as general anthropology, linguistics, and literature.

Basic Assumptions of Structuralism

Several basic assumptions inform structuralist studies. Structuralist critics assume that all social activity is governed by certain conventions, convictions, and rules. These foundational structures of all cultural systems manifest themselves in every form of human social activity. Humans have an innate capacity to structure their experiences into patterns of meaning. An important part of this structuring activity is creating polarities and binary oppositions, such as left/right, good/bad, up/down, subject/object, light/darkness, and male/female. Rather than being used as conscious categories, these structures may function at the unconscious or subconscious level. Some structural patterns are universal, shared by different cultures and expressed in all languages. All forms of social activity, even art and literature, reflect numerous structures. Easily perceived structures are referred to as "surface structures." Speech, for example, reflects certain surface structures that we ordinarily associate with proper use of language, such as correct grammar.

The use of any language, however, is also based on very complex linguistic structures, which are called "deep structures." We may use proper speech and be aware of the surface structures associated with our language but be unaware of the complex grammatical and linguistic structures—the deep structures—that shape our language.

Structuralists assume that literature reveals both surface and deep structures. Deep structures reflect patterns of thought that transcend time and space, but they can be extracted from literary texts. In structuralist interpretation, a text is viewed more as a mirror than as a window. As a mirror, the text reflects universally shared structures and concerns. Texts have their own integrity apart from the circumstances in which they originated. In structuralist analysis, a text stands on its own—it is autonomous—regardless of how it originated. It can be interpreted meaningfully without asking about the author's original intention. Generic considerations—the shape of the text—are more important than genetic considerations—how it originated. Structuralists do not deny the existence, or even importance, of genetic dimensions of a text, but they think historical/genetic issues can blur our perception of generic features of a text.

Structuralists are more interested in *how* texts communicate meaning than in *what* they communicate and mean. They ask the following questions: How does a text produced within particular cultural constraints express universal concerns? How does a reader decode the text? How do the deep structures of the text connect with those of the reader? Structural literary critics focus on the text, the reader, and the process of reading and understanding rather than the author's composition of the text and authorial intention.

Besides noting the differences between structuralist and other kinds of interpretation, we should look at some of the underlying exegetical assumptions of structuralism. Two major emphases are especially important: (1) ahistoricity and (2) universal ordering principles.

(1) Ahistoricity

According to structuralist criticism, any text is ahistorical, not in the sense that what is reported does not conform to historical reality, but in the sense that historical dimensions of a text—its origin, authorship, setting—are not the primary focus. It might be more accurate to say that their focus is atemporal, because they read texts without relating them to their time of composition or some other temporal framework outside the text. Every effort is made to exclude the dimension of time, unless it is a particular concern of the text.

This is in sharp contrast to earlier methods that emphasized the temporal distance between an ancient text and a modern reader. Structuralist critics do not frame interpretive questions by distinguishing between what a text meant and what it now means. When they read a text, they experience it as present to them—now. In this sense, a text—any text—is timeless. Whereas form critics, for example, ask questions about the origin of a text and how it functioned in its original setting, structuralist critics try to discern underlying assumptions of the text and how it expresses universal concerns. They concentrate on how the text "works" in the reader-text relationship.

Interpreters using more traditional methods of analysis may resist this atemporal approach, but understanding how structuralist critics tend to bracket questions relating to time helps explain two basic features of their interpretive approach.

(a) **The Final Form of the Text.** The completed text sets the agenda for structuralist critics. They do not inquire about the prehistory of the text, distinguish between earlier and later forms of the text, or try to identify later interpolations or editorial redactions of the text. They know, of course, that a text may exist in different recensions or versions. They are also aware of the complexities different versions of the same text pose for textual critics. But explaining why different forms of a text exist is not their main concern. Rather, they accept a given text as "received" and work with it. How a text originated and the process though which it reached the interpreter do not interest them. They focus instead on what lies before the reader—the finished text, waiting to be interpreted.

(b) **Structuralist Understanding of Time.** Structuralists' atemporal view of texts explains why they are not interested in its historical setting. They know that texts do not just happen: they were written by someone, at some time, in some place and setting. But they set aside questions related to author, original audience, and historical setting. They do not ask the usual historical questions: Who wrote it? To whom was it written? When? Where? How? Why? Under what circumstances?

Because structuralist critics work with a different theory of texts, they formulate a different set of interpretive questions. Rather than seeing a text as something through which an author conveys meaning to a reader, they think the text itself generates meaning.

One way to understand their approach is to distinguish between synchronic (literally, "with or at the same time") and diachronic (literally, "through time") analysis. *Diachronic analysis* conceives of a text as having developed over time. If we do a diachronic word study, for example, we may look at its etymology to determine the original root from which the term derived. Or we may trace how a word has been used in various historical periods and the meanings it has conveyed at different times. Diachronic analysis implies a linear form of investigation, in which we can chart development along a time line.

Synchronic analysis of texts, by contrast, is atemporal or ahistorical. It thinks of literary works suspended, as it were, in time. When we analyze texts synchronically, our first impulse is not to arrange them in chronological order. Regardless of when they might have been written, we experience all of them together—in the present. Synchronic analysis of two biblical themes from Genesis and the book of Acts would not approach one as earlier, the other as later. Structuralist critics would read both texts together in time. A better designation might be "achronic," that is, "without time" or without reference to time.

(2) Universal Ordering Principles

A second major emphasis in structuralist criticism is to see all forms of human experience and behavior as concrete manifestations of certain ordering principles or universal structures. This basic outlook has several implications.

(a) **Theory of Language.** Structuralist critics operate with a distinctive theory of language. For them, language is not simply a medium we use to communicate meaning but a complex set of ordered symbols, verbal and nonverbal, through which meaning is conveyed. All forms of social behavior have "languages." If customs of dress within a given society conform to well-established rules, we can speak of a "language of dress." The rules governing dress—what to wear, what not to wear, and when to wear what—resemble the rules of grammar and syntax that govern what, when, and how we speak or write.

Kinship patterns can be viewed in the same way. Within a given family or tribe within a society, relationships between persons are based on established principles. Informed by such principles, persons within a given social group relate to each other and make basic decisions, such as whom they may and may not marry. Persons within a social group may be thought of as the "words" of a language whose arrangement and placement are based on certain principles of "social syntax and grammar."

(b) **Surface and Deep Structures.** When structuralists read texts, they distinguish between surface structures and deep structures. Beneath the surface structures, a text reflects deep structures of conviction and world ordering. These deep structures are encoded within the text. Rather than trying to ascertain the meaning of particular words or phrases at the surface level, the exegete's task is to decode the text to identify the deep structures from which it ultimately stems and to which it points. Surface structure refers to contours of a text that we can visibly trace, such as the outline of an argument or the flow of a story. Deep structures, by contrast, are those underlying, ordering principles that are embodied within the text. They may not even be explicitly stated within the text.

To return to our earlier example, when we speak, we may use good principles of grammar without being conscious of these rules as we formulate our speech. Or we may decide not to wear our bathrobe to work without thinking about the underlying social grammar that informs our decision. And yet the underlying principles of grammar and syntax that govern what we say and wear can be deduced from our actual use of language and our customs of dress.

(c) **Binary Opposition.** A third basic structuralist principle used to interpret all empirical forms of social behavior and their deep structures is binary opposition. Structuralist critics work with interpretive categories of opposites, especially those they have observed in a wide variety of texts. Certain pairs of opposites are fundamental to all human experience and may be at work in producing any given text. This would include such binary opposites as light/darkness, good/evil, reconciliation/alienation, divine/human, and male/female.

The principle of binary opposition applies not only to deep structures but to structuralist method generally. Even in analyzing the surface structures of a text, we can look for pairs of opposites in the arrangement of the text.

Some Examples of Structuralist Exegesis of Biblical Texts

Now that we have discussed some of the general perspectives of structuralist criticism, we can consider some examples of how it has been applied to biblical texts.

Genesis 1–2

A well-known example is a structuralist interpretation of the OT creation story in Genesis 1–2. Instead of analyzing the opening chapters of Genesis using source criticism, which posits two creation accounts (Gen. 1:1–2:4a [P] and 2:4b–25 [J]) with their respective theologies, a structuralist analysis would see Genesis 1:1–2:1 as the basic unit in interpretation. This analysis is based on the following structuralist observations: (1) The unit is naturally defined this way since it begins with a reference to God's creating the heavens and earth (1:1) and concludes by noting that the "heavens and the earth were finished" (2:1). (2) The phrase "God said" occurs ten times (vv. 3, 6, 9, 11, 14, 20, 24,

26, 28, and 29). (3) The unit divides into two roughly equal parts with five uses of the expression "God said" in each: 1:1–19 (containing 207 Hebrew words) and 1:20–2:1 (containing 206 words). The first part describes the creation of the world's inanimate order; the second part describes the creation of the world's living beings. (4) Each half moves toward a similar climax: the first part concluding with a reference to the sun, moon, and stars to rule over the heavens, the second part with humanity to rule over the earth.

Here we see some of the principles of structuralist exegesis. First, the structures of the text reflect the subject matter and theology of the material. Second, the principle of binary opposition is evident through-out: two roughly equal literary units, inanimate orders/animate orders, rule of luminaries over the inanimate world/rule of humans over the animate world. Third, the focus is on how we read a text instead of how the author writes a text. How we perceive meaning in the text is more important than what the author originally intended.

The Parable of the Good Samaritan (Luke 10:30–35)

In the previous section, the structuralist interpretation of Genesis 1:1–2:1 focuses on the surface level of the text. Texts may be analyzed to reveal deeper structures, such as universal values and convictions. On the basis of folklore studies, a narrative grid has been developed to interpret narrative structures. The grid may be used to determine the structural relationships that appear in narratives. How many relationships appear in any given narrative depends on the story's complexity. Based on this grid, the following diagram identifies the typical roles (called actants by structuralists) present in the narrative structures of most stories, although not all roles are reflected in every story:

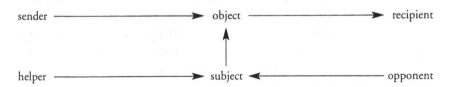

The sender is the originator of an action meant to communicate a mes-sage or transmit some object the recipient needs. This is done to ensure the recipient's well-being. The subject is the agent commissioned by the

sender to transmit the object to the recipient. The opponent attempts
to frustrate the action while the helper assists the subject in carrying out
the action.

An analysis of the narrative structure of the parable of the Good
Samaritan (Luke 10:30–35), for example, shows the following actants
in the narrative:

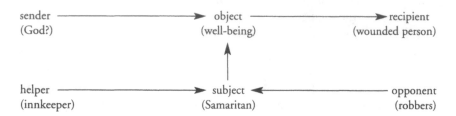

In most narratives (and also in many modern plots, such as the American Western or TV sitcoms), the characters and plots possess a remark-
able consistency. In most narratives, life's normalcy or equilibrium is
disturbed in some way. Anarchy or trouble develops. Some subject is
sent or takes action to restore order/well-being. This subject is opposed
by the creator of the anarchy or other opponents but is assisted by a
helper or helpers.

The Parable of the Prodigal Son (Luke 15:11–32)

The parable of the Prodigal Son (Luke 15:11–32) consists of two parts,
the first focusing on the younger son (vv. 11–24), the second on the elder
brother (vv. 25–32). Interpreters have often wondered about the relationship between these two parts, even speculating that the story originally
ended with the return of the prodigal. Some think that the elder brother
episode might have been added later as a way of addressing the Pharisees,
or some other group of opponents of early Christianity (see Luke 15:2).

Structuralist critics do not analyze the story by asking about the
story's prehistory. They focus on the story in its present form—the final
form of the text in Luke's Gospel. Since the story now exists with the
elder brother episode, it must be interpreted in that form. In this form,
the story reflects a basic folktale plot. It may also be seen as the story of
a character who moves through a sequence of being "at home," "away
from home," and "at home."

Binary oppositions are found in various sets of opposites: lost/
found, alienation/reconciliation, presence/absence. One way of structuring the story is to trace the movement from presence (the young

man at home) to absence (the young man away from home) to presence (the young man back at home) to absence (the elder brother ironically not "at home" with the father). In this way, the younger brother would typify "presence" or "foundness" while the elder brother would typify "absence" or "lostness."

By analyzing the story this way, structuralist critics are not concerned with how the story functions in the Gospel of Luke or with how it reflects the theology of the author of Luke. Instead, they try to discern how the structures of the story itself express meaning through universal categories.

Surprises

On occasion, plots and characters may startle us because they depart from what we expect. For example, in the parable of the Good Samaritan, the Samaritan is the outsider, the heretic, the opposite of what ancient Jewish culture would assume to be the ideal religious person. In the story, however, the Samaritan is the subject who brings aid to the wounded. In the story of Abraham's sacrifice of Isaac (Gen. 22), God plays two major roles: the deity is the opponent who demands the sacrifice of Isaac and thus produces anarchy; but the deity simultaneously acts as the subject who provides the substitute offering and alleviates the tension. In the narrative of Jacob's wrestling with the angel (God) at the ford of the Jabbok River (Gen. 32:22–32), Jacob is the hero on a quest. In the story, God appears not only as the originator of the quest but also as Jacob's opponent. As for the NT, in the overall structure of the Christ story, God is not only the sender and, in the son, the subject who brings salvation to the world, but also the world's opponent, since humankind has to be reconciled to God.

Structuralist Analysis of the Psalms

A structuralist interpretation of the book of Psalms has shown that the psalms can be understood through their deep structures. Practically all the statements in the psalms cluster around four actants. These are: (A) the protagonist, who may be the psalmist, the just person, the community, or the king; (B) the opposition, who may be the enemy, enemies generally, the wicked, or the nations; (C) God; and (D) others, including witnesses, the faithful, the just, and the nations.

In individual psalms these four elements assume various roles, generally with A as the recipient, B as the opponent, C as the helper and sender (although sometimes the opponent), and D as the corecipient. Various binary oppositions run throughout the psalms in the descriptions of persons, states of being, and expectations. These include life/death, joy/sorrow, lament/praise, weeping/dancing, blessing/curse, and so on. Using such structuralist insights, we can analyze particular psalms without trying to ascertain their actual life situations, the identity of the author or persons mentioned in the psalms, or the historical contexts in which they were written. Paradoxically, references in the psalms to disorder, evil, sin, and anarchy, which disrupt normal equilibrium, along with petitions for resolution and redemption, give the psalms a strong biographical/narrative flavor. Our ability to understand and identify, even subconsciously, with these universal structures in the psalms helps explain why over time they have appealed to people in every culture.

Mythic Structures and Narratives

Some biblical narratives lend themselves to even greater levels of abstraction that reflect mythical patterns of thinking and symbolic expression. Within some texts, mythical structures are found at an even deeper level of abstraction than narrative structures. We noted above how structuralists analyze the narrative structure of the parable of the Good Samaritan. At a deeper level of abstraction, the parable reflects mythical or paradigmatic structures. The story reflects polar opposites: life, order, health, and the kingdom of God set against death, disorder, woundedness, and the kingdom of Satan. At the surface level, the Samaritan as a religious outcast would have belonged in the camp of the disordered, while the Levite and priest occupied the arena of the ordered; but well-being in the story is produced by the Samaritan. The reader is challenged to venture outside the established order and ordinary religious boundaries and become, like the Samaritan, a "truly religious person." In the story Jesus challenges the normal mythical pattern by making the antihero into the hero. (We should note the parallels between such structuralist interpretations and medieval allegorical readings: see pp. 17–19.)

Concluding Observations

These brief examples illustrate some of the main principles of structuralist criticism. Rather than serving as detailed examples of structuralist exegesis, they are intended to show how exegetes using this interpretive method approach texts. The challenge for interpreters accustomed to historical-critical analysis is to resist asking the usual questions, such as, Who composed a text? When? Where? Under what circumstances? Instead, we must read biblical texts differently, attentive to both surface and deep structures, trying to discern such principles as binary opposition and how these deep structures convey universal truths and concerns.

BIBLIOGRAPHY

General

Barthes, Roland. *Writing Degree Zero, Elements of Semiology*. London: Jonathan Cape, 1984 (1968).

Calloud, Jean. *Structural Analysis of Narrative*. Philadelphia: Fortress, 1976.

Culler, Jonathan D. *Structuralism*. London: Routledge, 2006.

———. *Structural Poetics: Structuralism, Linguistics and the Story of Literature*. London and New York: Routledge, 2002 (1975).

———. *The Pursuit of Signs: Semiotics, Literature, Deconstruction*. Augmented ed. Ithaca, NY: Cornell University Press, 2002 (1981).

De George, Richard T., and Fernande M. De George, eds. *The Structuralists: From Marx to Lévi-Strauss*. Garden City, NY: Anchor, 1972.

Detweiler, Robert. *Story, Sign, and Self: Phenomenology and Structuralism as Literary Critical Methods*. Philadelphia: Fortress, 1978.

Greimas, Algirdas J. *Narrative Semiotics and Cognitive Discourses*. London: Pinter, 1990.

———. *Semiotics and Language: An Analytical Dictionary*. Bloomington: Indiana University Press, 1982.

Kermode, Frank. *The Genesis of Secrecy: On the Interpretation of Narrative*. Cambridge, MA: Harvard University Press, 1980 (1947).

*Lane, Michael, ed. *Introduction to Structuralism*. New York: Basic Books, 1970.

———, ed. *Structuralism: A Reader*. London: Jonathan Cape, 1970.

Leach, Edmund R. *Claude Lévi-Strauss*. Rev. ed. Chicago: University of Chicago Press, 1989 (1974).

Lodge, David. *Working with Structuralism: Essays and Reviews on Nineteenth and Twentieth-Century Literature*. London: Routledge & Kegan Paul, 1981.

*Propp, Vladimir. *Morphology of the Folktale*. 2nd ed. Austin: University of Texas Press, 1968 (1958).

Ricoeur, Paul. *The Conflict of Interpretations: Essays in Hermeneutics*. New ed. London: Continuum, 2004 (1974).

———. *Essays on Biblical Interpretation*. Philadelphia: Fortress, 1980; London: SPCK, 1981.

*Robey, David, ed. *Structuralism: An Introduction*. London and New York: Oxford University Press, 1973.

Scholes, Robert E. *Structuralism in Literature: An Introduction*. New Haven, CT: Yale University Press, 1974.

Biblical Structuralism

Barthes, Roland. *Structural Analysis and Biblical Exegesis: Interpretational Essays*. Pittsburgh: Pickwick, 1974.
*Barton, John. *Reading the Old Testament: Method in Biblical Study*. 2nd ed., rev. and enl. Louisville, KY: Westminster John Knox; London: Darton, Longman & Todd, 1996.
Greenwood, David C. *Structuralism and the Biblical Text*. Berlin and New York: Mouton, 1985.
*Keegan, Terence J. *Interpreting the Bible: A Popular Introduction to Biblical Hermeneutics*. New York: Paulist, 1985.
Patte, Daniel. *What Is Structural Exegesis?* Philadephia: Fortress, 1976.
Polzin, Robert M. *Biblical Structuralism: Method and Subjectivity in the Study of Ancient Texts*. Philadelphia: Fortress, 1977.
Tollers, Vincent L., and John R. Maier. *The Bible in Its Literary Milieu: Contemporary Essays*. Grand Rapids: Eerdmans, 1987 (1979).

Old Testament

Buss, Martin, ed. *Encounter with the Text: Form and History in the Hebrew Bible*. Philadelphia: Fortress, 1979.
Culley, Robert C., ed. *Classical Hebrew Narrative*. Missoula, MT: Society of Biblical Literature (Scholars), 1975.
———, ed. *Perspectives on Old Testament Narrative*. Missoula, MT: Society of Biblical Literature (Scholars), 1979.
Fokkelman, J. P. *Narrative Art in Genesis: Specimens of Stylistic and Structural Analysis*. 2nd ed. Eugene, OR: Wipf & Stock, 2004 (1991).
———. *Narrative Art and Poetry in the Books of Samuel: A Full Interpretation Based on Stylistic and Structural Analyses*. 4 vols. Assen: Van Gorcum, 1981–93.
Jobling, David. *The Sense of Biblical Narrative: Three Structural Analyses in the Hebrew Bible*. 2 vols. Sheffield, UK: JSOT Press, 1986–87.
Leach, Edmund R. *Genesis as Myth and Other Essays*. London: Jonathan Cape, 1969.
*Leach, Edmund R., and D. Alan Aycock. *Structuralist Interpretations of Biblical Myth*. Cambridge and New York: Cambridge University Press, 1983.
*Patte, Daniel, ed. *Genesis 2 and 3: Kaleidoscopic Structural Readings*. Chico, CA: Society of Biblical Literature (Scholars), 1980.

New Testament

Kodjak, Andrej. *A Structural Analysis of the Sermon on the Mount*. Berlin and New York: de Gruyter, 1986.

Patte, Daniel. *Narrative and Discourse in Structural Exegesis: John 6 and 1 Thessaloni-ans.* Chico, CA: Society of Biblical Literature (Scholars), 1983.

————. *Paul's Faith and the Power of the Gospel: A Structural Introduction to the Pauline Letters.* Philadelphia: Fortress Press, 1983.

*————. *Structural Exegesis for New Testament Critics.* Valley Forge, PA: Trinity, 1996 (1989).

————, ed. *Semiology and Parables: An Exploration of the Possibilities Offered by Struc-turalism for Exegesis.* Pittsburgh: Pickwick, 1976.

Patte, Daniel, and Aline Patte. *Structural Exegesis: From Theory to Practice. Exegesis of Mark 15 and 16. Hermeneutical Implications.* Philadelphia: Fortress, 1978.

Via, Dan. *Kerygma and Comedy in the New Testament: A Structuralist Approach to Hermeneutic.* Philadelphia: Fortress, 1975.

10

Canonical Criticism

The Sacred Text of Synagogue and Church

The Bible is the sacred Scripture of synagogue and church. This means that the writings comprising the Jewish and Christian Scriptures are endowed with a special authority that gives them a uniquely normative role within these communities of faith. Earlier, we noted some of the special problems related to interpreting sacred texts. We also observed the dynamic relationship between sacred texts and the religious communities in which they are revered. In one sense, the Scriptures were created by the communities of Israel and the Christian church; but in another sense, those communities were created by their Scriptures. Regardless of which came first, Scripture and community cannot exist apart from each other (see pp. 10–12). We now consider in more detail some of the implications of this symbiotic relationship.

The sacred texts—the canon—of a religious community are foundational documents. They play a key role in constituting the religious community and regulating its life and faith. Religious writings acquire such status because their communities of faith believe these texts reveal divine truth in a unique and unrepeatable manner. Such beliefs are reinforced by claims that these writings originated through special inspiration, which gives them revelatory character. This means that these writings reveal truth about God and the divine will in ways that other religious writings do not. As foundational texts, they embody, at least in embryonic form, the essence of the community's faith and practice.

Interpretive Strategies among Communities of Faith

Because a community's Scriptures are given such privileged status, they are different from all other texts, religious or nonreligious. Communities of faith not only revere their sacred texts, but they also read them using certain interpretive strategies. These strategies create several expectations among faithful readers.

First, believers read their Scriptures with expectations that differ from those brought to any other text. They read (or listen) to the Bible assuming that its message will be relevant to their lives. Through the words of Scripture, communities of faith expect to hear the voice of God, either directly or indirectly. If they do not hear God's actual voice in the words of Scripture, they at least expect to hear biblical writers witnessing to God's voice. Through reading, listening, and studying Scripture, believers anticipate, and often experience, deeply moving encounters with divine truth. Since God is so closely identified with Scripture, to read Scripture is to encounter God.

Second, the universe of the sacred text (or to use structuralist terminology, the semantic universe of the text) challenges believers to share its world and convictions. A canonical text confronts members of the community with an autocratic claim: accept the worldview of Scripture. Because of their unique status within believing communities, such texts impose themselves authoritatively upon readers and listeners.

Third, canonical texts are read with a degree of receptivity rarely extended to other texts. When believers read their own Scriptures, they already accept the vision of faith found in the text. With each new reading, they interpret the sacred text in light of their prior faith. Since these previous experiences with Scripture inform each reading, interpreters come to the text with a "preunderstanding." They have already made certain decisions about what they believe and how they understand Scripture to support those beliefs. Although believers may expect to learn new truths as they read their Scriptures, they usually come to the text with old truths—firm convictions about what the text means.

Because believers read Scripture with certain preunderstandings, which have been developed within the context of the community of faith, they tend to ignore or indulge differences, inconsistencies, and problems within the text. Out of respect, readers often minimize difficulties within the text. This may be done to honor their community's faith perspective. It also preserves the overall cohesion of the canon.

Distinctive Features of Canonical Criticism

In recent years, some scholars have challenged exegetes to read biblical texts explicitly as canonical Scripture. This approach has been designated in different ways, such as canonical/canon criticism, canonical hermeneutics, canonical exegesis, and canonical interpretation. Regardless of what we call this type of exegesis, it has several distinguishing features.

1. The canonical approach is synchronic (see pp. 142–43). Since all of the biblical writings constitute a single collection, they "stand together" in time. Canonical critics typically distance themselves from the diachronic questions that tend to preoccupy historical critics: the earliest or precanonical form of the text or tradition, the original intention of the writer, events and experiences behind the text, or the historical/sociological/psychological context that gave birth to the text. These questions may be given some consideration, but they are not the decisive factors for reading and understanding the text. Rather than thinking of the different biblical writings in their respective historical settings, and then arranging them along some reconstructed time line, canonical critics tend to think of them as a timeless collection. Instead of interpreting a given biblical book in light of its particular historical setting, canonical critics prefer to see how it relates to other books in the canonical collection. Their interpretive move tends to be horizontal—across the various biblical writings—rather than vertical—delving into the historical circumstances lying beneath the writings.

The tension between a canonical reading and the original author's intent was already an issue for Augustine (354–430). In the *Confessions*, he wrestled with how the "truth of things" relates to the "intention of the speaker [Moses]." By making this distinction, Augustine acknowledged that it was sometimes difficult to know whether "Moses meant this [interpretation] and wished this to be understood from his account" (Book 12, Chaps. 23–24). In cases where Moses' presumed intent was unclear, Augustine was inclined to look for the deeper truth—the "truth of things"—that lay hidden within an ambiguous text. Since these truths were derived from other parts of Scripture, Augustine was practicing a form of canonical criticism. He understood God to be speaking through the entire collection of biblical writings. Truth gained from reading one part of Scripture could be related to unclear or problematic texts in other parts of Scripture.

2. Closely related to canonical critics' synchronic view of biblical texts is their interest in the final form of the text. While they may

acknowledge that many biblical texts have been written and edited over long periods of time and comprise various layers of tradition, their interest lies elsewhere. Instead of looking for literary seams within a text and trying to decide how the various strands of material were edited into a coherent narrative, canonical critics deal with the text they find in their printed Bibles. They wish to interpret the "last edition" of a biblical book that was accepted into the canon. As noted earlier, they are especially interested in relating the "last editions" of all the biblical writings to each other: to hear them in concert with each other.

3. Canonical criticism also focuses on complete biblical writings rather than individual passages. Like redaction criticism, it opposes interpretive approaches, such as form criticism, that tend to isolate texts from their larger canonical setting. Canonical critics insist that a text should be read as part of the whole Bible, not as an independent, single unit. Each passage is read as part of a biblical book, and the biblical book is seen as part of the larger biblical canon. A single biblical book, no matter how important, has only penultimate authority. The Bible as a whole possesses final canonical authority.

Depending on the religious community and its Bible, this principle of relating parts to the whole can take different forms. For Jews, a passage from Isaiah must be read in light of the entire prophetic book, the prophetic writings as a group, and eventually the Torah and the Writings. The canonical horizon within which a particular passage is interpreted looks different in Christian communities. The same passage from Isaiah would also be read in light of the book of Isaiah, the OT Prophets, the Torah, the Historical Books, and the Writings; but the canonical horizon would also extend to the NT writings. Thus, for Christians, a passage from the OT read in the church will be heard in light of the NT.

Taking seriously the broad canonical horizon within which individual texts are read means that these texts are read and heard along with other biblical texts. The mutual interplay among texts has a cumulative effect that transcends any one text. This does not mean that the believing community should de-emphasize the plurality of the biblical writings and the diverse theological viewpoints expressed in them. The Christian church, for example, consistently opposed efforts to reduce the number of the Gospels from four to one or to combine the four into a single harmonization. Working with a defined canonical horizon, however, imposes limits on the interpretation of individual texts. Although a text may echo other biblical texts within the canon, it must eventually be constrained by the theological vision of the larger collection. There may be internal tensions among the biblical writings, but these tensions finally have to be worked out within the boundaries of a given canon, not beyond them.

4. Given their emphasis on the synchronic nature of biblical writings and the resulting interest in the final form of the text, canonical critics especially stress the relationship between the text and its reader(s) or listener(s). For them, the main interpretive focus is not how a reader interprets the text in order to discern the intent of the author. Instead, they are more concerned with how readers interact with a single biblical writing, and by extension, how they process what they learn from all the biblical writings across the canon.

By emphasizing the reader-text relationship, canonical critics are trying to be true to how Scripture has actually functioned within the communities of Israel and the Christian church. More important, they want to recover what has been lost when interpreters focus too narrowly on what texts meant in their original setting. Over time, the relationship that has persisted is the relationship between sacred text and believing community. Communities of faith in many different times and settings have read and interpreted Scripture—as a whole—in trying to make sense of their lives.

Rather than focusing narrowly on a single book or even one passage, interpreters have expected divine truth to be mediated to them through the different parts of Scripture. Seeing the collection of biblical writings as a chorus of voices, canonical critics are far more interested in hearing the entire chorus perform than hearing a soloist or even several soloists. Canonical criticism is just that: reading and interpreting the entire biblical canon critically for the life of faith.

5. Canonical criticism is overtly theological in its approach. In terms of our earlier diagrams (pages 22–24), canonical critics interpret the Bible as a vehicle for understanding the will of God. Since the Bible is seen as a mimetic reflection of reality, ascertaining the message of all the biblical writings enables readers to see God's true purpose for humanity: the divine reality. The Bible must be interpreted as Scripture. For Jews, it is the synagogue's Scripture; for Christians, it is the church's Scripture. In both cases, canonical critics are primarily interested in what the text means for the canonizing community—the community of faith whose predecessors produced the canon, that was called into existence by the canon and seeks to live by the canon. Construing the relationship between text and community in this way inevitably places a higher premium on what the text means now than on what it once meant.

Factors Affecting the Practice of Canonical Criticism

Different Biblical Canons

A canonical reading of a text will vary depending upon which believing community is doing the reading and which canon is being read. Jewish, Roman Catholic, Orthodox, and Protestant scriptural canons differ considerably from one another. Jewish Bibles do not include NT writings. Roman Catholic and Orthodox Christian Bibles include, along with the Jewish writings from the Hebrew Bible, the so-called apocryphal/deuterocanonical writings. Generally speaking, Protestant Christian churches operate with similar OT and NT canons. Not only does the list of canonical writings differ within these religious traditions, but also the content of individual books such as Esther and Daniel differs from one canon to another.

Since there are multiple canons within different religious traditions, canonical criticism will take different forms within each tradition. Roman Catholics, for example, allow such "apocryphal writings" as 1–2 Maccabees and Wisdom of Solomon a full canonical voice alongside the writings accepted by both Jews and other Christians, such as the Pentateuch.

Different Faith Perspectives

Also affecting how canonical criticism is practiced is the faith perspective within which canonical texts are read. This varies considerably, not only among the major religious groups themselves, but also among various denominations within the same religious tradition. Christians read the OT with different expectations and theological preunderstanding than Jewish readers. Even with Judaism and Christianity respectively, there is a broad spectrum of belief, ranging from fundamentalist to liberal. Not all Jews read their Bibles the same way; nor do all Christians interpret their Scriptures uniformly. Since Jews and Christians operate with different symbolic worlds, their reading conventions differ considerably.

Different Canonical Arrangements

Canonical criticism is also affected by the different ordering of books in the Jewish Bible and the Christian OT. How the biblical writings are arranged also reflects certain theological convictions and preunderstandings.

The books in the Jewish Bible are ordered into three divisions
—Torah, Prophets, and Writings. Priority is given to the Torah. The
medieval Jewish philosopher Maimonides (1135–1204) describes these
divisions as three concentric circles, with the Torah in the center and the
other two divisions as illustrative commentary arranged in descending
order of authority. This structure and its underlying assumptions indicate that the books in the second and third divisions are to be read looking backward. The Prophets and the Writings are read in the shadow of
the Torah.

The Christian OT canon, on the other hand, is structured into the
four following divisions: Torah, History, Poetry, and Prophets. The decision to make the Prophets the last section of the Christian Bible was
theologically significant. Since these writings were understood to contain predictions of the future, Christian readers naturally looked beyond
the OT to see how these promises were fulfilled in the NT. Since this
canonical arrangement arose in close connection with the NT canon,
readers were encouraged to read everything in the OT with a forward-
looking rather than a backward-looking orientation. Whereas Jews read
the Prophets and the Writings looking back to the Torah, Christians
read their OT looking forward to the NT. Theological preunderstanding not only determined canonical arrangement but also shaped how the
respective canonical collections were read and interpreted.

The Canonical Process: When a Writing Moves
from Its Historical Setting to Its Canonical Setting

Deciding which writings constituted the Jewish and Christian canons
of Scripture took place over several centuries. For the Jewish Scriptures,
this process began about the sixth century BCE and was not finalized
until about the second century CE. Within Christianity, two canonical
decisions were made: (1) the adoption of the Greek OT as the Christian OT and (2) the selection of twenty-seven writings comprising the
NT. Broadly speaking, the process of deciding on this two-part Christian canon occurred between the second and fourth centuries CE.

When Jews and Christians selected certain writings for their respective canons, they wanted these writings to be accessible to a wider audience through succeeding generations. Making these writings part of a
canonical collection also meant that they were detached from their historical settings and the communities of faith in which they were origi-

nally composed. Texts that were once rooted in particular communities now became available to the universal community. As a writing moved from a particular historical context to its canonical context, this affected how it was read and interpreted. Rather than being interpreted as a single writing, or even as part of a small group of writings, such as the Prophets or Psalms, it was now read as part of an entire canonical collection. In canonizing these writings, the believing communities declared the writings to be accessible to readers beyond their original setting and permanently relevant for all readers.

This shift in status was significant for interpretation. Through these decisions, both synagogue and church declared that the historically conditioned meaning of the Scriptures within their original context was no longer their only, or even most important, meaning. Prophetic preaching in the OT, for example, was originally addressed to specific historical situations; because the situations were known, explanatory details were not required. When this prophetic material became part of a later literary document and the memory of the original rhetorical situation had faded, the content of such speeches became generalized.

Isaiah's speeches in Isaiah 1:2–20 and 2:6–22, for example, were probably delivered in response to the devastating earthquake that had occurred recently under Uzziah in the eighth century BCE (Amos 1:2; Zech. 14:5). This material as we now have it, however, provides no clues that point unequivocally to such a setting. These two speeches, now severed from their original setting, have a more general cast. Now, in their new canonical setting, readers more easily interpret them as promises relating to an open future. In the canonical process, these speeches were dehistoricized—separated from their original historical setting. Even before being incorporated into the OT canon, however, these speeches had already undergone editorial changes that made them more open-ended in their orientation and less directly connected with their original historical setting. The modern reader now encounters this prophetic material in its canonical form, without specific clues to its original historical setting.

This same shift in orientation of biblical material can be seen in the OT psalms. Most if not all of the psalms were originally composed for use in services of worship. Over time, individual psalms were edited. Eventually these edited psalms were collected as a group, which became the book of Psalms. The editorial and canonical process that shaped the Psalter produced a book of compositions whose original association with Israel's worship is now almost totally obscured.

Some Examples of Canonical Criticism

Old Testament

The OT book of Isaiah provides one of the clearest illustrations of the impact of canonical reading. Historical criticism has demonstrated with a reasonable degree of certainty that large portions of Isaiah, at least chapters 40–55, come from the sixth century BCE. Second Isaiah, as this material is called, has been attached to a collection of prophetic oracles attributed to the prophet Isaiah, who lived during the eighth-century-BCE reigns of Kings Uzziah, Jotham, Ahaz, and Hezekiah (see Isa. 1:1). (Third Isaiah, chaps. 56–66, about which there is less certainty, has undergone a similar fate.)

In the editorial process that produced the canonical book of Isaiah, chapters 40–55 were detached from the events of the sixth century BCE. The canonical material no longer has explicit associations with this historical period. (References to Cyrus, e.g., Isa. 45:1, do not require chaps. 40–55 to be read with reference to the sixth century BCE.) When these chapters were added to the earlier section of Isaiah (chaps. 1–39), they were "rehistoricized" by being associated with the prophet Isaiah and the eighth century BCE. This shift gave chapters 40–55 a future-oriented perspective. In their new setting, these chapters also acquired a more redemptive character. A new interpretive horizon was also created: readers understood Isaiah's prophetic preaching as the prediction of future events. This reorientation is reflected in the second-century-BCE Jewish writing of Sirach:

> By his dauntless spirit he [Isaiah] saw the future,
>   and comforted the mourners in Zion.
> He revealed what was to occur to the end of time,
>   and the hidden things before they happened.
>   (Sir. 48:24–25)

As we already noted, in the editorial process, historically specific oracles of Isaiah assumed a generalized tone. Isaiah 9:2–7 and 11:1–9 once spoke about a particular contemporary ruler on the throne of David (in this case probably King Ahaz). In their more general form, however, such passages lent themselves to an idealistic, messianic interpretation. In their edited canonical form, the prophet did not appear to be speaking to his contemporaries; he appeared to be looking forward to one who would come. As part of a Christian canon, these texts from Isaiah naturally resonated with the early church's claims about Jesus.

Canonical exegesis must take into consideration not only the final form of the text but also how these "final editions" function as part of canonical Scripture. There are no First, Second, and Third Isaiahs in Scripture, only the book of Isaiah. Christian readers could hardly think of Yahweh's chosen leader in Isaiah solely in terms of Isaiah 9:2–7 and 11:1–9; they inevitably connected these passages with such texts as Isaiah 52:13–53:12. While historical critics would argue that these two sets of texts derive from different contexts and originally referred to different figures (although this is disputed), because these texts are now part of one biblical book, Christian readers naturally read them in light of each other. The common canonical setting of these originally diverse texts invites Christian readers to associate them with each other.

The book of Ecclesiastes provides another example. Its complexity invites different interpretations. Historical critics read Ecclesiastes one way, canonical critics another. Some scholars argue that the concluding paragraph (Eccl. 12:13–14) is a late editorial addition to the book. Most of the book adopts a rather pessimistic view of life. Some historical critics think the original book was completely skeptical in outlook. The final paragraph in the current canonical form of the book, however, suggests that one should not give in to doubt and unbelief. Because of its location at the end of the book, this paragraph mutes the preceding skeptical advice. The final canonical form of the text has overridden the pervasive skepticism of the earlier form of the text.

Whoever interprets the book of Ecclesiastes must explain the tension between the optimistic outlook expressed in Ecclesiastes 12:13–14 and the generally pessimistic outlook of the rest of the book. Rather than explaining the final paragraph as a later editorial redaction, added by someone who wanted to rescue the book by making it end on an upbeat note, canonical critics would take the final form of the text as it now stands, develop an interpretation that relates the final paragraph to the whole work, and then read the whole work in light of its current conclusion. Moreover, their interpretation would take into account relevant passages from other biblical books. It would be canonical in the fullest sense: an interpretation relating the part to the whole.

In developing a comprehensive interpretation of the book of Ecclesiastes, canonical critics would also encounter other problems. Ecclesiastes offers no hope of immortality or resurrection of the dead. On the contrary, Ecclesiastes 3:19 declares that humans suffer the same fate as animals; both die without hope. Canonical critics working with a Roman Catholic or Orthodox OT canon, however, would have to relate this rather pessimistic outlook with other biblical writings, such as the Wisdom of Solomon, which clearly affirms immortality and rewards after death (Wis. 3:1–9). Their problem is compounded further by the NT writings, which consistently uphold belief in the resurrection. Obligated to relate any single text to the entire Bible, canonical critics cannot limit their interpretation to the book of Ecclesiastes, or even to the OT. Eventually, they would discover that the pessimistic outlook, which typifies most of the book of Ecclesiastes, is a minority voice within the larger canonical chorus of voices.

New Testament

So far, we have illustrated canonical criticism primarily with reference to the OT, but it also has implications for NT interpretation. We have already noted that canonical critics, working with a Christian perspective, must take into account how interpretations of OT writings are influenced by the NT. But even among the NT writings themselves, canonical criticism can offer new interpretive perspectives. Here we can mention a few implications for the NT writings.

1. Canonical critics tend to interpret the teachings of Jesus within their canonical context, rather than in some historically reconstructed setting within the life of Jesus. Whereas form critics would try to trace a saying of Jesus found in one of the Gospels to its original setting within the life of Jesus, canonical critics would focus on its current canonical setting: its location within a particular Gospel and how the saying relates to other teachings of Jesus in the four Gospels.

By approaching the Gospels this way, canonical critics challenge many well-established assumptions of form criticism, tradition criticism, and redaction criticism. Much modern interpretation of the teachings of Jesus assumes that they must be freed from their present literary contexts and connected with the social, political, and religious circumstances of the historical Jesus. Canonical critics, however, would insist that such hypothetical reconstructions are of limited value. They are beneficial only if they contribute to an understanding of the present form of the text.

2. The status of biblical writings before they were recognized as canonical is of little interest to canonical critics. Rather than being inter-

ested in earlier forms of the four Gospels, or even in the reconstructed document Q, the hypothetical source used by Matthew and Luke, canonical critics focus on the final form of the four Gospels—the texts as we now have them. They also take seriously the current location of these writings within the NT canon. While NT scholars commonly link the Gospel of Luke and the book of Acts, because of their common authorship, and read Luke–Acts as a single, two-volume work, canonical critics would protest that this not only removes Luke from its position as one of the Synoptic Gospels, but also alters the way the book of Acts was read as a bridge between the four Gospels and the Pauline letters.

3. The chronological order in which biblical books originated is not decisive for exegesis. Modern scholarship tends to assume, for example, that 1 Thessalonians was the first letter Paul wrote. In the NT canon, however, Romans opens the collection of Pauline writings. In establishing this order, the early church predisposed the reader to interpret the remainder of Paul's writings in light of the book of Romans. The canonical arrangement of the Pauline letters separated them from their original historical settings. For canonical critics, it is more important that thirteen Pauline letters constitute the Pauline corpus, and for this reason they must be read in light of each other. How the letters relate to each other and how individual Pauline passages relate to the letter in which they occur, as well as other Pauline letters, are questions that preoccupy canonical critics. They are less interested in arranging the Pauline letters in proper chronological order and interpreting them accordingly than in seeing how they reflect a common theological vision.

Canonical critics are even less interested in ascertaining Paul's original intention or the circumstances in which the letters were composed. Instead, they focus on the Pauline texts in their final form and how they bear theological witness to the gospel. As we noted in looking at OT texts, canonical critics privilege how the NT writings are heard by the community of faith in their present context.

Concluding Observations

Many of the perspectives of canonical criticism, such as its focus on the final form of the text, whole writings instead of individual passages, and the theological message of the biblical writings, were also present in earlier forms of biblical criticism. There are clear similarities to redaction criticism and structuralist criticism. Some scholars have observed that canonical criticism reverts to precritical methods of biblical interpretation, which characterized the earlier patristic and medieval periods. To the extent that canonical criticism is trying to recapture the patristic and medieval emphasis on the message of the Bible as a whole, and how communities of faith relate to Scripture in settings of worship, devotion, and study—reading it expecting to hear and experience God's truth for their lives—it is trying to recover something that was lost in the rise and development of historical criticism.

Most canonical critics, however, have been trained in traditional methods of historical criticism. They are well aware of the historical complexities of the origin and growth of the OT and the NT. But they are also critical of the ways in which various methods of biblical criticism, especially in the twentieth century, were preoccupied with the "history behind the text" rather than with the "message of the text." Whereas historical criticism tended to "deconstruct" the biblical canon, analyze each writing historically, break up the canonical writings into smaller literary pieces, and analyze isolated passages, canonical criticism has tried to reverse this process. Freely admitting that individual writings, or parts of those writings, were formulated in earlier settings and were collected and edited into their present biblical form, canonical critics want to move beyond questions relating to the prehistory of the text to questions relating to the theological message(s) that resonate within the OT and NT canons as a whole. In this sense, canonical criticism is trying to correct some of the mistakes of earlier methods of biblical exegesis.

BIBLIOGRAPHY

The Development of the Biblical Canons

Aland, Kurt. *The Problem of the New Testament Canon*. London: Mowbray, 1962.

Auwers, Jean-Marie, and Henk J. de Jonge, eds. *The Biblical Canons*. Louvain: Peeters, 2004.

Barton, John. *Holy Writings, Sacred Text: The Canon in Early Christianity*. Louisville, KY: Westminster John Knox, 1997.

———. *Oracles of God: Perceptions of Ancient Prophecy in Israel after the Exile*. New York: Oxford University Press; London: Darton, Longman & Todd, 1986.

———. *People of the Book? The Authority of the Bible in Christianity*. Louisville, KY: Westminster/John Knox, 1988; London: SPCK, 1993.

Beckwith, Roger T. *The Old Testament Canon of the New Testament Church and Its Background in Early Judaism*. London: SPCK; Grand Rapids: Eerdmans, 1985.

Bruce, Frederick F. *The Canon of Scripture*. Downers Grove, IL: InterVarsity; Glasgow: Chapter House, 1988.

Ellis, Earle E. *The Old Testament in Early Christianity: Canon and Interpretation in the Light of Modern Research*. Eugene, OR: Wipf & Stock, 2003 (1991).

Farmer, William R., Dennis M. Farkasfalvy, and Harold W. Attridge. *The Formation of the New Testament Canon: An Ecumenical Approach*. New York: Paulist, 1983.

Evans, Christopher F. *Is "Holy Scripture" Christian? and Other Questions*. London: SCM, 1971.

Gamble, Harry Y. *Books and Readers in the Early Church: A History of Early Christian Texts*. New Haven, CT: Yale University Press, 1995.

———. *The New Testament Canon: Its Making and Meaning*. Eugene, OR: Wipf & Stock, 2002 (1985).

Gnuse, Robert. *The Authority of the Bible: Theories of Inspiration, Revelation, and the Canon of Scripture*. New York: Paulist, 1985.

Grant, Robert M. *The Formation of the New Testament*. New York: Harper, 1965.

Hahneman, Geoffrey M. *The Muratorian Fragment and the Development of the Canon*. Oxford: Clarendon; New York: Oxford University Press, 1992.

Helmer, Christine, and Christof Landmesser, eds. *One Scripture or Many? Canon from Biblical, Theological, and Philosophical Perspectives*. Oxford and New York: Oxford University Press, 2004.

Hengel, Martin. *The Four Gospels and the One Gospel of Jesus Christ: An Investigation of the Collection and Origin of the Canonical Gospels*. Harrisburg, PA: Trinity; London: SCM, 2000.

———. *The Septuagint as Christian Scripture: Its Prehistory and the Problem of Its Canon*. Edinburgh: T. & T. Clark, 2001.

Leiman, Shnayer Z. *The Canonization of Hebrew Scripture: The Talmudic and Midrashic Evidence*. 2nd ed. New Haven, CT: Connecticut Academy of Arts and Sciences, 1991.

*McDonald, Lee M. *The Biblical Canon: Its Origin, Transmission, and Authority*. 3rd ed. Peabody, MA: Hendrickson, 2006.

*McDonald, Lee M., and James A. Sanders, eds. *The Canon Debate*. Peabody, MA: Hendrickson, 2002.

Metzger, Bruce M. *The Canon of the New Testament: Its Origin, Development, and Significance*. New York: Oxford University Press; Oxford: Clarendon Press, 1997 (1987).

Miller, John W. *The Origins of the Bible: Rethinking Canon History*. New York: Paulist, 1994.

*Sundberg, Albert C., Jr. *The Old Testament of the Early Church*. New York: Kraus, 1969 (1964).

Trobisch, David. *The First Edition of the New Testament*. Oxford: Oxford University Press, 2000.

*von Campenhausen, Hans F. *The Formation of the Christian Bible*. London: Black; Philadelphia: Fortress, 1972.

Canonical Criticism

*Barr, James. *Holy Scripture: Canon, Authority, Criticism.* Oxford: Clarendon Press; Philadelphia: Westminster, 1983.

*Barton, John. *Reading the Old Testament: Method in Biblical Study.* Rev. and enl. ed. Louisville, KY: Westminster John Knox; London: Darton, Longman & Todd, 1996.

Brett, Mark G. *Biblical Criticism in Crisis? The Impact of the Canonical Approach on Old Testament Studies.* Cambridge: Cambridge University Press, 1991.

Brown, Raymond E. *The Critical Meaning of the Bible.* New York: Paulist; London: Chapman, 1981.

Brueggemann, Walter. *The Creative Word: Canon as a Model for Biblical Education.* Philadelphia: Fortress, 1982.

*Childs, Brevard S. *Introduction to the Old Testament as Scripture.* London: SCM; Philadelphia: Fortress, 1979.

*———. *The New Testament as Canon: An Introduction.* Valley Forge, PA: Trinity, 1994 (1985).

Coats, George W., and Burke O. Long, eds. *Canon and Authority: Essays In Old Testament Religion and Theology.* Philadelphia: Fortress, 1977.

Conrad, Edgar W. *Reading the Latter Prophets: Toward a New Canonical Criticism.* London and New York: T. & T. Clark, 2003.

Keegan, Terence J. *Interpreting the Bible: A Popular Introduction to Biblical Hermeneutics.* New York: Paulist, 1985.

Noble, Paul R. *The Canonical Approach: A Critical Reconstruction of the Hermeneutics of Brevard S. Childs.* Leiden: Brill, 1995.

O'Neal, G. Michael. *Interpreting Habakkuk as Scripture: An Application of the Canonical Approach of Brevard S. Childs.* New York: Peter Lang, 1998.

Roth, Wolfgang. *Isaiah.* Atlanta: John Knox, 1988.

Sanders, James A. *Canon and Community: A Guide to Canonical Criticism.* Eugene, OR: Wipf & Stock, 2000 (1984).

*———. *From Sacred Story to Sacred Text: Canon as Paradigm.* Eugene, OR: Wipf & Stock, 1999 (1987).

———. *Torah and Canon.* 2nd ed. Eugene, OR: Cascade, 2005 (1974).

Scalise, Charles J. *From Scripture to Theology: A Canonical Journey into Hermeneutics.* Downers Grove, IL: InterVarsity, 1996.

———. *Hermeneutics as Theological Prolegomena: A Canonical Approach.* Macon, GA: Mercer University Press, 1994.

Seitz, Christopher R., and Kathryn Greene-McCreight, eds. *Theological Exegesis: Essays in Honor of Brevard S. Childs.* Grand Rapids: Eerdmans, 1999.

Stuhlmacher, Peter. *Historical Criticism and Theological Interpretation of Scripture: Toward a Hermeneutics of Consent.* Eugene, OR: Wipf & Stock, 2003 (1977).

Wall, Robert W., and Eugene E. Lemcio, eds. *The New Testament as Canon: A Reader in Canonical Criticism.* Sheffield, UK: JSOT Press, 1992.

11

Exegesis with a Special Focus

Cultural, Economic, Ethnic, Gender, and Sexual Perspectives

During the second half of the twentieth century, a choral cacophany of voices came to be heard in the sanctuary of biblical interpretation. Some of these were old voices, previously suppressed or merely ignored, while others were new voices being heard for the first time. They all shared one major characteristic: they spoke from the shadows of the marginalized. These voices did not so much represent new methodologies in the exegetical discipline as much as new perspectives on and new goals for the entire enterprise. The practitioners of these new perspectives not only sensed themselves as but also were the unprivileged/ underpriveleged, the exploited, the downtrodden, the powerless, the oppressed, and the misunderstood.

At least six impulses contributed to these new perspectives that found expression in various forms: liberation theology, feminism, ethnicism, culturalism, and social criticism. (1) An almost global movement to change the status quo—to secure some power for the powerless, to promote justice in the civil sphere, to move toward equality in the social order, and to open the doors of expression and opportunity—characterized much of the period and became absorbed into biblical studies. (2) A weariness and boredom with the old approaches of the historical-critical method and its conclusions became widespread. The same old game seemed to be played over and over again with the biblical materials with slight shifts in the minutiae but nothing challenging in the conclusions. (3) The traditional practices of biblical interpretation came increasingly to be seen as dominated by elite white males with a Euro-American orientation that was judged less than representative of the world's population and of the Bible's readers. (4) New issues and problems in life came to the forefront during this period and there was a desire to allow the Bible to speak to these issues. (See, for example, the Earth Bible series, edited by Norman Habel, which highlights ecological issues.) (5) New developments in literary studies also influenced biblical interpretation. So-called New Criticism argued that the interpreter should focus on the text rather than on the "historical" author whose intentions remain unknown or at least uncertain. Reader-Response criticism focused attention on the reader as the creator of meaning in texts. Since readers are situated in time, place, and social context, these factors and the ideology of the reader have roles to play in interpretation. Subjectivity and various forms of ideology came to be recognized as appropriate, in fact as indispensable, elements in all interpretation. (6) Postmodernism has challenged practically all the certainties, foundations, methods, and conclusions of belief systems and epistemological methods while affirming that plurality and diversity characterize all things, including the interpretation of the Bible. This attitude has created an open playing field without predetermined boundaries in the interpretation of the Bible.

Liberation Theology

Beginning in the 1960s, and especially in Latin America, a movement arose that has sought to foster concern for and improvement of the status of the world's economically poor and impoverished, politically disenfranchised, and culturally deprived. This movement, called "liberation theology," was influenced by Vatican II, Marxist thought, and a greater recognition of the general living conditions prevailing in the so-called third world. This concern, acknowledged by the church, given expression by biblical scholars, and expounded in small local church base groups, found expression at the Medellin conference in 1968. This conference endorsed a theology of a "preferential option for the poor," manifested by God and proposed for the church. Biblical exegesis, it is argued, cannot be neutral but must take sides with the poor in the struggle against oppression

The liberation theologies have made extensive use of the Bible in their calls for the transformation of society. Various biblical texts and themes have been stressed by liberation exegetes. Most prominent is the utilization of the exodus story with its motifs of slavery, oppression, and liberation. Also of importance are the creation accounts with their monogenetic perspective. As is well known, both testaments stress the merciful disposition of the deity toward the oppressed and the poor. The actions and teachings of Jesus, especially the parables, also lend themselves to a liberation reading.

Liberation exegesis has become a staple of biblical interpretation not only in Latin American nations, but also throughout the two-thirds world. Approaches range from the minjung theology of Korea to the development of theology among dalit (casteless) Christians in India.

Feminist Interpretation

Although feminist interpretation of the Bible can be viewed as part of the liberation theology movement, its roots and development are somewhat different. Already in the nineteenth century, various female voices, especially in the United States, were highly critical of the male/patriarchal character of the biblical traditions and the use of these materials in the contemporary church and society. This move reached something of a pinnacle in the work of a committee published as *The Woman's Bible* (2 vols., 1885–88; reprinted several times since 1972). The driving force behind this project and the primary author was Elizabeth Cady Stanton (1815–1902). Behind these developments in the late nineteenth century lay a centuries-long debate and discussion in Protestantism concerning the role of women in the church and female ordination to the ministry.

The modern phase of feminist interpretation dates from the 1960s, when feminist issues became an important concern in the general culture. Since that time, women have sought to overthrow the legacy of social patriarchy, male dominance, and sexist exploitation.

Feminist readings and interpretation of the Bible have flourished in recent years with the increased number of female theological students, pastors, and academicians. Characteristic of their work are two series: Feminist Companion to the Bible, edited by Athalya Brenner, and Feminist Companion to the New Testament and Early Christian Writings, edited by Amy-Jill Levine. Feminist biblical interpretation is a widely diverse phenomenon, but may be said to encompass the following methodological processes.

1. Texts—stories and laws—about women are approached from a "hermeneutic of suspicion." Both the texts and their interpretations are subjected to close scrutiny as to their meanings under the suspicion that these have been produced with biases based on gender. Often here the language and the translation may be examined with questions as to their implicit content and whether sexual bias is present. Whether a text or interpretation is fundamentally biased, reflecting ancient patriarchal culture and mores or the previous male-dominated processes of the academy, or whether it contains some insights valid across differences of gender, has to be determined. Many texts can be interpreted with a positive legacy ("retrieved"), whereas others must be considered irretrievable, critiqued, and relativized.

2. Feminists tend, of course, to highlight stories and episodes in which women play significant roles or texts in which gender plays little role. Significant also are those texts in which the treatment of women is so subhuman that they are called "texts of terror." The highlighting of the male chauvinist character of the Bible can in and of itself be corrective. Reading the backgrounds of a text, listening to its silences, and imaginatively recreating the roles and speeches of female characters can be informative. Often the depiction of females in independent stories may be much more positive than the editorial framework within which they appear.

3. Feminist exegetes approach the text without pretense about some undefinable objectivity. Feminists are quite willing to acknowledge that they are reading the text through the lens of feminism. Conscious identification with the feminine provides a means of resonating with biblical texts and avoids the fakery of claiming a disinterested posture.

Underneath the umbrella of feminist readings of the Bible are *mujerista* (from Spanish *mujer,* "woman") and womanist interpretations. The former is used to designate Latina feminist readings; the latter offers the particular perspective of African American women. Both express a theology and interpretation of the female in an alien and oppressive society.

Postcolonial Interpretation

The last century has seen the breakup of the empires founded by European states. Many countries in the world were subject to colonization and domination by foreign states and empires. The attitudes and worldviews of the colonizers were imposed on the colonies. Colonizing powers often read themselves into the biblical story. For example, New World settlers saw themselves as reenacting the exodus from Egypt and migrating to a new promised land. In such a scheme, Native Americans became the "Canaanites" of the new world order. In the colonies, indigenous culture was generally ignored or devalued. In many cases, the attempts of the colonies to develop their own expressions were also discounted as inferior to those of the homeland.

Postcolonial biblical interpretation consciously attempts to take into account the influences of colonization. It encompasses a wide variety of processes—interpretation subsequent to the time of initial colonization, interpretation after independence, then as the dominating international power changes, incorporation of indigenous thought into interpretation, and critiques of the exotic worldview.

Postcolonial interpretation of the Bible—as varied and diverse as it is—has as its goal not only to deconstruct the imperialist interpretation imposed upon native populations and to free them from such worldviews (so-called guerilla exegesis) but also to find means and methods for drawing upon and integrating indigenous culture and experience into biblical readings. It is now recognized that much of the Bible itself is "colonial literature," that is, texts produced by people living under colonizing powers—Assyrian, Babylonian, Persian, Syrian, Greek, and Roman. Postcolonial biblical interpretation has taken its place in the ever-growing world of postcolonial thought and literature.

African and African American Interpretation

In a strictly technical sense, African and African American interpretation of the Bible may be described as a recent phenonenon. This however would be a misconstrual of the evidence. Black slaves in the Americas who had received their Christian religion from white Europeans found an outlet for their hopes and dreams by reading their experiences into and through biblical materials. These then found expression in their spirituals, an early form of African American biblical interpretation.

The modern, self-conscious phase of "the blackening of the Bible" has as its goal not only the acquisition of liberation from oppression and marginality but also the correction of deficient and misguided forms of interpretation.

1. There has been a strong drive among this community of readers and interpreters to recover the role, importance, and contribution of

Africa to world and biblical history and culture. This effort has been labeled "corrective historiography." Proponents charge that the role of Mesopotamian and Greco-Roman civilizations has been overstressed at the expense of African-Egyptian civilization. The political and cultural impact of Africa thus needs to be reevaluated. An interesting point in this regard is the fact that the Negroid kingdom of Cush on the Upper Nile controlled the entire Nile Valley and was a major international power for almost a hundred years in the late eighth and early seventh centuries BCE, but this is seldom stressed in biblical studies.

2. In the history of Jewish and Christian interpretation of the Bible, black peoples have been depicted negatively. The effort to counter this has been designated "corrective interpretation." The account of the cursing of Ham/Canaan in Genesis 9:20–27, for example, has been seen for centuries, without foundation, as the origin of human blackness. Another example illustrates this tendency. In 1655, Isaac de La Peyrère (1596–1676) sought to explain the origin of "New World" peoples not mentioned in the Bible. His book *Man before Adam* argued for the creation of some humans before Adam. These "preadamites" were considered subhuman. Many people claimed that blacks and other indigenous people were descended from these preadamites and thus less than fully human. Such skewed interpretations have been used to subordinate blacks in the world.

3. Africans and African Americans have sought to de-Europeanize biblical interpretation. Art and literature have depicted biblical events, places, and persons as if they were European. Attempts to rectify this practice have argued that people of ancient Palestine were probably more similar to people of Africa than people of Europe.

4. African interpreters have sought to demonstrate that much in the Bible—rituals, culture, thought and theology—has analogies in African culture.

5. Africans and especially African Americans have stressed many themes that they have in common with diverse forms of liberation theology—oppression, marginalization, slavery, and the elements that point to redemption and freedom.

Queer Commentary

Gays and lesbians are beginning to play a more significant role in culture studies in general and biblical interpretation in particular. Queer theory shares many of the perspectives of postmodernism. Gender identity and roles are viewed as social constructs rather than ontological realities. As in all social constructs, social power and politics are viewed as integral features in society's ordering of sexual roles.

In biblical studies, queer theory has stressed several issues: (1) The reexamination of society's views on sexuality, sex, and gender and their claim to biblical warrants has sought to challenge and resist these traditional views and interpretations. (2) A strong emphasis is placed on the biblical teachings about justice in society, thus challenging the injustice shown against homoeroticism. (3) The shape and character of Jesus' life and ministry have been stressed to present him as a "prophetic outsider" who refused to adopt and live by the sexual and marriage standards of his day.

Conclusion

Biblical interpreters with interests in matters discussed in this chapter now have a wealth of literature available. Persons whose concern in exegesis does not focus on these perspectives in particular should nonetheless gain some acquaintance with these approaches and keep them in mind when reading and studying the Bible.

BIBLIOGRAPHY

General

*Adam, A. K. M. *Faithful Interpretation: Reading the Bible in a Postmodern World.* Minneapolis: Fortress, 2006.

———. *Postmodern Interpretations of the Bible: A Reader.* St. Louis: Chalice, 2001.

Clines, David J. A. *Interested Parties: The Ideology of Writers and Readers of the Hebrew Bible.* Sheffield: Sheffield Academic Press, 1995.

Collins, John J. *The Bible after Babel: Historical Criticism in a Postmodern Age.* Grand Rapids: Eerdmans, 2005.

Fredriksen, Paula, and Adele Reinhartz, eds. *Jesus, Judaism, and Christian Anti-Judaism: Reading the New Testament after the Holocaust.* Louisville, KY: Westminster John Knox, 2002.

Hayes, John H., ed. *Methods of Biblical Interpretation.* Nashville: Abingdon, 2004.

Levison, John R., and Priscilla Pope-Levison. *Return to Babel: Global Perspectives on the Bible.* Louisville, KY: Westminster John Knox, 1999.

Perdue, Leo G. *Reconstructing Old Testament Theology: After the Collapse of History.* Minneapolis: Fortress, 2005.
Rogerson, J. W. *According to the Scriptures? The Challenge of Using the Bible in Social, Moral, and Political Questions.* London: Equinox, 2006.
Scholz, Susanne, ed. *Biblical Studies Alternatively: An Introductory Reader.* Upper Saddle River, NJ: Prentice Hall, 2003.
Segovia, Fernando F., and Mary Ann Tolbert, eds. *Reading from This Place.* 2 vols. Vol. 1: *Social Location and Biblical Interpretation in the United States.* Vol. 2: *Social Location and Biblical Interpretation in Global Perspective.* Minneapolis: Fortress, 1995.

Liberation Theologies

*Boff, Leonardo, and Clodovis Boff. *Introducing Liberation Theology.* Maryknoll, NY: Orbis, 1987.
Brown, Robert McAfee. *Gustavo Gutiérrez: An Introduction to Liberation Theology.* Maryknoll, NY: Orbis, 1990.
Croatto, J. Severino. *Exodus: A Hermeneutic of Freedom.* Maryknoll, NY: Orbis, 1981 (1978).
Gutiérrez, Gustavo. *A Theology of Liberation: History, Politics, and Salvation.* Maryknoll, NY: Orbis, 1973.
———. *We Drink from Our Own Wells: The Spiritual Journey of a People.* Maryknoll, NY: Orbis, 1984.
Míguez Bonino, José. *Doing Theology in a Revolutionary Situation.* Philadelphia: Fortress, 1975.
———, ed. *Faces of Jesus: Latin American Christologies.* Maryknoll, NY: Orbis, 1984.
Tombs, David. *Latin American Liberation Theology.* Leiden: Brill, 2002.
van Iersel, Bas, and Anton Weiler, eds. *Exodus: A Lasting Paradigm.* Edinburgh: T. & T. Clark, 1987.

Feminist Theology

Bach, Alice, ed. *Women in the Hebrew Bible: A Reader.* London and New York: Routledge, 1999.
Bird, Phyllis A. *Missing Persons and Mistaken Identities: Women and Gender in Ancient Israel.* Minneapolis: Fortress, 1997.
———, ed. *Reading the Bible as Women: Perspectives from Africa, Asia, and Latin America.* Semeia 78. Atlanta: Scholars, 1997.
Brenner, Athalya, ed. *A Feminist Companion to Reading the Bible: Approaches, Methods and Strategies.* London and New York: Routledge, 2001.
Cannon, Katie. *Katie's Canon: Womanism and the Soul of the Black Community.* New York: Continuum, 1995.
Choi, Hee An, and Katheryn P. Darr, eds. *Engaging the Bible: Critical Readings from Contemporary Women.* Minneapolis: Augsburg Fortress, 2006.

Clifford, Anne M. *Introducing Feminist Theology.* Maryknoll, NY: Orbis, 2001.

Day, Linda, and Carolyn Pressler, eds. *Engaging the Bible in a Gendered World: An Introduction to Feminist Biblical Interpretation in Honor of Katherine Doob Sakenfeld.* Louisville, KY: Westminster John Knox, 2006.

Day, Peggy L., ed. *Gender and Difference in Ancient Israel.* Minneapolis: Fortress, 1989.

Frankel, Ellen. *The Five Books of Miriam: A Woman's Commentary on the Torah.* New York: G. P. Putnam, 1996.

Frymer-Kensky, Tikva. *Reading the Women of the Bible: A New Interpretation of Their Stories.* New York: Schocken, 2002.

Grant, Jacquelyn. *White Women's Christ and Black Women's Jesus: Feminist Christology and Womanist Response.* Atlanta: Scholars, 1989.

*Lapsley, Jacqueline E. *Whispering the Word: Hearing Women's Stories in the Old Testament.* Louisville, KY: Westminster John Knox, 2005.

Newsom, Carol A., and Sharon H. Ringe, eds. *The Women's Bible Commentary.* Expanded ed. Louisville, KY: Westminster John Knox, 1998.

Pardes, Ilana. *Countertraditions in the Bible: A Feminist Approach.* Cambridge, MA: Harvard University Press, 1992.

Plaskow, Judith. *Standing Again at Sinai: Judaism from a Feminist Perspective.* San Francisco: Harper & Row, 1990.

Russell, Letty, ed. *Feminist Interpretation of the Bible.* Philadelphia: Westminster, 1985.

Sakenfeld, Katherine Doob. *Just Wives?: Stories of Power and Survival in the Old Testament and Today.* Louisville, KY: Westminster John Knox, 2003.

Schüssler Fiorenza, Elisabeth. *Bread Not Stone: The Challenge of Feminist Biblical Interpretation.* Rev. ed. Boston: Beacon, 1995.

*———. *Wisdom Ways: Introducing Feminist Biblical Interpretation.* Maryknoll, NY: Orbis, 2001.

———, ed. *Searching the Scriptures: A Feminist Commentary.* 2 vols. New York: Crossroad, 1993–94.

Taylor, Marion Ann, and Heather E. Weir, eds. *Let Her Speak for Herself: Nineteenth-Century Women Writing on Women in Genesis.* Waco, TX: Baylor University Press, 2006.

Trible, Phyllis. *God and the Rhetoric of Sexuality.* Philadelphia: Fortress, 1978.

*———. *Texts of Terror: Literary-Feminist Readings of Biblical Narratives.* Philadelphia: Fortress, 1984.

Weems, Renita J. *Just a Sister Away: A Womanist Vision of Women's Relationships in the Bible.* San Diego: LuraMedia, 1988.

African and African American Interpretation

Adeyemo, Tokunboh. *African Bible Commentary.* Grand Rapids: Zondervan, 2006.

Blount, Brian K., gen. ed. *True to Our Native Land: An African American New Testament Commentary.* Minneapolis: Fortress, 2007.

*Brown, Michael J. *Blackening of the Bible: The Aims of African American Scholarship.* Harrisburg, PA: Trinity, 2004.

Cleage, Albert B. *The Black Messiah.* New York: Sheed & Ward, 1968.

Dube, Musa W., ed. *Other Ways of Reading: African Women and the Bible.* Atlanta: Society of Biblical Literature, 2001.

Felder, Cain Hope. *Race, Racism, and the Biblical Narrative.* Minneapolis: Fortress, 2002.

———. *Troubling Biblical Waters: Race, Class, and Family.* Maryknoll, NY: Orbis, 1989.

———, ed. *Stony the Road We Trod: African American Biblical Interpretation.* Minneapolis: Fortress, 1991.

Mosala, Itumeleng J. *Biblical Hermeneutics and Black Theology in South Africa.* Grand Rapids: Eerdmans, 1989.

Oduyoye, Mercy Amba. *Introducing African Women's Theology.* Sheffield: Sheffield Academic, 2001.

Ukpong, Justin S. *African Interpretations of the Bible.* Atlanta: Society of Biblical Literature, 2006.

West, Gerald O., and Musa W. Dube, eds. *The Bible in Africa: Transactions, Trajectories and Trends.* Leiden: Brill, 2000.

*Wimbush, Vincent L., ed. *African Americans and the Bible: Sacred Text and Social Textures.* New York: Continuum, 2000.

———. *The Bible and African Americans: A Brief History.* Minneapolis: Fortress, 2003.

Postcolonial Interpretation

Boer, Roland. *Last Stop before Antarctica: The Bible and Postcolonialism in Australia.* Sheffield: Sheffield Academic, 2001.

Fabella, Virginia, and Rasiah S. Sugirtharajah. *Dictionary of Third World Theologies.* Maryknoll, NY: Orbis, 2000.

Kwok, Pui-Lan. *Postcolonial Imagination and Feminist Theology.* Louisville, KY, and London: Westminster John Knox, 2005.

*Sugirtharajah, Rasiah S., ed. *The Postcolonial Bible Reader.* Oxford: Blackwell, 2006.

———. *Voices from the Margin: Interpreting the Bible in the Third World.* Maryknoll, NY: Orbis, 1991.

Trible, Phyllis, and Letty M. Russell, eds. *Hagar, Sarah, and Their Children: Jewish, Christian, and Muslim Perspectives.* Louisville, KY: Westminster John Knox, 2006.

Queer Commentary

*Brooten, Bernadette J. *Love between Women: Early Christian Responses to Female Homoeroticism.* Chicago: University of Chicago Press, 1996.

Guest, Deryn, Robert Goss, Mona West, and Thomas Bohache, eds. *The Queer Bible Commentary.* London: SCM, 2006.

Guest, Deryn. *When Deborah Met Jael: Lesbian Biblical Hermeneutics.* London: SCM, 2005.

Martin, Dale B. *Sex and the Single Savior: Gender and Sexuality in Biblical Interpreta-
tion.* Louisville, KY: Westminster John Knox, 2006.
Moore, Stephen D. *God's Beauty Parlor: And Other Queer Spaces in and around the
Bible.* Stanford, CA: Stanford University Press, 2001.
———. *God's Gym: Divine Male Bodies of the Bible.* New York: Routledge, 1996.
Moxnes, Halvor. *Putting Jesus in His Place: A Radical Vision of Household and Kingdom.*
Louisville, KY: Westminster John Knox, 2003.
Nissinen, Martti. *Homoeroticism in the Biblical World: A Historical Perspective.* Min-
neapolis: Fortress, 1998.
Stone, Ken. *Practicing Safer Texts: Food, Sex and Bible in Queer Perspective.* London and
New York: T. & T. Clark, 2004.
———, ed. *Queer Commentary and the Hebrew Bible.* London: Sheffield Academic;
Cleveland: Pilgrim, 2001.

12

Integrating Exegetical Procedures

The goal of exegesis is an informed understanding of a text. All of the exegetical procedures and types of criticism discussed in the preceding chapters have this as their aim.

At this point, the reader may feel a bit overwhelmed by the many different approaches and their complexities. One might ask, Is all of this necessary merely to understand a text? How is it possible to use and integrate all of these procedures? Such questions are especially pressing for students in colleges, universities, and seminaries, who are required to write exegesis papers for courses related to the Bible. For this reason, the discussion in this chapter is aimed primarily for students in academic settings. Before discussing some of the more practical aspects of exegesis, we offer several suggestions.

Some Preliminary Observations

1. The task of biblical exegesis is closely related to other aspects of theological education. Many theological courses require students to read and analyze texts, whether primary or secondary. For this reason, theological students have many opportunities to practice exegesis other than in courses related to the Bible. Whenever you encounter a text in any of your courses and ask such questions as, How should I read this text? What does it mean? Why is it said this

way? How can I express what this text says in my own words? you are doing exegesis.

You should remember that most theological work is exegetical in orientation. As you develop your exegetical skills in other areas, such as church history, systematic theology, ethics, sociology of religion, and the various arts of ministry courses, you should use this learning in your Bible courses. It also works in reverse. What you learn as a biblical exegete is transferable to other theological courses and settings.

2. Practically all biblical studies, even if they are not designated as "exegetical," are relevant to the task of exegesis. Introductory and other courses on the Bible explore the nature and content of biblical documents, the history and religion of Israel and the early church, and the culture and background of biblical texts. Many of these areas of study provide valuable data and insights needed in exegetical work. As you become more informed about the Bible, you become a better exegete. Connections between what you learn in more general, thematic courses about the Bible and exegesis courses may not always be obvious. You may have to make these connections yourself. Integrating your biblical learning requires conscious—and consistent—effort.

3. Not every exegetical procedure we have discussed is relevant to every text. Some texts present no significant text-critical problems. Although there are thousands of textual variants within the manuscript tradition of the NT, relatively few of them will significantly affect your understanding of a passage. As you study a biblical passage, some exegetical approaches will be more significant than others. Seldom will you use every method of biblical criticism in analyzing a single passage.

4. Exegesis frequently occurs unconsciously. As we have noted, many exegetical approaches are based on common sense. They may have technical names and use complex methods, but they usually operate with a simple logic. Even if certain methods seem abstract and complicated, the scholars who developed them were often trying to answer basic questions. As you employ these methods, often the challenge is to follow your own intuition and exercise good judgment in framing interpretive questions and formulating answers to those questions.

In practice, this means that when you read a biblical passage and try to make sense of it, you may be doing grammatical analysis or be engaged in canonical criticism without even realizing it. Your task is not so much applying each type of criticism we have discussed to a biblical passage but rather letting the passage dictate the kinds of interpretive methods you need to use. Doing exegesis is less about applying methods and more about seeking meaning. As you engage in the latter, you will do the former.

5. You stand on the shoulders of earlier exegetes. It is important to remember that, while many of the types of biblical criticism we have discussed were developed in the last two or three centuries and acquired technical terminology of relatively recent vintage, most of them have earlier precedents. Throughout our discussion, we have tried to illustrate how biblical interpreters in earlier periods anticipated modern interpretive methods. In some cases, such as textual criticism, our modern methods actually originated in the early centuries of the Common Era. Remembering these connections with your predecessors will help you to see that many of the questions you ask as a modern reader have occurred to Bible readers throughout the centuries in many different historical and cultural settings.

6. You should not use the different types of biblical criticism as though you were cooking from a recipe. You will not necessarily employ them in the order in which they were discussed in this book. Although we have tried to introduce them in a logical fashion and show how certain methods led to the development of other methods, we do not think of them as steps you should take along a preset path.

For the beginning exegete, it might make sense to apply each type of criticism to a passage in the order in which we have introduced them. Asking whether a passage contains textual variants that significantly affect your interpretation is a natural first step. Doing text-critical analysis would be the place to begin. Then moving to methods of analysis discussed in the following chapters, such as historical criticism, grammatical criticism, and so on, would also be a logical approach.

In practice, however, it usually works differently. You may begin by reading a biblical text several times, trying to follow its logic, establish its historical frame of reference, place it within its larger literary context, and identify its form or genre. While doing these things, you may discover an important textual variant that requires you to employ textual criticism. Or, as you try to understand a passage, you may begin to notice its composite literary character. This, in turn, might prompt you to ask whether different strands of earlier tradition have come together. If so, you would then employ tradition criticism.

As a general rule, you should allow the passage to dictate which methods you use, and the order in which you use them, rather than "applying" them in some mechanical, stair-step fashion. You will often find that the various types of criticisms are interrelated. Text-critical conclusions, for example, may depend upon what you have decided about form-critical questions. Whether a particular textual variant is more original may depend on decisions that relate to the literary form of the passage. Sometimes, text-critical conclusions are closely related to how you analyze a passage grammatically.

Getting Started

We have emphasized the importance of letting the questions and exegetical issues arise from the text itself. But how is this done? A way to start is by reading and rereading the passage in its context several times. It often helps to read the passage in several different modern translations or versions. As you reread the passage, you can formulate questions of various kinds. But they should be questions that arise from your reading, rather than questions that you bring to the text. If the same questions or the same types of questions keep surfacing, make a list of them and classify them into appropriate categories.

If certain words or phrases remain obscure, and their meaning does not register with you in subsequent readings, you can make them part of your interpretive agenda. You might list the ones that require specialized word study. Or, if all the words and phrases themselves are clear, but they are still puzzling, you may find that the syntax of the sentence—how the words and phrases are arranged in relation to each other—needs to be untangled. Such questions would move you into some form of grammatical analysis. After reading a passage several times, you may notice a significant variation of wording that is referred to in a footnote. If the note refers to "other ancient authorities" who report a different wording, you will need to do text-critical analysis.

When we encourage beginning exegetes to let the text itself set the interpretive agenda, we are not suggesting that you can approach a text with a mind that is a "blank tablet." Every time you read a text, you bring to that experience what you already know, your life experiences, your general outlook, your individual concerns, and your biases and prejudices. This is what scholars mean when they observe that each of us approaches a biblical text with a certain "preunderstanding." Another way of putting it is that each of us reads biblical texts within our given "social location." A peasant farmer and a corporate lawyer read the Bible asking different questions. In each case, where the reader is located socially and culturally shapes the questions that are raised by a biblical text.

It has been said that a literary work is like a picnic—the author brings the words and the reader brings the meaning. This observation may be an exaggeration, but it has a kernel of truth. Rather than assuming that you can read texts with complete objectivity, that is, without any preunderstanding or underlying presuppositions, you should recognize that you have a particular social location, which should be taken into account in your interpretation. Your interpretation will be more convincing if you admit that you have presuppositions, identify them, understand how you developed them, and then allow for them as you interpret a passage.

You should not simply read your own interpretation into a passage. As we noted earlier, this is "eisegesis" not exegesis. You can, however, read a passage through the understanding you bring to a text. But you should allow this understanding to be broadened, modified, or deepened with each new reading of a text.

The Autonomy of the Text

Letting a text speak for itself implies that it is autonomous. Once a text has been written (or edited), reached its final form, and been included in a canonical collection, it has a life of its own. No longer is it attached to its original author. Like a newborn child, it is now a separate being.

Respecting the autonomy of a text requires you to stand back, as it were, and give it space. Frequently, interpreters crowd the text, even insinuate themselves into the text. They are too eager to speak to the text rather than listen to it. Interpretations that result from reading a text this way tend to privilege the reader's voice rather than the voice of the text. But if you respect the autonomy of a text by allowing it to speak for itself, you will find that it will provide a full interpretive agenda.

When we encourage readers to respect the autonomy of the text, to listen first and speak later, we do not exclude the possibility of coming to a text with our own agenda. Perhaps you are trying to reconstruct the history of a particular period of biblical history. You may identify the biblical passages that relate to your investigation. Your job may be to determine how these texts can be used as reliable evidence for your historical reconstruction. With a clearly defined interpretive goal, you can come to these texts with some already formulated questions. You can bring these questions to the text and still respect its autonomy. This means refusing to make these texts conform to your previous expectations. You can listen to what the text says, evaluate it using widely accepted exegetical tools and methods, and draw your conclusions accordingly.

Exegesis: Primary Research or Secondary Reporting?

Throughout our discussion, we have emphasized the importance of readers engaging biblical texts directly. By this we mean trying to listen to a text first, rather than letting its meaning be mediated to you through secondary treatments, such as biblical commentaries or scholarly articles. For this reason, we have introduced you to primary research tools, such as dictionaries, concordances, encyclopedias, and other resources that scholars themselves use in writing commentaries or scholarly articles.

We have taken this approach because we think exegesis is too often seen (and taught) as research that is drawn from secondary sources. Consulting such resources can be informative at many levels, but we do not think exegesis is an exercise in which you mainly consult different commentaries, sift through their various interpretations, and develop an interpretation of a passage from them. Doing exegesis this way may appear to be very scholarly, even erudite, but it produces only a mosaic of commentaries. It also means that you engage the text through the commentaries—indirectly. We prefer you to engage the biblical text directly. Before consulting any other resources, you should read a text, struggle with it, formulate questions out of this struggle. Let the text, rather than commentaries, set the interpretive agenda.

To use a crude example, if exegesis is primarily cutting and pasting quotations together from commentaries and other secondary treatments, the exegete is like an artist who paints a picture by cutting up other artists' pictures and pasting them together. Exclusive dependence on commentaries results in derivative rather than original interpretations. Granting such dominance to biblical commentators also produces a kind of exegetical tyranny in which the beginning interpreter assumes that the commentators' questions are not only the right questions to be asked of a text, but also the important ones, or even the only ones.

Beginning exegetes often consult commentaries and other secondary treatments because they are reluctant to ask their own questions of a text. A beginner's questions may turn out to be ill-formulated, even naive, but they are the questions a beginner must ask. As you gain experience in doing exegesis, your questions become more refined and your confidence to ask good questions increases. We encourage beginning exegetes not to be intimidated by the erudition of biblical commentaries and scholars. Respect them? Yes, but do not allow them to set your interpretive agenda completely. We think you are better off reading the text for yourself and formulating your own questions. Once you have developed your own sense of the major interpretive issues from your own reading of the text, consult commentaries and other secondary resources.

We do not minimize the work of biblical commentators and the members of scholarly guilds. We have written commentaries and belong to those guilds. We believe biblical scholars render a valuable service to those who read, study, and interpret texts, both beginners and experienced interpreters. But we want to encourage beginning exegetes to use their own imaginations and develop a sense of independence.

For the purpose of learning to do exegesis, commentaries and other secondary sources are most valuable for consultation at later stages of investigation rather than at the earliest stage of research. Commentaries are valuable, especially in providing controls for beginning exegetes. Once you have read a text, formulated your questions, and developed your own hunches about which issues must be addressed, you can consult commentaries to test your perceptions against those of more experienced biblical interpreters.

Deciding which commentaries to consult is also important. Lists of commentaries on individual books are usually found in the standard OT and NT introductions. Evaluations of individual commentaries and commentary series can also be found in standard biblical bibliographies (see the bibliography in chap. 1 on p. 29).

Writing an Exegesis Paper

In many college and university Bible courses, as well as courses in postbaccalaureate theological schools and seminaries, exegesis usually results in an exegesis paper. The paper may be a short, focused study of a text, or it may be a major research paper twenty-five or thirty pages in length. Typically, these papers are written according to the accepted conventions for writing research papers in colleges and universities. Whether the papers are written using *The Society of Biblical Literature Handbook of Style*, *The Chicago Manual of Style* (15th ed.), *The Modern Language Association* style, or some other style handbook usually depends on the professor's preference. Here we are not concerned with the style in which the paper is written; we are more interested in the compositional strategy you adopt in writing the paper.

As we have already noted, we view exegesis as more than the compilation of statements and opinions of various commentators. Exegesis is also more than a report of your research. Beginning exegetes sometimes assume—incorrectly—that an exegesis paper consists of systematically organizing all of the research they have conducted. Some of this occurs, to be sure, but exegesis is more than this. Rather than collecting and organizing all the *data* you have uncovered, you must develop a coherent *interpretation* of the passage based upon a careful review of the data. Exegesis is not so much a report on your research as it is an informed, competent reading of a passage based on your research.

The difference between a research report and a coherent interpretation is an important one. The latter requires you to deploy rather than just report information you have gathered. You also have to decide on a strategy for presenting your interpretation: How should I introduce my interpretation? What point(s) do I want to argue for? How should I arrange my arguments? How should I conclude my interpretation? In writing up the results of your exegesis, you should remember that your research informs rather than constitutes your interpretation.

It is also important to distinguish between information and understanding. Papers written by beginning exegetes may contain a lot of historical, lexicographical, and grammatical information, along with biblical references. These papers can be packed full of information, but this does not necessarily mean that they reflect a deep understanding of the interpretive issues in the passage. The real challenge is to organize the detailed research you have accumulated into a coherent, interesting interpretation of the passage. The paper should argue for a particular point of view—a thesis that embodies your interpretation of the passage. An exegesis paper may be filled with correct information yet fail to illuminate the passage.

You also have to decide how to organize the exegesis paper. The simplest, most straightforward way is to write an introduction, treat the passage in a verse-by-verse manner, and write a conclusion. This organizational scheme is found in many commentaries. Some biblical passages lend themselves to this kind of treatment, but others do not. In some cases, a thematic arrangement might be preferable. The most important consideration is whether the paper is organized in a way that does justice to the crucial interpretive issues in the passage. The main question here is whether your organizational framework is pliable enough to unfold a well-organized, convincing interpretation of the passage.

Here again, you should take your cue from the text itself. Some texts unfold an argument in a sequential, step-by-step fashion. In these cases, your paper might be structured so that you trace the steps in the argument and discuss them one by one. Or a passage may fit into a well-defined genre, such as a prophetic oracle or a parable. The challenge here is to use an organizational structure in your paper that does justice to that genre. Parables, for example, often reflect certain plots or highlight certain types of persons (villain, hero/heroine, etc.). In this case, your paper may be organized using these literary structures rather than a verse-by-verse outline. Narrative texts may require a structure uniquely suitable to them. With some texts, the paper can be organized around certain themes that are prominent within the passage. The general rule is that the structure of the paper should fit the structure of the passage.

Some Practical Suggestions

So far, we have discussed the practical steps of doing an exegesis only incidentally. We now summarize our main suggestions.

1. Allow the text to set the agenda. You should let the questions arise out of your dialogue with the text itself. As you read and reread a biblical passage, preferably in the original but in at least more than one translation, you should formulate questions that are appropriate to the text. But they should also be your own questions—what you find problematic, intriguing, or challenging about the text. As you formulate these questions, you can begin to sift through them and decide which ones should be addressed first.

2. Let the questions point to the appropriate methodology, exegetical technique, or type of criticism. For this to occur, you must have a basic understanding of how biblical texts have originated and developed over time. You should be generally aware of the different dimensions of biblical texts, or the different perspectives from which previous interpreters have viewed them: historical, literary, social, canonical, etc. Given this broader understanding of the Bible, you are in a position to decide which tools are suitable for addressing each dimension. For example, if the text contains references to historical persons, places, or events with which you are unfamiliar, you should instinctively know to employ historical criticism.

3. Use the tools appropriate to a given exegetical technique. As we have seen, certain types of biblical criticism make use of certain reference tools. In some cases, special reference works have been developed in connection with certain exegetical techniques. The synopsis, which displays the Gospels in parallel columns, was developed by scholars engaged in various forms of literary and source criticism. It is now an indispensable tool for form criticism, tradition criticism, and redaction criticism. A critical edition of the Bible, which supplies information about variant readings, is essential for addressing text-critical questions.

Beginning exegetes must know what tools are available, what information they can supply, and how they should be used in relationship with each other. Such knowledge is best gained through firsthand experience in using them.

4. Once you have formulated some basic questions and developed some tentative answers, do a preliminary synthesis of these findings. As you raise questions from different perspectives, you will discover that different lines of questioning are interrelated. Literary questions about the formal arrangement of a text may be related to historical questions about the circumstances in which it originated. Theological questions about how the text relates to certain doctrines or religious issues can sometimes be answered only in connection with literary and historical questions.

As you see different connections in your questions, you will employ different exegetical techniques or types of criticism. This, in turn, often enables you to refine your questions or pose new, even more sophisticated, questions. The interpretive cycle is repeated. With these freshly formulated questions, you should read the text again, discover other dimensions that you have not seen before, and employ the appropriate exegetical techniques or types of biblical criticism, trying all the while to formulate your own understanding of the passage. And so it goes.

5. Set a time to conclude the analysis. The term "analysis" derives from a Greek word, *analyō*, which literally means to "break up." Analysis is an intellectual process in which we break something up (or break it down) into its component parts. These initial stages of exegesis are analytical in this sense. You read a passage, examine its language and grammatical structure, trying to figure out how it was put together. You look at its component parts, such as the different sections of a passage or its prominent themes. You try to isolate these different parts but also to relate them to each other.

You sometimes discover that using one exegetical procedure will lead to another. But you may also find that you must use separate techniques that have no clear connection with each other. Either way, you try to make sure that you have identified the parts of a passage that are important for developing an informed interpretation of it. You may spend a lot of time pursuing questions that prove to be irrelevant or unimportant. But this is the nature of exegetical research. As you try to understand a passage, you will find that some things about the passage are central, and others are peripheral. Exegesis helps you sort through these in order to determine what questions really need to be addressed.

Exegesis papers of beginning theological students often resemble a potpourri of miscellaneous facts and observations. This usually occurs because the passage was poorly analyzed or because insufficient time was allowed to synthesize the results of the exegetical investigation. To remedy this, we suggest that you decide on a definite time to conclude the analysis stage. This is sometimes difficult, because analysis can go on forever. Exegesis can be so engaging that you find there is literally no limit to how far you can investigate a passage. But eventually analysis must end. You can conclude the analysis if you have established appropriate time limitations and have learned to focus on important questions.

6. Synthesize your findings into a coherent interpretation of the passage. The term "synthesis" derives from a Greek word, *syntithēmi*, which literally means "to bring together." This is the stage of exegesis in which you try to bring together what you have learned. This is the most difficult stage of an exegesis, primarily because it requires you to make some hard decisions.

In the analysis stage, you generally uncover a lot of information—far more than you can incorporate into an exegesis paper (or a sermon). You may have discovered many interesting things about the passage. At some point, however, you have to conclude your analysis, survey what you have found, assess the relative importance of the various things you have learned, and then decide how all of this information can be put together into an illuminating, coherent interpretation of the passage.

Deciding how to organize your information is what ancient rhetoricians referred to as "arrangement." It often happens that the sequence in which you gathered the information—the process of exegesis—differs from the sequence in which you present the information in a formal paper. You may decide that something you discovered last should come first in the paper; or that what you first learned about the passage should form the conclusion. The order in which you conducted your exegetical research may not correspond to the order in which you arrange your exegetical findings.

Synthesis requires you to weigh each part of your exegetical investigation in light of other parts. During analysis, you may have spent a lot of time answering certain questions, but in formulating your interpretation you may find that you can compress a lot of this information into a very short space. Or the reverse may be true. You may have spent a relatively small amount of time researching a particular issue but decide to devote several paragraphs to it in the exegesis itself. All of these are judgment calls that you must make as an exegete. Deciding how much space to devote to different issues is often a matter of balance and emphasis. Usually, you will have developed enough familiarity with a passage to know the aspects of a passage that need full elaboration and those that require shorter treatment.

7. Allow ample time for synthesis. Beginning students often fail to allow enough time to "put the pieces back together." This often results from poor planning or postponing synthesis to the last moment. It is advisable to allow some time between concluding the analysis and developing a synthesis of your research. You will find that certain things will jell during this interim. With some time, you get a better sense of what is important and what is not.

Concluding Observations

As we have emphasized throughout our discussion, *exegesis is a systematic process through which we reach an informed interpretation of a passage of Scripture.* We think it should be a process in which readers directly engage the biblical text. First, we read the text for ourselves and let it speak to us on its own terms. Next, we develop our questions out of the text and use appropriate exegetical techniques to answer them. As we gather information and seek to understand the text, we try to formulate our own interpretation of the text.

As we move from analysis to synthesis, we decide on a strategy for presenting our interpretation. We include insights and information from our research that informs and advances our interpretation. We write a paper that argues for a point of view rather than merely reports on our research. We try to convince the reader of our point of view. We write a concluding paragraph or section in which we summarize our interpretation and its theological significance.

As we develop our interpretation, we must make some choices. Some will be rather obvious; others will not. Through it all, we should use our imagination. Exegesis, after all, is an exercise in seeing. We read the text in order to see it; or we listen to a text in order to hear its message. Either way, we try to convey what we have seen and heard in a convincing, imaginative interpretation. Somewhere in the exegetical process, we may even experience artistic creativity: see things that other interpreters have not seen, hear things they have not heard, and experience new meanings that change us.

13
Employing the Fruits
of Biblical Exegesis

The Bible is read and interpreted in many different contexts in contemporary culture. These range from individual reading for general knowledge to college and university literature courses. Individuals may read the Bible as one of the classical documents every educated person should know. The Bible is included in academic curricula as a writing from classical antiquity that has exercised enormous influence throughout history.

Although the exact content of the Bible differs in Judaism and various Christian churches, it is a sacred text for both Jews and Christians. Since the Bible occupies a place of unique authority in both religious traditions, it plays a normative role in shaping their life and faith. The Bible exercises this normative role in different ways, depending on the context in which it is used. Even with this variety of functions, however, the Bible's use within religious communities differs from the way in which it is read by the general public or studied in a comparative literature course in college.

Exegesis is employed in all of these settings in which the Bible is read and studied. Whether the setting is public or private, secular or religious, formal or informal, Bible readers engage in exegesis. It may be practiced in different ways, but serious readers of the Bible in each setting generally share a common purpose: to reach an informed understanding of the biblical text.

While we recognize the Bible's popularity within the broader culture, our special interest is how it is currently used within the two religious traditions of Judaism and Christianity. Among the many ways the
Bible functions for these communities, four are especially prominent:
(1) one of its most important uses is as a source for reconstructing the
early history of Judaism and Christianity; (2) it is a foundational document used to formulate theological beliefs; (3) it has a central role in
their public worship, in which it is read and proclaimed as sacred Scripture; (4) it serves as a source of inspiration and guidance for living a
meaningful, moral life.

For Historical and Archaeological Reconstruction

One of the results of post-Enlightenment investigations of Scripture
was the change in perspective toward biblical texts and how they should
be used for historical reconstruction. Prior to the Enlightenment, the
story of Israel and the early church as reported in the Bible was assumed
to be "the way it happened." Readers of the Bible generally assumed
that the actual course of historical events corresponded to the biblical
narrative—the story line of the text.

This equation of biblical history with actual history was modified
for several reasons. The rise of modern science posed a serious challenge
to biblical chronology. Biblical chronology, understood literally, suggested that the earth was 6,000 years old. Geological studies of fossils
and dinosaur bones revealed a much earlier origin of the universe. As
biblical scholars examined the Pentateuch and the historical books of
the Bible, they found not one but several "stories of Israel" embedded
within the text. Analysis of the biblical writings revealed various sources
within the Pentateuch, each reflecting a somewhat different theological
viewpoint. Scholars now saw that the early biblical narratives should be
read as theologically constructed stories rather than as literal history.
They were religious writings rather than merely historiography.

Similar changes occurred in how the NT was read. For centuries it
had been assumed, more or less uncritically, that the story of the life of
Jesus and the early church as unfolded in the four Gospels and the book
of Acts was "the way it happened." The NT biblical story, it was
thought, reported the actual course of events. From the eighteenth century forward, however, differences among the four Gospels received
closer attention. It became more difficult to harmonize the Fourth

Gospel with the Synoptic accounts of Matthew, Mark, and Luke. It also became clear that Acts is a highly selective account of the origin and growth of the early church. Scholars began to see the pervasive theological tendencies of these NT narratives. They could no longer be read as simple, straightforward historical accounts, as they once were.

One of the lasting legacies of the Enlightenment was the emergence of history as a major category of thought. Ancient writings that reported historical events had to be read critically rather than naively. "Critical history" emerged as a new discipline, with its own perspectives and methodologies. Like other scholars who studied ancient history, biblical scholars now read their ancient sources differently. They became more attuned to the historical dimensions of the Bible: it originated in certain historical settings and developed over time. They saw that the Bible not only reports history, but it also *has a history*. Historical study of the Bible also underscored the distance—chronologically and culturally—between its ancient setting and modern readers. Readers became more aware of the differences between their worldview and that of the biblical writers. Scholars increasingly saw the Bible as an anthology of ancient writings that should be subjected to scrutiny just as other ancient sources were.

Today, historians of Israelite and early church history, like their "secular" counterparts, view the Bible as an indispensable source for reconstructing history. Unlike their earlier counterparts, however, especially those before the Enlightenment, they adopt a more critical stance toward the biblical sources. Rather than reading the biblical narratives as straightforward, factual reporting, biblical scholars now acknowledge the Bible's heavy theological emphases. They are also more aware of the many different historical contexts in which the various biblical writings originated and developed. Rather than taking biblical texts relating to historical persons and events at face value, biblical scholars now submit such texts to critical scrutiny. They look for theological motives that account for what they find in the texts. Rather than harmonize differences among the historical narratives of the Bible, biblical scholars now evaluate them critically as they reconstruct their critical histories.

Another shift in perspective relates to the role of divine intervention within history, especially reports of miraculous occurrences that altered the course of events. The rationalistic outlook that characterized Enlightenment thought caused scholars to be more skeptical about divine revelation and supernatural explanations of events. This represents a radical break with the outlook of the biblical writings, which

speak of divine involvement in historical events. Modern biblical historians acknowledge this explicit theological perspective within the Bible,
but see it as a reflection of the faith and theology of the early Israelite
and Christian communities rather than a datum of history itself.

Modern historians realize they are not writing a definitive history—
"the history"—and narrating once and for all how things actually happened. As children of their age, they acknowledge their own biases,
limited knowledge, and ideological perspectives. They view history as a
reconstruction of the past based on our knowledge and experience of
the present—often informed by a lot of intuition.

Just as historians no longer write the history of Israel and the early
church by retelling the biblical story, neither are they any longer bound
exclusively to the evidence of the Bible. In recent years, archaeological
evidence has become increasingly important for biblical historians. Beginning in the nineteenth century, archaeological excavation of sites around
the Mediterranean Sea got under way and has continued almost without
interruption. These efforts have yielded an abundance of evidence related
to biblical history. Some of these discoveries are written sources—inscriptions and other texts—but most are nonwritten artifacts.

Texts can usually be dated on the basis of the material on which they
were written and other matters related to their content, such as the language used, style of writing, and references to historical persons and
events. Other artifacts—such as pottery, remains of buildings, skele-
tons, and jewelry—provide valuable information about styles of life,
levels of culture, means of livelihood, and types of habitation.

All of the unwritten archaeological evidence comes out of the ground
uninterpreted. Archaeologists and historians must interpret the data,
generally in light of other evidence and particularly the written sources,
especially the Bible. Contrary to much popular opinion, the purpose of
archaeology is neither to prove nor to disprove the Bible. Archaeology is
by nature a neutral discipline. While archaeology can illumine the actual
course of Israelite and early Christian history, it can neither validate nor
invalidate the theological claims of the biblical record.

To reconstruct the history of ancient Israel and the early church, it is
now necessary to correlate what is reported in the Bible with written
and nonwritten archaeological evidence. All who undertake such historical reconstructions must remember several things.

1. Exegesis of all written material is required. The historian must
answer such questions as these: To what genre of literature does the text
belong? What type of historical information can we expect to gain from

such a genre? To what source or sources does the text belong? What theological tendencies may have influenced what is reported in the text? From what historical period does the text come? How might this context have influenced the text? What cultural and sociological knowledge might be gained from the text? If the text does not provide explicit historical evidence, does it provide any implicit evidence that is useful for historical reconstruction?

2. All texts relevant to a particular event or time period must be considered. The same episode is often reported in separate accounts. This is the case, for example, with many narratives, such as those about the conquest of Canaan (Josh. 1–12 compared with Judg. 1) and some events in the reign of Jehoshaphat (1 Kgs. 22:48–49 compared with 2 Chr. 20:35–37). Exegetes must compare these parallel accounts and evaluate their historical probability.

3. Relevant nonbiblical written material should be taken into consideration. This too must be submitted to exegesis, using the same procedures that apply to biblical writings. Since most surviving inscriptions are royal inscriptions, they are often filled with propaganda that "puts a spin" on events in order to praise the monarchy and exaggerate royal achievements.

The Assyrian king Shalmaneser III, who reigned from 858 BCE until 824 BCE, for example, in a number of inscriptions reports how he fought a coalition of twelve kings at Qarqar in northern Syria in 853 BCE. In all of these, he claims to have completely annihilated the coalition that included King Ahab of Israel. At best, he seems only to have fought his opponents to a standstill. His inscriptions note that he had to fight the same group several times over the next decade. Interestingly, no reference appears to any of these battles in the Hebrew Bible even though, at Qarqar, Ahab's forces were extremely large.

4. When nonwritten archaeological material is relevant to the discussion, it should be incorporated. Or it might be necessary to report the absence of such data. These nonwritten materials can supplement the written archaeological evidence and the biblical texts. If, for example, you are working on 1 Kings 9:15–22, which lists those who assisted King Solomon in building the temple, archaeological material from Hazor, Megiddo, and Gezer would be relevant.

In some cases, archaeological evidence raises questions about the historical reliability of a biblical report. For example, Joshua 7:1–8:29 reports on the Israelite capture of a large, fortified city at Ai. Excavations at the site of ancient Ai (et-tell in modern Palestine) have shown that the site was unoccupied from about 2000 to 1150 BCE and that after reoccupation, it was actually a small village not a major city. Here the archaeological evidence requires us to reassess how we can use the biblical account.

We see that reconstructing an event in biblical history requires correlating various forms of evidence: biblical and nonbiblical literary evidence and nonliterary archaeological evidence. Each form of evidence must be evaluated on its own merits. Exegesis, however, plays a vital role in these evaluations, especially of the written materials. Exegesis lies at the heart of all historical reconstruction. Although many nonbiblical sources figure into reconstructing biblical history, the Bible remains a primary source. Sometimes it is the only source that reports an event. In every case, however, exegesis is indispensable for sound historical reconstruction.

For Doing Theology

The task of theology, as a specialized discipline, is to articulate the faith of the synagogue and the church for each new generation of believers. Professional theologians, both academic and ministerial, do this on a sustained, regular basis. Professional theologians, however, are not the only ones who engage in theological reflection. Nonprofessional or lay theologians also do so. All who make a conscious, concerted effort to reflect on their faith and give organized shape to these reflections are doing theology.

While the work of professional theologians—usually professors working in academic settings—has much in common with the theological reflections of ministers, rabbis, teachers, and lay persons, professional theologians have a unique calling. Since they do theology full time, they are responsible for formulating fresh theological visions for their generation. In their constructive theological work, they seek to relate faith to every aspect of life. This requires them to draw on many fields of knowledge as they develop their theological systems.

As theologians reflect upon the multiple dimensions of faith and the various settings in which it is experienced, they work at both theoretical and practical levels. Much of their work involves abstract thinking— intellectual work—in which they construct systems of thought. Within theological studies, this is the field of systematic theology. Typically, systematic theologians construct their systems using well-established topics, or loci. These include such topics as the doctrine of God (theology in its narrow sense), human nature (anthropology), doctrines of salvation (soteriology), doctrines of Christ (Christology), doctrines of the Holy Spirit (pneumatology), and views of the end time (eschatology).

There is also a practical side to the work of systematic theologians. Even those who focus on theoretical questions and spend their time developing systems of thought are usually interested in the practical implications of their constructive work. They may be interested, for example, in the problem of evil, but they are often passionately concerned with the forms evil takes in modern life. Moreover, their theological writing and teaching typically seek to address concrete manifestations of evil in the world—and mitigate if not eradicate them.

Working from a bifocal perspective—theoretical and practical— theologians attend to the cognitive and experiential dimensions of faith. They construct ways of thinking and talking about God's presence and activity within the world, but they also take into account the "lived lives" of believing communities. Theologians seek not only to inform communities of faith; their work is also informed by those same communities.

The work of theologians is bifocal in another respect: they deal with both the present and the past. Their aim may be to articulate the faith for their own generation, but they draw on the work of previous theologians. Since theology has been a central element in Jewish and Christian history, modern theologians look to earlier formulations for guidance and inspiration. How earlier theologians, such as Augustine, Maimonides, and Thomas Aquinas, developed their systems of thought is the special provenance of historical theologians. Their field of study is the history of doctrine or the history of Jewish and Christian thought.

Whether theologians focus on the present or past, the interpretation of Scripture figures prominently in their work. As we noted earlier, the Bible is a foundational document in both Judaism and Christianity. In each tradition, many other writings have been produced that relate to the Bible. They may contain stories and traditions about the Bible; or they may contain teachings that explain how the Bible should be interpreted and lived. Many of these writings play an influential role within Jewish and Christian communities. And yet the Bible remains the core text around which these other interpretations and writings have been developed. Because of its unique role as an inspired text, it possesses an authority within the community that exceeds that of other influential writings.

Because of the central role the Bible plays in Judaism and Christianity, it cannot be ignored by theologians. Usually the biblical witnesses, such as the OT prophets or the NT Gospels or letters, are given primacy as theologians construct their theological systems. This occurs partly because they are the earliest witnesses to the faith of Jews and Christians, but also because of the normative role they have played in shaping basic beliefs and behaviors.

This close relationship between the Bible and theology makes biblical exegesis indispensable to the work of theologians. As they do their theological work, they draw on the scholarship of biblical exegetes. Since the fields of theological studies and biblical studies are themselves academic specialties within the broader field of theological and religious studies, theologians must rely on the work of biblical specialists. Because the Bible has figured so centrally in theology through the centuries, modern theologians must also themselves become exegetes. Many of them have received specialized training in biblical languages, exegesis, history, and theology, although they themselves may not be biblical specialists. When theologians appropriate material from the Bible in constructing their systems, they too employ the exegetical methods we have discussed.

In an earlier period, theologians often used the Bible as a source for proof texts. They might, for example, adduce biblical passages relating to one of the theological loci, such as God, Christ, or the Holy Spirit. If they could cite all the biblical texts supporting a particular theological view, they could incorporate "the biblical view of x" into their theological discussion. Some contemporary theologians still do this, but most academically trained theologians now understand the shifts in perspective toward the Bible that have occurred over the last two or three centuries. It is usually evident whether they have taken into account the results of historical-critical study of the Bible. If they draw on the OT book of Isaiah, for example, they are well aware of the differences between Isaiah 1–39, 40–55, and 56–66 and the critical issues related to the interpretation of this material. Similarly, for the NT, they well understand the interpretive issues related to how the four Gospels witness to the historical figure Jesus, both his life and teachings.

Because modern theologians typically include Scripture as a central part of their work, beginning exegetes can benefit from reading them. You may be doing an exegesis of a biblical passage for a seminary course in Bible, but you may discover rich, illuminating discussions of your passage in the books and scholarly articles of systematic or historical theologians. Along with biblical commentaries, then, systematic theologies can become a valuable resource for you.

Since seminary students usually do exegesis in Bible courses while also enrolled in courses in systematic or historical theology, the possibilities for making connections between these different theological disciplines are great. We urge you to integrate what you learn in theology courses with your biblical exegesis. Discussions of different Christologies through the ages, for example, can enrich your understanding of important christological texts, such as Philippians 2:5–11 and 2 Corinthians 5:17. In theology courses dealing with modern environmental issues, and our responsibility toward the care of the earth, you will probably consider how Genesis 1–3 can be used in formulating a meaningful doctrine of creation for contemporary believers.

We urge you to make such connections as a reminder that biblical exegesis is more than the study of (ancient) biblical texts. It also relates to other fields of theological studies in which scholars and students are trying to discern how Scripture should inform how we think about the world and live in it.

For Preaching

The Bible plays a central role in the preaching of both Jewish synagogues and Christian churches. For this reason, preachers must learn to do exegesis.

Books on homiletics (the study of preaching) frequently distinguish between exegesis and proclamation. This is a vital distinction, which calls attention to important differences between these activities.

As we have seen in our earlier discussion, while the terms "exegesis," "interpretation," or even "hermeneutics" are often used interchangeably, they usually describe a fairly well-defined set of activities. We have spoken of different exegetical methods or types of biblical criticism. We have also distinguished between doing exegetical research—compiling information about a passage from various resources—and developing an informed interpretation of a passage of Scripture. By the latter we mean more than rehearsing the information we have uncovered about a passage. Interpretation is a different intellectual exercise. It requires us to ask at the most basic level, What does this text mean? How can I talk about it meaningfully to other people? How, for example, can I summarize the theological message of such important passages as Genesis 1–2?

In biblical commentaries, we often find scholars honoring this distinction by using such headings as Exegesis or Exegetical Analysis for

the data and information they accumulate about a text. In a separate
section, often called Theological Reflection, biblical commentators will
unfold their interpretation of the passage, or at least spell out some of
the theological implications of their exegetical work.

The move from exegesis to proclamation represents another distinct
intellectual move. Preparing a sermon is different from preparing an
exegesis. Sermon preparation will often involve biblical exegesis, although
it may not entail a full-fledged exegesis paper like one written for a seminary course.

One of the basic differences between doing exegesis and preparing a
sermon relates to audience. In exegetical work, sometimes the main
audience is the exegete. I may do exegesis of a passage in order to develop
a fuller understanding of it for my own personal benefit. Even when
you write an exegesis paper for a college or seminary course, it is often
written for your own benefit rather than that of the professor. In one
sense, the intended audience is your professor, but as a rule the exegesis
does not significantly broaden your professor's knowledge of the text.
You are the one who benefits. You write the exegesis for yourself—to
deepen your own understanding of the passage.

A sermon, by contrast, has a different audience: the preacher's synagogue or church. Preachers may prepare sermons in their private study;
they may even do exegesis to deepen their understanding of a passage of
Scripture. But they do so knowing that within a few days they will
"deliver it" to the community of believers they serve. Even if the sermon
is recorded and broadcast to a wider audience, or circulated in printed
form, initially it is meant for a particular audience on a given occasion.
This liturgical context—the synagogue or church service—with its distinctive features, such as readings, hymns, prayers, announcements, and
other celebrations, is the primary setting in life for a sermon.

Within this context, the preacher is speaking to others. The sermon
may be based on a lectionary text read just before the sermon or earlier
in the service. And yet the sermon is more than reading the lectionary
text. It is even more than an expanded paraphrase of a biblical text. The
preacher's unique role is to proclaim the text or, rather, to proclaim the
good news to which the text bears witness. Preaching a sermon is different from standing in the pulpit and reading an exegesis paper, even
a stimulating paper. Preaching from a biblical text will require the
preacher to make exegetical moves, perhaps to move in and out of the
text as the sermon unfolds. Still, preaching is a unique act of communication in which someone, who has studied, wrestled with, and prayed

over a biblical text, presents "the message of the text" to a group of listeners, usually with whom the preacher is in some form of covenant
relation or whom the preacher knows well.

As we have emphasized, biblical texts yield different levels of meaning. Most of them are so rich that no one can presume to have grasped
"the meaning" of the text. But in preparing a sermon on a text, the
preacher can do exegesis in order to develop an informed interpretation
of the text. This interpretation can have a single, sharp profile. It can be
one strand of the text developed into a full interpretation. It can take
many different forms. The sermon may even draw on the interpretation
the preacher has developed in preparing an exegesis on the text. But the
sermon still represents a different move.

It is more than just the audience that distinguishes preaching from
exegesis. It is what the audience represents: people who live in the
world, connected with their families, employers and employees, con-
stituents, clients, customers, friends, and enemies at many levels and
in many different ways. They live in many different contexts: home,
school, work, gym, athletic fields, community associations, to name
just a few. They experience the world they know through computers,
research, sales deals, counseling settings, and in many other different
ways. And yet they leave all of these contexts behind when they come
to worship. Or, rather, they bring all of these contexts with them. They
are connected with many different worlds in many different ways, and
the preacher's unique obligation is to connect the biblical text and its
message with them and their worlds.

This is often described as making the text relevant to the parish-
ioner. What this implies is that the believer comes to worship knowing
that at some point the Bible will be read and proclaimed. The believer
will listen to these words—and listen for the word of God coming
through them. But more than this, the believer will expect the preacher
to talk about these words from the biblical text—to explain them, make
sense of them, proclaim them. Preachers use illustrations as a way to
connect the message of the text with people's lives. Sometimes they are
entertaining and clear. At other times, they are muddled and not even
funny. But preachers know that they must do more than talk about the
past, as interesting as that might be. Even the biblical past, for all of
its intriguing features, remains remote for many modern believers.
The preacher and the group of believers gathered for worship live in
the present. They may love the past, even prefer to live there. But their
lives are anchored in the present. And the preacher's weekly challenge is

to help modern believers make sense of their lives by making sense of the Bible.

One way of helping you relate exegesis to preaching is to recall that biblical texts have tended to function in three ways: constitutively, prophetically, and advisorily. These three functions may be related to the three basic forms of ministry: priest, prophet, and sage (or teacher). This division is, of course, somewhat artificial and is offered merely as a lens through which to view the various ways a text can be used. Just as the various functions of ministry overlap and are frequently embodied in the same person, so also a single text can function in different ways, depending on how it is used in its context.

To speak of a *constitutive* or *priestly* function of a text refers to how it is used to support, enhance, and celebrate life. This function deals with human existence by reenacting past experiences and traditions, engaging in ritualized sacred practices, and negotiating the routine demands of life. These functions often take the form of festivals and rituals, which orient people to their past, anchor them in their present, and offer them a meaningful future. Ancient revered texts are read to remind people of the charters of their faith and to recall the many faithful women and men who have preceded them in their journey of faith. They hear words of salvation and hope, along with words of judgment and warning. Through all of these words, their identity is reinforced even as they face new realities. In these functions, traditions and rituals play a vital role. They establish and reestablish the daily, weekly, monthly, and annual rhythms that establish the contours of the community's existence.

The *prophetic* function challenges the present, its commitments, and its orientation. It also calls for new and sometimes radical revision of the present. The prophetic perspective views the present critically. It invites people to consider new viewpoints and different orientations. Sometimes these new visions challenge a people's identity, threaten its self-understanding, and question its customary behavior. The prophetic voice may issue its challenge by drawing upon earlier traditions and views of the past. It may also sketch a new vision of the future. It may pronounce a word of judgment or offer words of hope. It may announce death or life. It evaluates present conditions, asking how they can be better. It seeks not to constitute but to reconstitute.

The *advisory* function—the function of the sage or the wise person—has as its goal the offering of instruction, wisdom, or insight. It has no overt desire to confirm the present and its conditions or to reform and reconstitute it. The voice of the sage draws on general human experience. It seeks to illuminate rather than create new conditions. Such illumination may be catalytic by opening up new perspectives that can lead to reconstitution. This function tends to be reflective, even introspective. It looks inward rather than backward or forward. It trades on insight rather than dramatic new revelation or traditional beliefs. It probes the human condition more deeply, convinced that deeper, reflective lives are more meaningful lives.

For Personal Appropriation

Just as the Bible belongs to historians, theologians, and preachers, it also belongs to all who read it for moral guidance, spiritual edification, or pleasure. The person who reads the Bible for these purposes may not be motivated by professional interests, but this does not mean that exegesis is any less necessary. If exegesis is the systematic process through which we come to an informed understanding of a biblical text, it becomes as essential for the nonprofessional as for the professional reader. Even the professional reader who reads the Bible for personal appropriation does not stop doing exegesis.

Rather than viewing the work of biblical scholars and other professional theologians and historians as preliminary work to be laid aside when reading the Bible for personal profit, it is better to see the everyday reader as part of a larger circle of interested readers and interpreters who share a common goal. Those who devote themselves to full-time study of the Bible usually do so in order to benefit those who cannot. Even if the work of scholars sometimes challenges cherished assumptions about the Bible, it cannot easily be ignored. Scholarly work becomes part of a public conversation, in which communities of faith themselves participate.

When we read the Bible for moral and spiritual guidance, we assume the position of a first-time hearer. We relate to the text much as the original hearers to whom the writings were originally addressed. Since we are separated from the original events by many centuries, we cannot avoid the third-party perspective discussed earlier. As later readers, we overhear rather than hear directly. It is not as though we intrude ourselves into an earlier conversation, however; Israel and the church canonized these writings because of their capacity to transcend the settings they originally addressed and to speak to future generations of believers. What distinguishes those who read the Bible for moral and spiritual

guidance from those who read it in the service of history, theology, or
preaching is the immediacy of the relationship between text and reader.
Rather than reading the Bible for some other purpose, we are reading it
for our direct benefit.

This does not mean that we should read the Bible any less rigorously,
certainly not any less critically. Even when we read the Bible for personal benefit, there is no reason to suspend our critical judgment. We
should still interrogate the text, and do so rigorously. The questions we
bring to such a reading may differ greatly from those the historian
brings. Our questions are not any less pressing or important. We should
remember that many of the types of biblical criticism we have discussed
were developed because of the high personal investment scholars had in
these texts. They too were often reading the Bible for moral and spiritual guidance. Critical methods were developed to make these texts
more, not less, understandable.

Someone has suggested that when we read the Bible for spiritual
guidance, we read it sympathetically. By this we mean that we align ourselves with the biblical authors and their theological visions. We stand
with them, as it were, and look out on the world as they saw it. By
adopting their vantage point, we "look along with" rather than "look at"
the text. The former phrase suggests that we stand inside the text, within
the tradition as it were, adopting the perspective of the text, at least pro-
visionally. On later reflection, we may embrace the viewpoint of the text,
or we may reject it. But we are willing, at least initially, to place ourselves
within the text, listen to its voice, and be open to its message.

"Looking at" the text suggests the picture of someone standing outside the text "looking in." This is not necessarily a negative stance or
even a detached, disinterested relationship to the text, but it is a different perspective. In one sense, critical historians adopt this stance. They
are viewing the biblical text as any other ancient writing or archaeological artifact. Knowing that ancient writings reflected ideological tendencies and were rarely, if ever, neutral in their outlook, historians
operate with a hermeneutic of suspicion. Even critical historians, however, can "look along with" the text, especially if they align themselves
confessionally with the communities of faith that produced them.
To do so does not mean that they must embrace the point of view
expressed in the text, but they may still be generally supportive of its
overall intention.

Theologians may read the Bible for the purpose of constructing new
systems of thought and addressing ever-changing situations. Like histo-

rians, they too read the Bible critically. In one sense, they use it for some other purpose. But scholars now recognize that the Bible makes theological claims from start to finish. It sketches theological visions in many different situations. Even if these are archaic in many respects and may not address modern readers directly, theologians can still "look along with" the biblical text as sympathetic readers. They may find aspects of the biblical vision, such as its prescientific outlook or its patriarchal view of the world, highly problematic. Scholars have developed different strategies for dealing with these features of the Bible. Some strategies reject such views outright; others find ways of mitigating them; still others find ways of embracing them without significantly changing them.

We soon discover that we can adopt many different stances toward the Bible, and they may not be mutually exclusive. It is possible, for example, for a literary critic to read Shakespeare's writings through a scholarly lens, subjecting them to all kinds of literary and source criticism. The same critic, however, can still read Shakespeare for pleasure and enjoy seeing his plays performed. Scholars also read the Bible critically, recognizing the different ways it can be used, but also experience intellectual stimulation and moral edification.

Reading the Bible for personal appropriation should not be conceived in a narrowly individualist sense. The Bible may belong to Jews and Christians, but it also belongs to the larger culture. So pervasive has been the Bible's influence, especially in Western culture, that it has become a cultural icon. Artistic appropriation of the Bible underscores this point. The arts broadly speaking—visual, musical, dramatic, literary—have been profoundly shaped by the Bible. When the Bible is appropriated through artistic creativity, we can see exegesis at work. Artistic works as different as Handel's *Messiah* and MacLeish's *J.B.* reflect exegetical strategies for reading the Bible. This is also true in popular culture, especially when the Bible is portrayed in film, drama, and popular music. Biblical stories have provided Hollywood a rich source of narratives for producing movies. Every Bible-based movie is based on exegesis. It may be poor exegesis, but it is exegesis nevertheless. These interpretations may be presented in different modes from historical reconstruction, theological appropriation, and sermons, but the difference is one of form rather than essence. As exegetes, we can often learn much from these artistic appropriations of the Bible and biblical themes.

The beginning exegete should be alert to the various ways the Bible is used in modern culture. We might ask whether Mel Gibson's *The Passion of the Christ* is historical reconstruction or artistic appropriation, or even theological reconstruction and biblical proclamation. It is probably some of each. This should not surprise us. We have seen that even the historian who deals with the biblical texts at certain junctures must also deal with literary, theological, homiletical, moral, and artistic dimensions of the texts. Modern readers of the Bible often find themselves sensitive to the many dimensions of the biblical text. The beginning exegete who wishes to read the Bible with an informed understanding can do no less.

BIBLIOGRAPHY

Exegesis and Historical-Archaeological Reconstruction

Abraham, William J. *Divine Revelation and the Limits of Historical Criticism.* Oxford and New York: Oxford University Press, 2000 (1982).

Bartholomew, Craig G. *"Behind" the Text: History and Biblical Interpretation.* Carlisle, UK: Paternoster; Grand Rapids: Zondervan, 2003.

Brettler, Marc Zvi. *The Creation of History in Ancient Israel.* London and New York: Routledge, 1995.

Davies, Philip R. *In Search of 'Ancient Israel': A Study in Biblical Origins.* 2nd ed. Edinburgh: T. & T. Clark, 2004.

Davis, Thomas W. *Shifting Sands: The Rise and Fall of Biblical Archaeology.* New York: Oxford University Press, 2004.

*Dever, William G. *Archaeology and Biblical Studies: Retrospects and Prospects.* Evanston, IL: Seabury-Western, 1974.

―――. *What Did the Biblical Writers Know, and When Did They Know It? What Archaeology Can Tell Us about the Reality of Ancient Israel.* Grand Rapids: Eerdmans, 2001.

―――. *Who Were the Early Israelites, and Where Did They Come From?* Grand Rapids: Eerdmans, 2003.

Evans, Craig. *Jesus and the Ossuaries.* Waco, TX: Baylor University Press, 2003.

Finkelstein, Israel, and Neil A. Silberman. *David and Solomon: In Search of the Bible's Sacred Kings and the Roots of the Western Tradition.* New York: Free Press, 2006.

Grabbe, Lester L., ed. *Can a "History of Israel" Be Written?* London: T. & T. Clark, 2004.

Greenspoon, Leonard J., M. Dennis Hamm, and Bryan F. LeBeau. *The Historical Jesus through Catholic and Jewish Eyes.* Harrisburg, PA: Trinity, 2000.

Harvey, Van A. *The Historian and the Believer: The Morality of Historical Knowledge and Christian Belief.* Urbana, IL: University of Illinois Press, 1996 (1966).

Hendel, Ronald S. *Remembering Abraham: Culture, Memory, and History in the Hebrew Bible.* Oxford and New York: Oxford University Press, 2005.

Hoffmeier, James K., and Alan R. Millard, eds. *The Future of Biblical Archaeology: Reassessing Methodologies and Assumptions.* Grand Rapids: Eerdmans, 2004.

Jeremias, Joachim. *The Problem of the Historical Jesus.* Rev. ed. Philadelphia: Fortress, 1980 (1964).

Johnson, Luke T. *The Real Jesus: The Misguided Quest for the Historical Jesus and the Truth of the Traditional Gospels.* San Francisco: HarperSanFrancisco, 1997.

Kitchen, Kenneth A. *The Bible in Its World: The Bible and Archaeology Today.* Eugene, OR: Wipf & Stock, 2002 (1977).

Lapp, Paul W. *Biblical Archaeology and History.* New York: World, 1969.

Laughlin, John C. H. *Archaeology and the Bible.* London and New York: Routledge, 2000.

Lemche, Niels P. *The Israelites in History and Tradition.* London: SPCK; Louisville, KY: Westminster John Knox, 1998.

Long, V. Philips, Gordon J. Wenham, and David W. Baker. *Windows into Old Testament History: Evidence, Argument, and the Crisis of "Biblical Israel."* Grand Rapids: Eerdmans, 2002.

McArthur, Harvey K. *In Search of the Historical Jesus.* New York: Scribner, 1969; London: SPCK, 1970.

———. *The Quest through the Centuries: The Search for the Historical Jesus.* Philadelphia: Fortress, 1966.

*Miller, J. Maxwell. *The Old Testament and the Historian.* Philadelphia: Fortress; London: SPCK, 1976.

*Moore, Megan B. *Philosophy and Practice in Writing a History of Ancient Israel.* London: T. & T. Clark, 2006.

Richardson, Peter. *Building Jewish in the Roman East.* Waco, TX: Baylor University Press, 2004.

Schweitzer, Albert. *The Quest of the Historical Jesus: First Complete Edition.* Minneapolis: Fortress, 2001 (1906).

Vermès, Géza. *Jesus in His Jewish Context.* Minneapolis: Fortress; London: SCM, 2003.

Wenthe, Dean O., Paul L. Schrieber, and Lee A. Maxwell, eds. *Hear the Word of Yahweh: Essays on Scripture and Archaeology in Honor of Horace D. Hummel.* St. Louis: Concordia, 2002.

Exegesis and Doing Theology

Achtemeier, Paul J. *An Introduction to the New Hermeneutic.* Philadelphia: Westminster, 1969.

*Adam, A. K. M., Stephen E. Fowl, Kevin J. Vanhoozer, and Francis Watson, eds. *Reading Scripture with the Church: Toward a Hermeneutic for Theological Interpretation.* Grand Rapids: Baker Academic, 2006.

Barth, Karl. *Church Dogmatics* 1/1. Edinburgh: T. & T. Clark; New York: Scribner, 1936. Pages 98–212.

Bartlett, David L. *The Shape of Scriptural Authority*. Philadelphia: Fortress, 1983.

Childs, Brevard S. *Biblical Theology in Crisis*. Philadelphia: Westminster, 1970.

Curran, Charles E., and Richard A. McCormick. *The Use of Scripture in Moral Theology*. New York: Paulist, 1984.

Dauphinais, Michael, and Matthew Levering. *Holy People, Holy Land: A Theological Introduction to the Bible*. Grand Rapids: Brazos, 2005.

Donfried, Karl P. *Who Owns the Bible? Toward the Recovery of a Christian Hermeneutic*. New York: Crossroad, 2006.

*Fowl, Stephen E. *Engaging Scripture: A Model for Theological Interpretation*. Oxford: Blackwell, 1998.

Frei, Hans W. *Eclipse of Biblical Narrative: A Study in Eighteenth and Nineteenth Century Hermeneutics*. New Haven, CT: Yale University Press, 1974.

Hanson, Paul D. *The Diversity of Scripture: A Theological Interpretation*. Philadelphia: Fortress, 1982.

Johnston, Robert K., ed. *The Use of the Bible in Theology: Evangelical Options*. Eugene, OR: Wipf & Stock, 1997 (1985).

*Kelsey, David H. *Proving Doctrine: The Uses of Scripture in Modern Theology*. Harrisburg, PA: Trinity, 1999 (1975).

Mahoney, Edward J., ed. *Scripture as the Soul of Theology*. Collegeville, MN: Liturgical Press, 2005.

Marshall, I. Howard, Kevin J. Vanhoozer, and Stanley E. Porter, eds. *Beyond the Bible: Moving from Scripture to Theology*. Grand Rapids: Baker Academic; Milton Keynes, UK: Paternoster, 2004.

McKim, Donald K., ed. *A Guide to Contemporary Hermeneutics: Major Trends in Biblical Interpretation*. Eugene, OR: Wipf & Stock, 1999 (1986).

———. *What Christians Believe about the Bible*. Nashville: Nelson, 1985.

Nineham, Dennis E. *The Use and Abuse of the Bible: A Study of the Bible in an Age of Rapid Cultural Change*. London: SPCK, 1976.

O'Collins, Gerald, and Daniel Kendall. *The Bible for Theology: Ten Principles for the Theological Use of Scripture*. New York: Paulist, 1997.

Patte, Daniel. *Ethics of Biblical Interpretation: A Reevaluation*. Louisville, KY: Westminster John Knox, 1995.

Pleins, J. David. *The Social Visions of the Hebrew Bible: A Theological Introduction*. Louisville, KY: Westminster John Knox, 2001.

Smart, James D. *The Past, Present, and Future of Biblical Theology*. Philadelphia: Westminster, 1979.

Wainwright, Arthur W. *Beyond Biblical Criticism: Encountering Jesus in Scripture*. Atlanta: John Knox; London: SPCK, 1982.

Watson, Francis. *Text and Truth: Redefining Biblical Theology*. Grand Rapids: Eerdmans, 1997.

*———. *Text, Church, and World: Biblical Interpretation in Theological Perspective*. Grand Rapids: Eerdmans, 1994.

Wenham, Gordon J. *Story as Torah: Reading Old Testament Narrative Ethically*. Grand Rapids: Baker Academic, 2004.

Whybray, R. Norman. *The Good Life in the Old Testament*. London: T. & T. Clark, 2002.

Exegesis and Preaching

Achtemeier, Elizabeth R. *The Old Testament and the Proclamation of the Gospel*. Philadelphia: Westminster, 1973.

———. *Preaching Hard Texts from the Old Testament*. Peabody, MA: Hendrickson, 1998.

Barclay, William. *Communicating the Gospel*. Edinburgh: St. Andrews Press, 1978 (1968).

*Barrett, Charles K. *Biblical Preaching and Biblical Scholarship*. London: Epworth, 1957. Repr. as *Biblical Problems and Biblical Preaching*. Philadelphia: Fortress, 1964.

*Best, Ernest. *From Text to Sermon: Responsible Use of the New Testament in Preaching*. 2nd ed. Edinburgh: T. & T. Clark, 1988.

Cox, James W. *A Guide to Biblical Preaching*. Nashville: Abingdon, 1976.

Craddock, Fred B. *As One without Authority*. Rev. and with new sermons. St. Louis: Chalice, 2001.

———. *Overhearing the Gospel*. Rev. and exp. ed. St. Louis: Chalice, 2002.

———. *Preaching*. Nashville: Abingdon, 1985.

Davis, Ellen F. *Wondrous Depth: Preaching the Old Testament*. Louisville, KY: Westminster John Knox, 2005.

Davison, Lisa Wilson. *Preaching the Women of the Bible*. St. Louis: Chalice, 2006.

Fuller, Reginald H. *The Use of the Bible in Preaching*. Philadelphia: Fortress; London: Bible Reading Fellowship, 1981.

Gowan, Donald E. *Reclaiming the Old Testament for the Christian Pulpit*. Atlanta: John Knox, 1980; Edinburgh: T. & T. Clark, 1981.

Greidanus, Sidney. *Preaching Christ from the Old Testament: A Contemporary Hermeneutical Method*. Grand Rapids: Eerdmans, 1999.

Kaiser, Walter C. *Preaching and Teaching from the Old Testament: A Guide for the Church*. Grand Rapids: Baker Academic, 2003.

Keck, Leander E. *The Bible in the Pulpit: The Renewal of Biblical Preaching*. Nashville: Abingdon, 1978.

———. *Taking the Bible Seriously: An Invitation to Think Theologically*. Nashville: Abingdon, 1962.

Klein, George L. *Reclaiming the Prophetic Mantle: Preaching the Old Testament Faithfully*. Eugene, OR: Wipf & Stock, 1998 (1992).

Kysar, Robert. *Preaching John*. Minneapolis: Fortress, 2002.

Kysar, Robert, and Joseph M. Webb. *Preaching to Postmoderns: New Perspectives for Proclaiming the Message*. Peabody, MA: Hendrickson, 2006.

Long, Thomas G. *Preaching and the Literary Forms of the Bible.* Philadelphia: Fortress, 1989.

*———. *The Witness of Preaching.* 2nd ed. Louisville, KY: Westminster John Knox, 2005.

Long, Thomas G., and Edward Farley, eds. *Preaching as a Theological Task: World, Gospel, Scripture, in Honor of David Buttrick.* Louisville, KY: Westminster John Knox, 1996.

McKim, Donald. *The Bible in Theology and Preaching: A Theological Guide for Preaching.* Eugene, OR: Wipf & Stock, 1999 (1994).

Murphy, Roland E., ed. *Theology, Exegesis, and Proclamation.* New York: Herder & Herder; London: Burns & Oates, 1971.

O'Day, Gail R. *The Word Disclosed: Preaching the Gospel of John.* Rev. and exp. ed. St. Louis: Chalice, 2002.

Sanders, James A. *God Has a Story Too: Sermons in Context.* Eugene, OR: Wipf & Stock, 1998 (1979).

Smart, James D. *The Strange Silence of the Bible in the Church: A Study in Hermeneutics.* Philadelphia: Westminster; London: SCM, 1970.

Smith, D. Moody. *Interpreting the Gospels for Preaching.* Philadelphia: Fortress, 1980.

Thiselton, Anthony C. *The Two Horizons: New Testament Hermeneutics and Philosophical Description.* Exeter, UK: Paternoster, 1979; Grand Rapids: Eerdmans, 1980.

*Thompson, James W. *Preaching Like Paul: Homiletical Wisdom for Today.* Louisville, KY: Westminster John Knox, 2001.

Thompson, William D. *Preaching Biblically: Exegesis and Interpretation.* Nashville: Abingdon, 1981.

Williams, Michael E., et al., eds. *The Storyteller's Companion to the Bible.* Nashville: Abingdon, 1991–.

Wilson, Paul S. *God Sense: Reading the Bible for Preaching.* Nashville: Abingdon, 2001.

Exegesis and Personal Appropriation

Barr, James. *The Bible in the Modern World.* London: SCM; Philadelphia: Trinity, 1993 (1977).

*Brueggemann, Walter. *The Creative Word: Canon as a Model for Biblical Education.* Philadelphia: Fortress, 1982.

Capps, Donald. *Biblical Approaches to Pastoral Counseling.* Eugene, OR: Wipf & Stock, 2003 (1981).

Davis, Ellen, and Richard B. Hays, eds. *The Art of Reading Scripture.* Grand Rapids: Eerdmans, 2003.

Davidson, Robert. *The Bible in Religious Education.* Edinburgh: Handsel, 1979.

Gottwald, Norman K., and Richard A. Horsley, eds. *The Bible and Liberation: Political and Social Hermeneutics.* Rev. ed. Maryknoll, NY: Orbis; London: SPCK, 1993.

Gustafson, James M. *Christ and the Moral Life*. Chicago: University of Chicago Press, 1979 (1968).

*Hays, Richard B. *The Moral Vision of the New Testament: Community, Cross, New Creation: A Contemporary Introduction to New Testament Ethics*. Edinburgh: T. & T. Clark, 1996.

Holmer, Paul L. *The Grammar of Faith*. San Francisco: Harper & Row, 1978.

Rogerson, John W., and M. Daniel Carroll R. *Theory and Practice in Old Testament Ethics*. London: T. & T. Clark, 2004.

Rogerson, John W., Margaret Davies, and M. Daniel Carroll R., eds. *The Bible in Ethics: The Second Sheffield Colloquium*. Sheffield, UK: Sheffield Academic Press, 1995.

Rogerson, John W., Christopher Rowland, and Barnabas Lindars, eds. *The Study and Use of the Bible*. Basingstroke, UK: Pickering; Grand Rapids: Eerdmans, 1988.

Roncace, Mark, and Patrick Gray, eds. *Teaching the Bible: Practical Strategies for Classroom Instruction*. Atlanta: Society of Biblical Literature, 2005.

*Wink, Walter. *The Bible in Human Transformation: Toward a New Paradigm for Biblical Study*. Philadelphia: Fortress, 1973.

———. *Transforming Bible Study: A Leader's Guide*. 2nd ed. Nashville: Abingdon, 2001.

Appendix
Using Electronic Technologies
in Exegesis

The arrival of information technology over the last few decades has greatly affected how interpreters of the Bible read and experience texts. While many Bible readers still prefer the printed page, others enjoy having the Bible readily accessible in electronic form, whether on their desktop or portable computer or in a compact, handheld electronic device. Electronic databases now enable readers to do sophisticated, speedy searches of bibliographical resources that were unimaginable just a few years ago. The availability of such electronic resources has produced greater efficiencies in time and energy. It is no longer necessary, for example, for biblical interpreters to be near libraries to have access to technical research tools.

Here, we consider some of the new possibilities this electronic revolution offers biblical exegetes. We also consider some of the special problems these new technologies pose for biblical interpretation. Given the rapidity of change within electronic media, any introduction, however elementary, becomes quickly outdated. Even so, we think it worthwhile to survey some of the basic options currently available. Our treatment falls into two broad categories: (1) biblical software and (2) use of the Internet.

Biblical Software

No survey of biblical software can be truly comprehensive or up to date in a publication such as this; that would require a Web site updated on a continual basis. Indeed, by the time this review has been published, it will be out of date. Nevertheless, despite rapid changes in technology, there are some enduring qualities to look for in a biblical software package.

We will mention some important criteria, then apply them to some of the popular software packages now available. We now consider some of the most important questions to ask in choosing software.

1. *What Bible versions are available?* Many software packages emphasize the large number of Bible versions they contain. But a crucial consideration for exegetes is the quality of these Bible translations. Given the widespread use of English, a package should contain the major translations in use by Christian and Jewish readers in the English-speaking world. These include the New Revised Standard Version, which is widely used in mainline Protestant churches; the New International Version, because of its prominence in evangelical circles; the New American Standard Bible, which has been adopted officially by the Roman Catholic Church; and the Tanakh, which is published by the Jewish Publication Society as the accepted text for Jewish readers. The King James Version (or Authorized Version) is still preferred by many Christians, especially those born before 1950 and many people of all ages in conservative and fundamentalist churches.

Using these four or five texts in parallel columns will give exegetes who know only English some idea of the various translation choices implicit within the original text. Students who read the original biblical languages will need the latest scholarly editions of the Bible in those languages. For the Hebrew Bible, the main scholarly edition is the *Biblia Hebraica Stuttgartensia*; for the Greek OT (Septuagint), Alfred Rahlfs's *Septuaginta* is the most convenient edition available; for the Greek NT, the twenty-seventh edition of *Novum Testamentum Graece* edited by Eberhard Nestle and Erwin Nestle and Barbara Aland and Kurt Aland (= N-A 27) and the fourth edition of *The Greek New Testament*, edited by Kurt Aland and Barbara Aland and published by the United Bible Societies (=UBS 4), are the standard critical editions.

Other important biblical texts, which are especially important for the history of biblical interpretation, include the Latin Vulgate and its English translation, the Douay Version; the German Bible translated by Martin Luther (or modern German translations); and the Anglican Coverdale Bible.

Some software packages contain a multiplicity of English-language Bibles, which are often included primarily because their copyright has expired. This enables the software publisher to reproduce them at little or no cost. Many of these English translations are included with little, if any, attention given to how faithfully they render the original languages. This is also true of many of the modern-language Bibles included in these packages. They may present the Bible using simple language, but their quality varies greatly.

2. *How well does the concordance function work?* One of the greatest strengths of a computerized Bible is the ability to search for words or phrases quickly and efficiently. But such computerized searches are not necessarily simple.

The most basic search is the "simple string search," which browses a document for a particular set of characters in a designated order. A search for "sin" will produce all of the occurrences of the word "sin." But it will also yield the occurrences of "sinner," "single," or "cousins," since these terms also contain the three designated letters. If the search is limited to these three letters in this order, it might omit occurrences of "sins."

A "complex string search" consists of "partial strings" (a designated group of letters), which may be separated from each other by several letters or words. This type of search is generally more effective than a simple string search. For example, a complex string search for "forgiv sin," which allows an interval of two words, should find phrases like "forgive my sin," "forgive us our sins," "forgiving sin," and "forgiveness of sins." We can immediately see the possibilities offered by a complex string search.

When we move from searches in English to those using Hebrew and Greek, we encounter some difficulties. Simple string searches in the original languages are more difficult for several reasons.

First is the use of different alphabets. A good search engine should have fonts for the original languages built into the program's interface. If we were using a program without Hebrew fonts, for example, and wanted to search for "bereshit," the first word of the Hebrew Bible, first, we would have to remember that Hebrew characters are written from right to left. Then, we would type (from left to right) the equivalent string of English characters. Our entry would look as follows: tyÙi$)"r:B. But if our program included Hebrew fonts, we could type the Hebrew characters using the "qwerty" keyboard (striking keys assigned to different Hebrew letters and symbols) or click on them on a virtual keyboard on the screen.

The second problem with simple string searches in the original languages is the amount of information that a single word in the original language contains. This occurs because Hebrew and Greek are highly "inflected" languages: The form of a word changes depending on how it functions within a sentence. The core of the word—its word stem—can acquire prefixes and suffixes that reflect whether it is a singular or plural form, its case (nominative, genitive, accusative, etc.), and other changes that affect its meaning. These various changes in the form of a word, depending on how it is used in a sentence, are referred to as its morphology (literally, the "study of forms"). For these reasons, each Hebrew and Greek word in the biblical text is associated with a small packet of information that includes the lexical form of the word (the so-called root form) and its grammatical characteristics. The technical term for grouping this information together is "morphological tagging."

Because of the complexity of Hebrew and Greek, basic string searches are often insufficient. More powerful search engines allow the user to perform "morphological searches." This process makes it possible to find words when they appear in particular grammatical configurations. If we wished, we could search for a single inflected form of a Greek word, for example, every instance of the Greek verb *anoigō* that occurs in a plural aorist passive form. But if we wanted to know where the verb *anoigō* occurs, regardless of how it is inflected—its tense, voice, mood, or number—we could also conduct this broad search.

For evaluating computerized concordances, the general rule is, The more sophisticated the engine, the more you can accomplish.

3. *How user friendly is the software package?* This criterion involves two major topics, "interface" and the learning curve.

"Interface" refers to how the screen looks in the program: how much information is displayed at one time, the quality of that information, and how easily new information is displayed. Evaluating the program's interface is partly a question of aesthetics—how the screen looks—and partly functionality—how it serves individual user preferences. Some programs allow users to customize the interface, thereby responding to each user's needs.

The two most important interface questions are (1) How easily can one view the biblical text and change between texts? and (2) Does the screen easily display grammatical and lexical information when one is working with the original languages? A good interface will allow students who do not know the original languages to find the basic morphological information that will enable them to use more sophisticated original language tools.

The second consideration is the learning curve. The main question here is, How difficult is it to use the program? Can a first-time user intuitively understand how to use the software? Or will it require some study to figure out how to accomplish basic tasks? Most software packages have an internal logic to them; they make sense, given the approach of the programmers and certain technical limitations with which they are conceived. But how accessible or obvious is that logic for the ordinary user? Some complex packages include a set of learning tools or videos to help first-time users learn the logic of the program. The best way to determine the learning curve of a particular program is through its concordance or search function. This tends to be the most commonly used function and potentially the most difficult.

4. *What is the quality of the other resources that accompany the biblical texts?* Some questions to ask here are, What other tools and resources are included in the package? How pertinent are they to modern scholarly research? How good are they?

In evaluating specific tools, we can ask, What lexical and lexicographical tools are included in the package? What commentaries and dictionaries are bundled in the package? When were they originally published? How current is the scholarship represented in them? What theological tendencies are reflected in the resources?

As with biblical versions, more is not always better. Less expensive packages tend to include older resources that are more readily available because they are free of copyright restrictions. Once a certain amount of time has passed, a text enters the public domain and can be reproduced for sale at little or no cost to the publisher. A publisher must pay a licensing fee in order to reproduce more current works still under copyright. While some works have enduring value despite their age, the exegete must carefully assess the quality of these resources and exercise discernment in using them. Many of the resources included in these software packages have a heavy doctrinal bias, which must be taken into account by discriminating users.

A Select List of Some Current Software Packages

Bibloi 8 (fomerly Bible Windows)

This program is the newest version of what was formerly called "Bible Windows." After a threatened lawsuit from Microsoft over the name "Windows," the software has adopted a new name and includes several new features. The major Bible versions that come with this program are minimal (Revised Standard Version, New Revised Standard Version, and King James Version). The full production version should include links to online versions of the New American Standard Bible and the New International Version. Nevertheless, it comes fully stocked with the appropriate original language texts including an analytical Greek NT, Rahlfs's Septuagint (LXX), and the *Biblia Hebraica Stuttgartensia*. Other important inclusions are the complete Latin Vulgate and Luther's German Bible. The program also includes an English translation of the Apostolic Fathers and the OT Pseudepigrapha. The Hebrew and Greek convert to an interlinear mode with a single click. While the search functions for the English, Latin, and German texts are nothing more than sophisticated string searches, the Hebrew and Greek texts are fully searchable by dictionary entry and can be customized grammatically. Its powerful search engine is quite intuitive, requiring little time to begin conducting complex searches. Unfortunately, this program does not have the ability to search across different biblical language editions and modern translations of the Bible.

The on-board reference works are equally minimal and restricted to lexicographical tools. While the publishers of this program have limited their choices, they have selected solid reference works: the Liddell-Scott Greek lexicon and the Louw-Nida *Greek-English Lexicon of the New Testament* for Greek, and the Brown-Driver-Briggs *Hebrew and English Lexicon* for the Hebrew. The most exciting feature is a direct link to the full edition of the Liddell-Scott lexicon, which is located on the Perseus Web site. Not only is this a great tool, but it presages the inherent potential in connecting local software with the best Internet resources.

BibleWorks 7

This software package contains an abundance of material. The packaging states that it contains more than 112 Bible editions in thirty languages. A quick look at the offerings confirms that this is no exaggeration. As one would expect, all of the major English versions are available. The Greek texts include the major eclectic texts (texts based on many manuscripts rather than mainly following one manuscript) since Stephanus's Textus Receptus (1550). The *Biblia Hebraica Stuttgartensia* and Latin Vulgate are also included, along with Greek and Hebrew interlinear texts. Unless the user is a professional Bible translator or a skilled linguist who knows several languages, most of these versions will remain unused. The lexicographical resources are equally rich: the major lexicons, including the Louw-Nida *Greek-*

English Lexicon of the New Testament, the Liddell-Scott Greek lexicon, the older Thayer's Greek lexicon, the Brown-Driver-Briggs *Hebrew and English Lexicon*, and the concise version of the Koehler-Baumgartner Hebrew-Aramaic lexicon. The most recent program also includes the complete works of Philo and Josephus (in Greek and English), the Apostolic Fathers (in Greek and English), and Metzger's *Textual Commentary on the Greek New Testament*.

BibleWorks 7 has the most powerful search engine of all the software packages surveyed in this review. The Advanced Search Engine feature allows truly intricate search specifications not only within, but also across, specific versions and editions of the Bible. Unfortunately, doing advanced searches in this program is confusing and time consuming, even for an experienced computer user performing a moderately difficult search. Partly, this results from the program's use of three different boxes and various connecting lines to display the search. With practice, users will eventually become more familiar with advanced searches, but they must overcome a significant learning curve to take full advantage of the impressive capabilities of the search engine.

The well-designed interface presents a lot of useful information on screen at any given time. It can also be fully customized to fit the user's needs. One of the strengths of the interface is its ability to present a verse or set of verses from different versions or editions in parallel columns. By simply positioning the mouse pointer over each Hebrew or Greek word, the user can obtain the relevant morphological information. This enables users to identify or "parse" inflected forms.

The accompanying resources are mostly limited to lexicographical tools, although some biblical aids of lesser value are also included. The core application includes several commentaries, time lines, and Bible dictionaries. These resources are valuable mainly as quick references. For the most part, they are dated (and thus free of copyright restrictions) and for this reason have limited value. Users should not depend on such resources exclusively in doing biblical research.

BibleWorks is built on a module paradigm. This means that the core program comes with a set of resources, and additional resources, which "plug in" to the core application, may be purchased. While all of the above features are part of the "core" application, several important modules are available for purchasing. These include the Bauer-Danker *Greek-English Lexicon of the New Testament* (BDAG), the complete Liddell-Scott-Jones (LSJ) Greek lexicons, the Blass-Debrunner-Funk *Greek Grammar of the New Testament*, and Kittel's *Theological Dictionary of the New Testament.* There are also modules for introductory Greek, Hebrew, and Aramaic grammars. The ability to expand BibleWorks is an attractive feature of this software program.

Overall, BibleWorks is an excellent program. One of its strengths is the amount of material included in the program. The core program, however, is relatively expensive, and costs compound as one adds modules. First-time users might also find the abundance of information a bit overwhelming. In order to harness the program's full capabilities, a user must be willing to invest a considerable amount of time to learn the program. Recognizing this steep learning curve, the programmers have included a number of instructional videos to expedite the learning process. This is the most powerful of the packages surveyed, but also the most complex and difficult to use.

Logos Bible Software Series X: Scholar's Library

This is also an excellent package. The heart of the package is the Libronix Library engine which organizes the massive number of resources that either come with the program or are available for separate purchase. Many of these resources are older works—often devotional writings—whose copyright protection has expired. Nevertheless, some of them are primary sources that are valuable in doing exegesis, such as the Amarna letters, a forthcoming electronic edition of the Dead Sea Scrolls in both the original languages and English translation, and the complete works of Philo and Josephus. This is certainly a strong collection of resources with more becoming available all the time.

The biblical portion of the program is also very strong. It contains the major English-language Bibles and a number of others (except the Douay Version, an English translation of the Vulgate used by Roman Catholics). The original language editions include the *Biblia Hebraica Stuttgartensia* and the major eclectic Greek texts since Stephanus's Greek edition (1550). The Latin Vulgate is also included, along with Hebrew and Greek interlinears. The search engine is very strong and conducts complex string searches in English and Latin. Complex morphological searches can be conducted in the original languages. The program, however, does not support cross-version searches. This search engine requires some study in order to conduct complex searches.

The interface is fairly intuitive—following a Web page paradigm— and may be fully customized. Morphology for original language words is available by moving the mouse pointer over the word, although the lexical form of the word and definition are not included in this feature. The latter are available, however, with a right click of the mouse.

Overall, this package is a very strong resource. The integration of the electronic book resources is its major advantage over the other packages, although the search engine is not quite as powerful as that of BibleWorks. It too comes with with helpful instructional videos. Like BibleWorks, this software package is available in several different versions. The advanced packages, though, are more expensive than any other software reviewed.

The Essential IVP Reference Collection

This package is a collection of reference works that plugs into Logos's Libronix Library engine. Identifying itself as a "complete electronic Bible study resource," this package is light on the Bible and heavy on the resource. Its strength is the wide array of reference works on the Bible that come with it; as for actual Bible editions, it comes only with the King James Version and four other English texts available through separate purchase. As stand-alone biblical software, it is not up to the task. As a reference work, it contains many of InterVarsity's popular works, all of which are heavily biased toward conservative evangelical theology.

Zondervan Pradis 5.0

This package has a helpful interface, which places text, morphology, and "helps" in an easily accessible format. The "helps" reflect a consistent conservative-evangelical perspective, which limits their usefulness. The number and editions of texts are also limited, though they include the major English versions and a Hebrew and Greek text. The search feature is a simple string search for the English but the Hebrew and Greek feature is a more sophisticated search that allows lexical searches. Complicated grammatical searches are not possible. The lexicographical aids are limited, featuring analytical lexicons for both Hebrew and Greek. None of the major dictionaries is included.

Overall, this is an acceptable package featuring an attractive interface, sufficient texts, and a sufficient search engine. While complex original language searches are not possible, this package would be adequate for students with limited or no access to original languages.

BibleSoft PC Study Bible 4

This package is primarily designed for users whose primary exegetical language is English. It contains the major English Bibles. It also includes Hebrew and Greek texts, but these are not well supported. Searching for Hebrew and Greek terms is most easily accomplished through the antiquated Englishman's Concordance rather than searching with the original languages themselves. The commentaries bundled with the package are quite old and theologically slanted. The one exception is the United Bible Societies *New Testament Handbook*. The concordance feature is a simple string search, which means that searches for more than a single word are difficult. The search feature poses some problems. In our tests, even simple single-word searches had to be tried under a variety of conditions before they would actually run. The user interface is simplistic and designed to prevent several different actions from occurring at once. This limits the amount of information displayed on the screen at any one time.

Overall, this package is suitable only for basic reference. Compared with the other packages reviewed here, it is lightweight.

Accordance (for Apple Users)

The introductory package for Accordance 7 is produced by Oak Tree Software (http://www.accordancebible.com/). It includes a number of public-domain English Bibles and one modern English translation of the user's choice. Users are also able to purchase and "unlock" additional Bible modules. The developers offer more advanced modules in their Scholar's Collection. These include *Biblia Hebraica Stuttgartensia*, Nestle-Aland's *Novum Testamentum Graece* (N. A 27), Liddell-Scott's *Greek-English Lexicon*, Louw-Nida's *Greek-English Lexicon of the New Testament*, and Brown-Driver-Briggs's *Hebrew and English Lexicon* (with Bauer-Danker's *Greek-English Lexicon of the New Testament* [BDAG] available separately). The Scholar's Collection also contains modules for the Septuagint (LXX), OT Pseudepigrapha, Philo, and Josephus, among others. Many of these texts are grammatically tagged for quick translation helps. Other available collections include the Church Fathers, individual Greek manuscripts, a Greek NT apparatus, and the *Anchor Bible Dictionary*.

The interface is more intuitive and less cluttered than other Bible programs. Organized around the search function, the main window consists of a "search entry" field and a "results display" beneath it. If multiple Bible versions have been installed, they can be displayed side by side, with the number of linked modules limited only by the size of the user's screen. An Instant Details floating window displays lexical information when the mouse passes over a Hebrew or Greek word. Multiple searches and lexicons can be organized through a tabbed interface on the main window.

One of Accordance's main strengths is original language searching. Users can search for exact words, words tagged to dictionary entries, or all words with a common root. Complex searches (called "constructs") can be entered directly into the search field, through the Search menu or by means of an interface that graphically depicts the search parameters. Any search result can also be analyzed statistically via a Details button, which offers charts, graphs, tables, and concordance lists.

The modular design of Accordance is both a strength and weakness, mainly because major English translations and original language versions are not available in the same collection. The introductory collection is a good starting point, but it is not comprehensive. The library of available modules is extensive, however, and more are being added regularly. In addition, students and pastors are eligible for a discount. Another strength is the quality and responsiveness of customer support. The company's Web site provides a plethora of support options including a weekly blog, flash demos, and a user forum moderated by experienced users as well as Accordance developers. Accordance also schedules one- and two-day hands-on workshops in the U.S. and Canada to demonstrate the software's capabilities.

Web Sites and the Internet

Valuable resources for biblical interpretation are available on the Internet, but users must exercise caution. Resources that have been published in conventional printed form, such as encyclopedias, other general reference works, scholarly monographs, and journals, can be evaluated by several established criteria, such as the publication date and the reputation of the publisher, and the author(s) or editor(s) under whose name they appear. Similar criteria exist for Internet resources, but they are not as well established in every case. If a Web site has been prepared under the auspices of a well-known university, generally the user can be confident of its reliability. This is especially the case if the Web site has been in use for several years, is regularly maintained, and has attached to it the name of someone whose credentials can be checked. This is also true of Web sites prepared by established scholars, whose reputations have been confirmed through their publications and other peer-review structures within their universities or scholarly guilds. Just as interpreters must use critical judgment in deciding on the quality and credibility of printed books or articles, even moreso is this the case with Internet resources.

Some special considerations in evaluating Web sites and Internet resources include the following:

1. *Reputation of the originator or sponsor of the Web site.* Was it created under the auspices of an established college, university, or research center? What are the scholarly credentials of the person(s) responsible for creating and maintaining the Web site?

2. *Date and scholarly value of the resources to which the Web site provides access.* As in the case of software packages, copyright issues often dictate which materials are chosen as resources for biblical interpretation. A commentary or Bible dictionary may show a recent reprint date, but it may have been published years, even centuries, earlier. Translations of ancient writings, such as patristic authors, may be useful for general reference, but these may not be satisfactory for more specialized use. In this case, it may be necessary to acquire more up-to-date translations that may not be readily available on the Internet.

3. *Theological viewpoint.* While some Web sites provide a wide range of resources reflecting diverse theological points of view, others are more narrowly defined. As with printed books and reference works, it is generally possible to determine whether the overall viewpoint of the Web site is theologically liberal or conservative, whether it represents the extreme of either perspective or some variation in between.

4. *Age and probable duration of the Web site.* Since Internet resources are more ephemeral than printed resources, how long the Web site has been in existence and the likelihood of its continued maintenance become important considerations. This may be related to its institutional affiliation, for example, whether it is sponsored and supported by a university or research center. But other considerations may come into play as well. Even here, some poorly conceived and badly maintained Web sites may have been in existence for a long time, and some very good Web sites may be only a few years (or months) old. As with most things, however, track record matters.

BIBLIOGRAPHY: SELECTED WEB SITES RELATING TO BIBLICAL STUDIES

General

Ancient World Mapping Center Links
http://www.unc.edu/awmc
Links to major ancient mapping sites on the Web.

The Bible Tool
http://www.crosswire.org/study/index.jsp
This powerful online tool allows users to view the Biblical text in parallel columns in hundreds of versions, including the older English translations (RSV, NASB, not the NRSV or NIV) and some original language versions (the Westcott Hort Greek New Testament and Rahlf's Septuagint). Users can click on original language terms for brief definitions and quick concordance (simple) searches. The site also includes several older, theologically-slanted commentaries. The site is clean and user-friendly, but does not include many of the newer, copyrighted translations and resources.

Blue Letter Bible
http://www.blueletterbible.org/
A solid content site, this Bible site presents the Bible text in a number of translations. It contains some valuable features, for example, a biblical concordance. It also contains valuable interlinear editions of the OT and the NT, which correlate each Hebrew and Greek word or phrase with its corresponding English translation. Especially helpful is the numbering system for each term, which enables users to get to the relevant entry in a Hebrew or Greek lexicon, encyclopedia (Kittel), or wordbook. Other supporting resources, for example, commentaries, are quite dated.

Classics and Mediterranean Archaeology
http://www.umich.edu/~cfc/resources.htm
Extensive list of classics links and links to archaeological site pages.

Biblical Interpretation
http://www.earlham.edu/~seidti/iam/interp_mss.html
Great primer on manuscripts, manuscript transmission, and textual criticism; contains many good pictures (including an animated sheet of papyrus constructing itself) and a helpful exercise that illustrates the process using an English text.

Catholic Resources
http://catholic-resources.org/
Bible information and links by Felix Just; very thorough, especially on basics; this site could be considered a hypertext introductory handbook.

United Kingdom Resources

http://www.intute.ac.uk/artsandhumanities/

Web resources for education and research created by a network of universities and partners in the United Kingdom. The section on Historical and Philosophical Studies includes valuable subsections on Archaeology and Religion and Theology.

Religious Texts

http://www.religion-online.org/

A massive site for online scholarly essays and books on Christianity organized by seminary-type categories. (New Testament includes books by Dibelius, Keck, Jeremias, Perrin, and articles by Johnson, Fitzmyer, Mitchell; Old Testament includes a book by Napier and articles by Brueggemann and Koptak.)

Textual Criticism

http://rosetta.reltech.org/TC/TC.html

An electronic journal sponsored by The Society of Biblical Literature devoted to textual criticism. Contains large numbers of transcriptions and facsimiles(!) of the great Uncials (א is represented by Tischendorf's diplomatic edition; B is Tischendorf's transcription; D is Tischendorf's facsimile [often a bit dark for viewing like Matt. 1 Latin]); a transcription collation of f^{13}; and a transcription of sy^s. Also, several old modern critical editions—the Cambridge Septuagint (LXX), Field's Hexapla, von Gall's Samaritan Pentateuch, 1873 Textus Receptus, von Soden's NT, Tischendorf's *Novum Testamentum Graece* 8th ed., and volume 2 of Westcott and Hort's Greek NT.

Wabash Center

http://www.wabashcenter.wabash.edu/Internet

Collection of electronic resources related to religious study and practice, with a particular interest in teaching religion. Topics are grouped by subject matter as well as resource type. Of particular interest is the collection of syllabi from courses taught on specific topics.

ZHubert

http://www.zhubert.com

This site was specifically created for students learning the original biblical languages (in particular Greek). Users can view texts in parallel in most free English versions (NASB, RSV) and the original languages. The user can also view the text critical apparatus alongside each verse. Advanced tools include a Greek concordance with links to the Liddell-Scott lexicon (via Perseus) and a search tool that allows morphological searches, although such searches must be entered in Unicode and thus are difficult for the first-time user. Overall, the site is very user-friendly, as one can hover the cursor over a word and see instant lexical and parsing information. Several study tools are included, including vocabulary lists and a helpful flashcard tool.

Sites Related to the Old Testament and the Ancient Near East

Achaemenid Royal Inscriptions

http://www-oi.uchicago.edu/OI/PROJ/ARI

Includes transliterations and translations of inscriptions in Old Persian, Elamite, and Akkadian.

Casco Bay Assyriological Institute—Digital Maps—Java Version

http://www.cba-inst.org/DigiMap/Index_Java.html

Digital maps identifying all known Assyriological locations; based on the *Helsinki Atlas*.

Cuneiform Digital Library Initiative

http://early-cuneiform.humnet.ucla.edu

Presents transliterated texts and, when possible, images from the cuneiform collections of participating libraries. It also contains information of cuneiform scripts, their development and translation. Established by the University of California at Los Angeles (UCLA) and the Max Planck Institute, this should be a stable site.

Dead Sea Scrolls and Qumran

http://orion.mscc.huji.ac.il

Sponsored by the Orion Center for the Study of the Dead Sea Scrolls, which is part of the Institute for Jewish Studies at Hebrew University in Jerusalem. It is generally considered the best site for the Dead Sea Scrolls.

http://www.flash.net/~hoselton/deadsea/deadsea.htm

Solid site on the Dead Sea Scrolls. Reflecting indebtedness to Golb, this site challenges some of the consensus views on the sources of the scrolls.

http://www.ao.net/~fmoeller/qumdir.htm

Facsimile of Qa, the Qumran Great Isaiah Scroll.

The Electronic Text Corpus of Sumerian Literature

http://www-etcsl.orient.ox.ac.uk/

The name says it all. The texts are in transliteration and translation, and bibliographical data are also included.

ETANA

http://www.etana.org/

The most valuable site on the Web relating to the ancient Near East (ANE). This site contains classic scholarship on the ANE, including 135 scanned-in key primary and secondary sources (often in German or French). It also contains links to current archaeological sites and includes searchable current secondary literature.

iTanakh

http://www.itanakh.org

A collection of electronic resources related to the study of the Hebrew Bible and related ancient Near Eastern texts. The site includes links to other sites, articles, and online resources, grouped by topics such as archaeology, languages, and texts.

Okeanos: Ancient Near Eastern Studies

http://faculty.washington.edu/snoegel/okeanos.html

A site with links to scholarly periodicals, excavations, and other resources.

Postmodern Bible Amos

http://www.bible.gen.nz/amos

Experimental hypertext commentary.

Sites Related to the New Testament and Early Christianity

Centre for the Study of Ancient Documents

http://www.csad.ox.ac.uk/

Contains links to the Vindolanda Tablets and the Oxyrhynchus Papyri.

Duke Papyrus Archive

http://scriptorium.lib.duke.edu/papyrus/

Offers online images and reference material regarding over 1,400 papyri. Texts are organized by topic, language, and chronology. The site also includes helpful articles on topics related to the study of papyri and links to other papyri-related sites.

Early Christian Writings

http://www.earlychristianwritings.com/

Both a gateway and a primary source site, this site focuses on the literature produced by early Christians and their opponents from the beginnings to Origen (ca. 185–254 CE). One hundred fifty-six texts or authors are listed in provisional chronological order. Clicking on the text or author opens a page for each entry that gives links to online texts and resources and bibliographical information for offline resources. Often a short description of the significance of the entry accompanies it. The Historical Jesus section has good summaries of players in the so-called Third Quest. The site is operated by Peter Kirby but does not list his credentials or affiliations.

Early Jewish Writings

http://www.earlyjewishwritings.com

Another resource of texts collected by Peter Kirby.

Encyclopedia of NT Textual Criticism

http://www.skypoint.com/~waltzmn/

Extensive and very well done; a valuable reference for matters related to textual criticism.

The Five Gospels Parallels

http://www.utoronto.ca/religion/synopsis/

This site presents the Gospels (RSV) in parallel, allowing the user to pull up a passage in one Gospel and see the corresponding parallels. The site allows various permutations, including the four canonical Gospels, the three Synoptic Gospels, the four Gospels plus the *Gospel of Thomas,* and the Gospels and Paul.

Into His Own

http://virtualreligion.net/iho/

Site on the background and environment from which Jesus and early Christianity came; many translations of primary texts; choice of texts and overall framework reflects outlook of the Jesus Seminar.

Jewish Roman World of Jesus

http://www.religiousstudies.uncc.edu/JDTABOR/indexb.html

Scholarly articles and essays in NT backgrounds.

New Testament Gateway

http://www.ntgateway.com/

A very professional site operated by Mark Goodacre, a NT professor in the department of religion at Duke University. As a gateway, it is a collection of links grouped under a variety of topics bringing together some of the best NT scholarship on the Web. Especially interesting is the collection on the Synoptic problem, which reflects Goodacre's support for a neo-Griesbachian explanation of the origin of the Gospels (Luke used Matthew; Mark used Matthew and Luke).

New Testament Transcript Prototypes

http://nttranscripts.uni-muenster.de/

Allows a user to work through the Nestle-Aland Greek text (N-A 27) verse by verse and explore the textual apparatus. For each verse the apparatus is provided (along with a basic definition of the Greek words via Perseus), and the user can click on each manuscript to see a transcription of the Greek text. The site also has detailed information on twenty-six major Greek manuscripts. This project, under the auspices of the University of Münster, is still a work in progress. Users are required to download (for free) Greek fonts.

Paul and Pauline Studies

http://www.paulonpaul.org/
Introductory site on Paul that uses the letters to sketch a history of his missionary work; includes cautionary sections on why Acts is not as reliable historically as the letters themselves.

http://www.thepaulpage.com/
A good scholarly page on the new perspective on Paul (Wright, Dunn, et al.) containing articles and essays reflecting various viewpoints, along with bibliography.

http://www.luthersem.edu/ckoester/Paul/Main.htm
Craig Koester's introductory page on important Pauline cities; suitable for introductory students. Also valuable is his page on the cities of Revelation with images and introductory information on the cities addressed in the letters to the seven churches.

Perseus

http://www.perseus.tufts.edu
Valuable resource for the classical world.

http://www.tyndale.cam.ac.uk/tyndale/Perseus.htm
Good introduction to overlooked Perseus resources.

Synoptic Problem Home Page

http://www.mindspring.com/~scarlson/synopt/
Lists all the major solutions proposed (throughout the history of scholarship) to the Synoptic Problem and includes helpful diagrams of each solution. The site also contains links to other sites related to the Synoptic Problem.

W. Wilker Bible-Links Page

http://www1.uni-bremen.de/~wie/bibel.html
Wonderful collection of links; includes links to thirty-nine photographs of NT papyri; valuable resource for textual criticism.

Index of Scriptural References

Biblical passages discussed in some detail are indicated by italicized page numbers.

Index of Subjects and Names